Anna C. Johnson

The Cottages of the Alps

Or, life and manners in Switzerland

Anna C. Johnson

The Cottages of the Alps
Or, life and manners in Switzerland

ISBN/EAN: 9783337102296

Printed in Europe, USA, Canada, Australia, Japan

Cover: Foto ©ninafisch / pixelio.de

More available books at **www.hansebooks.com**

THE

COTTAGES OF THE ALPS;

OR,

Life and Manners in Switzerland.

BY THE AUTHOR OF "PEASANT LIFE IN GERMANY."

NEW YORK:
CHARLES SCRIBNER, 124 GRAND STREET.
M DCCC LX.

ENTERED according to Act of Congress, in the year 1860, by
CHARLES SCRIBNER,
In the Clerk's Office of the District Court of the United States, for the Southern District of New York.

W. H. TINSON, Stereotyper.   GEO. RUSSELL & CO., Printers.

TO

MADAM DORA D'ISTRIA,

𝔗his 𝔙olume is 𝔍nscribed,

IN

TESTIMONY OF THE FRIENDSHIP

OF

THE AUTHOR.

PREFACE.

WHILE the independence of Switzerland, so often assailed, yet so long providentially maintained, appears to be again threatened by the advances of a powerful neighbour, it is hoped that a picture of the social and political life of the Swiss people, from recent personal observation, may not be unacceptable to the English people who have evinced so warm an interest in the events now passing in Southern Europe.

The name upon our dedicatory page may not be familiar to our readers; and as we have placed it there for the purpose of making known to them the life and works of a woman who is becoming a bright and shining light amid the darkness of Eastern despotism, it is due that we say a few words to prove her title to the slight tribute we thus pay her, and her claim to the attention of the English public.*

She is an Eastern princess of the ancient and noble family of Ghika. Her ancestors originated in Macedonia, and emigrated centuries ago to Wallachia, where since 1658 they have been the family from which the *Hospodars* have been mainly elected, under the Ottoman rule, and characterised always by bravery, intrepidity, and love of liberty.

Wallachia is one of the Danubian principalities which

---

* This work was first published in London, by Messrs. Sampson Low, Son & Co., 47 Ludgate Hill.

have been so long the object of strife between Russia, Austria, and Turkey; and the Ghikas are the indomitable native princes who have resisted them, and rebelled against their tyranny, unto death.

After the first Russian occupation, Gregory Ghika the Seventh was the restorer of the throne of Wallachia, and the resuscitator of their beloved Roumanic language and literature. He instituted many reforms, relieved the country of a debt which had weighed upon it for a century, and formed a plan of national education. But neither Russia nor Austria wished to see the Roumaini revive in their native strength and glory, and contrived to plunge them anew into misfortunes.

From 1828 to 1834 the throne of Bukarest was vacant, and since that period only once have they been ruled by a native prince. This was Alexander Ghika, brother of Gregory, equally noble and equally unfortunate. This brings us to the princess of our story, Helena Ghika, the niece of these two princes, and daughter of Michael Ghika, a long time " Minister of the Interior " to his brother. She was born on the 22d of January, 1829, and during all her life in the East saw her country struggling, resisting, and conquered but never subdued. Before the revolution of 1842 her father had removed his family to Dresden to complete their education, and her cousin, Alexander Gregory Ghika, has, in these latter days, commenced the struggle anew to throw off the foreign yoke. One of her books is entitled the "Heroes of Roumaini;" and those who are familiar with the history of her country will understand her enthusiasm for liberty, and love of her people.

But it is owing to the resolution of her father that she

should not be nurtured in the supineness which characterises the lives of Eastern ladies, that she received an education which would be considered masculine even in England and America. In her childhood she had an English *bonne*, and at seven years of age was placed under the tutorship of the renowned Professor Papadopulos, who not only taught her the rich languages of the East, Greek, Latin, and French, but imbued her with the spirit of the ancient philosophers and heroes, and initiated her into all the learning of the schools.

Her father said, " All the progress of later years in literature was owing to the blending of masculine intelligence and vigour with a proper development of feminine tact and perception. These are continually reacting on each other, so that every new subject is handled with a profound investigation and artistic detail, which leave no room for fallacy. Uneducated women in any country are the dupes of intriguers and the strongest enemies of progress, whether in Church or State; and in every country those who oppose their elevation, by the use of the cant of " woman's rights " and " woman's sphere," and other terms of scorn and ridicule, know very well that while they can be kept floating in saloons, insipid and thoughtless, society will remain corrupt, and the pillars of freedom be continually tottering."

We commend these sentiments of an Eastern prince to the consideration of some of our fellow-countrymen; and we have not forgotten once hearing an American lady in a saloon express the utmost contempt for another, whom she had been invited to meet, and yet to whom she refused to be introduced, because she despised a woman who made literature her study, and was an authoress!—or another, who said, "A woman who became public in any way was only worthy of contempt." To such ladies we need not present the subject of our story. They will despise her for having voluntarily renounced the "life of saloons," as she herself expresses it, to devote herself to literature and the effort by her pen to do something for the freedom of her beloved country. It will be useless for us to say to such paragons, how beautiful is her daily life, how spotless her character, how noble her enthusiasm, and how severe her labour—she is by these very virtues public, and her name becoming familiar in every tongue.

Her father not only insisted that she should be thoroughly disciplined in mind, but in body; and among various other exercises, she was taught to swim, and became so expert that in late years she saved the life of a lady in her family, the instructress of her sister, who fell into the water when no one was near to save her but herself. Music and painting were not neglected, nor an acquaintance with general literature. She speaks and writes Russian, German, Italian, French, and English; and at an exhibition of fine arts in St. Petersburg, obtained the prize for two of her paintings. Her invocations of the Muses have not been less successful; and that she is the only person who has ascended the *Mönch*, one of the highest mountains in Switzerland, proves that these graces are not incompatible with energy and heroism.

At the age of twenty years she was married to a Russian prince, Koltzoff Massalsky, a descendant of the old Vikings of Moldavia, who entered Russia in the days of Vladimir in 988, and have never been especially popular with the reigning dynasty. She resided six years at the Russian Court, during which time her health failed, and the influence of a northern climate threatened to sink her into an early grave. Physicians said she must leave or die. The invasion of Wallachia by Russia in 1853 seemed to her a crime, against which she ventured a remonstrance.* This made her unpopular, and her passports were freely given to exile herself in whatever land she chose. She had no children to link her to the land of her adoption, and she went forth to wander, at least till her health should be restored, and it may be for ever, unless oppression should cease, and the peace which can only be the consequence of justice on the part of the stranger, should be restored between the Empire and the dependent province.

We heard of her everywhere in Switzerland as the quiet, unassuming lady, benevolent to the poor and kindly to all, acting the part of godmother to a peasant's child in a cottage, the beloved of children, sympathizing with all sorrow, and yet living entirely apart from the gay world. The first months of her exile were spent in Ostend, in 1855, and there she published her first book, "Monastic Life," which appeared at Brussels. The next year she resided in Canton Tessino, to enjoy the delicious climate on the borders of Lago Maggiore. In quick succession since this period have appeared the volumes entitled severally, German, French, and Italian Switzerland—books which fill a void in literature that, we cannot understand why, has been left so long unfilled. But we are consoled with the thought that

* The old Russian party would have preferred to send her to Siberia with two other noble ladies whose crimes were the same, and who are now exiles among the eternal snows, but for some reason the Emperor did not comply with their demands.

no one could have done it better, and it may be well that the task was left to her. Those who would know the history, the heroes, the authors, the reformers, and philanthropists of Switzerland, can find them portrayed nowhere else in their true light, indeed, nowhere else at all except in their own chronicles.

It struck us as a curious coincidence that a lady should have come from the far east, and another from the far west, to meet in the little republic with the same object, the same opinions, and the same enthusiastic love of liberty, one being born subject of a despot and the other of a free government. We did not succeed in obtaining her books till our own was finished, and when we first heard of them feared we might be upon common ground and one pen rendering the other unnecessary. But we found, without knowing it, that we began just where she had left off, and the end of her books and the beginning of ours could not have been better fitted together had it been done by design. Hers are of the past and ours of the present, and Switzerland must be viewed in both these relations in order to be understood. There are striking resemblances in thought, in facts, and in expression even, but which can only be the result of similarity of views, as we had no knowledge of each other in any way till the works of both were finished.

In her preface to this work she says, " I have travelled through great kingdoms without finding anything to make a noble feeling. There we see only such victories as spiritual tyranny or worldly despotism can exercise over the healthy understandings of men; but you, fruitful plains of Thurgovie, peaceful valleys of St. Gall, renowned mountains of Appenzell, how different the feelings which you call up!

You walk with a fearless step and lift an independent brow to heaven, while the people of the great nations around you still bow their necks to the yoke. You are a free people, and the banner on which glitters the federal star can with just pride wave near the Lion of free, happy England, and the star-spangled banner of unconquerable America."

For these principles she and her books are interdicted in Austria and in Russia, though they come freely into France and Belgium, and also are allowed in Germany. The reviews and journals of the different countries notice her according to their ideas of liberty; her genius and her talent are never gainsaid.* She forbade us to name her titles in our dedication, and though we have given them here in order to explain her life, we forget them always in our intercourse with her, for it is the woman only that we know. She has won for herself a title more noble than accident bestowed upon her, like England's noble queen, who immortalises the throne instead of allowing the throne to immortalise her.

We have written of the people of Switzerland as we did of those of Germany, but we cannot say we have described the "peasant life," because there is, legitimately speaking, no such thing in Switzerland. According to the 4th article of their constitution, "All Swiss are equal before the law. There are in Switzerland no subjects; none who enjoy privileges on account of birth, person, or family." Every peasant may look forward to the highest honours in the gift of the

---

* Besides contributing to journals in Paris, Athens, Italy, Switzerland, and Germany, she has written in these last six years, "The Women of the East;" "The Ionian Isles," under the rule of Venice and British protection; "Nationality of Roumanie;" "The Orientals and the Papacy," &c., &c., which, our readers will see, leaves her little time for saloons.

republic, if he will make himself worthy of them, and it is the occurrence of every day that the upper ranks are filled by accessions from the lower.

In Germany the mercantile class and mechanics are as far below the nobility as the peasantry are, and their life and occupations come as legitimately within our sphere.

In Switzerland the president and council, the senate and deputies, are also a part of the people, and thus is given us a still wider range, without departing from our subject.

Here the mountains are the castles, and nature constructs all the palaces. In the cities there is nothing princely, and nothing feudal except the ruins; we shall therefore indulge ourselves in saying whatever we think is new and interesting, whether of high or low. But though a greater experience and additional language have increased our facilities for observation and study, we do not here, any more than there, confine ourselves to what we can learn by personal effort. What others, with larger acquaintance and better opportunities, have learned, may be more valuable than anything we may collect ourselves, whatever may be our fitness or capacity. Of the reliability of these sources, we, of course, must be the judge. We cannot enlarge our book to unwieldy dimensions, or mar our pages with "authorities" and "statistical proofs," which not ten persons among those for whom we write would take the trouble to examine or care to know.

We are influenced by the "spirit of truth," and have no cause of malice or unkindness towards the country we have left, or the one in which we are.

We could transcribe many letters, written voluntarily by

German friends, assuring us that our representations have not even the fault of exaggeration.

But we have since heard that many things are not German merely, but *continental*. In Switzerland we have relied wholly upon the people and their own chronicles. The Swiss are all *chroniclers*, and remarkably faithful in writing of themselves. We have found them always ready to open their stores for our researches, and never manifesting any fear of our pen.

We are particularly indebted to Dr. Prof. Osenbrugg, of Zurich University, for a series of observations made by himself in various tours in Switzerland to see the country and to write about the people. The descriptions of prisons, court trials, and various facts in jurisprudence, were furnished us by him, and we are only sorry that we cannot do justice to the original, in which law and poetry are blended in an unusually happy manner. Dr. Oesterler, of the same city, and the librarian of the Biblioteke, were invaluable assistants in our studies.

The "American Minister Resident," at Berne, furnished us cordially with introductions and special passports, to enable us to travel with profit and pleasure, and we are especially indebted to the firm of "Dalp & Co." for any courtesy to facilitate us in our work.

Whether we travelled alone, or in what sort of company, we do not this time inform the public, as it does not essentially concern them, and we will not subject others to the reproach of the evil-minded and vulgar, but may say it is no such marvellous thing in these days to travel in any tolerably civilized country. There is sufficient law and sufficient honour among men for the protection of all who need it, and it may be something to the credit of Germans and Swiss that we have never, in a single instance, during three years among them, required more than our own dignity could furnish, and now, as before, can say we have had no experience that has caused us to regret having come among them.

In both books we have only aimed at giving a good general idea of the people. Names and dates, localities and masses of details, only clog the memory, and answer no useful purpose in a book like this. Specialties may be interesting to those who have travelled extensively, but to those who cannot identify each event and scene with the spot where it occurred, by personal observation, it is only tedious to attempt it. Geographies and guide-books are made especially for those who would trace heights and distances with exactness, and there are plenty of authors with a different plan to fill the chasms we have left.

That the portraits of life and manners are faithful, we know, and we have been gratified in reading the letters of two German travellers, editors of a St. Louis journal, who had been twenty-five years in America, and returned to the fatherland to receive the same impressions as a stranger, from the lack of progress, and the sluggishness of all enterprise, where despots rule, and the comparative sluggishness of everything in the old, time-honored world.

That our suggestions will be of any use we cannot have the vanity to hope, but there is just now a general awakening throughout the Continent that bids fair to result in promoting the interest of the governed. The day of blind obedience is past, and a tremulous fear has seized the sovereigns of every state, that unless they rule more wisely and beneficently, they will soon cease to rule at all. Whether it be kingdom, or empire, or republic, we care not, provided Justice and Mercy sit on the throne and walk hand-in-hand among the people.

CONTENTS.

CHAPTER I.

First Impressions—People, past and present—Cars and Diligences—Berne and its Bears—Prisoners—Federal Palace—Promenades—Mountains, ... 21

CHAPTER II.
URI.

Travellers at Fluelen—Description of Villages—Houses—Elections—Grütli—Costumes—Calamities, ... 33

CHAPTER III.
SCHWYTZ.

Origin of People — Brunnen—Diligence — Hotels—Costumes—Improvements—Einsiedeln—Pilgrims—Legends, ... 48

CHAPTER IV.
UNTERWALD.

Alpine Pastures—Sennhutten—Cheese-making—Cows and their Bells—Alpine Festivals—Agriculture—Fêtes, ... 63

CHAPTER V.
LUCERNE.

Ancient Laws and Customs—City of Lucerne—Social Life—Ascent of the Righi—Ancient Procession—Weddings, ... 78

CHAPTER VI.

ZUG.

Pleasant Custom—Churchyard—First Battle for Freedom—Home Sickness of Swiss Soldiers—Witchcraft—Forms of Punishment, 93

CHAPTER VII.

VALAIS.

Crossing the Furka—Rhone Glacier—Inn—Manufactures and Agriculture—Love of Liberty—Cretinism, ... 104

CHAPTER VIII.

VAUD.

Cheese Societies—Union Dairies—Wine-presses—Blacksmiths' Shops—Lace-making—Vintage Festival of Vevay—Shepherd Songs, . 119

CHAPTER IX.

GENEVA.

Calvin—Jews—Lake Leman—Watch-making—Social Life—Swimming Schools for Girls, ... 138

CHAPTER X.

FRIBURG.

Gruyère Cheese—Gessenay Shepherds—Cheese Aristocracy—Swiss Song—Influence of Amusements—Legends, ... 152

CHAPTER XI.

NEUCHATEL.

Queen Bertha—Trouble with Prussia—Military System—Watch-making—Language, ... 166

CHAPTER XII.

SOLEURE.

Patricians—Material Interest—Journalism—Old Laws—Houses—First Agricultural Societies—Costumes, ... 180

CHAPTER XIII.
ZURICH.

Modern City—Old Laws—Silk Manufacture—Happy Homes—Frogs and Snails—Great Shooting Festival, ... 192

CHAPTER XIV.
SCHAFFHAUSEN.

Old City—Pride and Exclusiveness—Jews—Costume—Rhinefall—Distinguished Men, ... 216

CHAPTER XV.
BASLE.

Social Life—Opinions of Old Authors—Revolutions—Jews—Robbers—Looms—Celebrated Men, ... 229

CHAPTER XVI.
ST. GALL.

Money-making—Vices of Material Life—Embroideries—Swiss Muslins—Cherry Water—City Life, ... 244

CHAPTER XVII.
APPENZELL.

Spirit of Liberty—Murder by a Young Girl—Stickstube—Costume—Alps—Amusements, ... 257

CHAPTER XVIII.
GLARUS.

Scene in Street—Old Families—Zwinglius—Brotherhood—Schabzieger Cheese—Alpine Tea—Calico—Incident on Railway—Elections—Superstitions—Old Laws and Customs, ... 275

CHAPTER XIX.
THURGOVIE.

Talk in a Diligence—Coachman's Livery—Thurgovian Village—Post Office—Napoleon in Thurgovie—Custom-house—Schools—Weddings, ... 298

CHAPTER XX.
GRAUBUNDEN.

Splügen—Via Mala—Grey League—Vale of Disentis—Italian Shepherd—Castasagna Chestnuts—Alpine Fête—Kiltgang—Engadine—Dances, ... 312

CHAPTER XXI.
ARGOVIE.

Roman City—Convents—Quarrels—Jews—Dark Days of Old—Schools—Three Cantonal Divisions—Homeless People—Peasant Dinner Festivals, ... 340

CHAPTER XXII.
TESSINO.

Italian Skies—Governments—Clergy—Education—Church Bells—Peasant Houses—Costumes—Fairs—Mines—Agricultural Fête Days—Marriages—Distinguished Men, ... 353

CHAPTER XXIII.
BERNE.

Interlaken—Empress-Mother of Russia—Sunrise from the Grimsel—Story of Peter Zeibach—Old Customs—Bernese Boys—Fellenberg—Country Life, ... 368

CHAPTER XXIV.
CONCLUSION.

Attachment of the People to their Government—Federal Assembly—Council of State—Federal Council—Tribunal—Constitution—Officials—Postage—Nationality, ... 389

APPENDIX, ... 403

THE COTTAGES OF THE ALPS.

CHAPTER I.

FIRST IMPRESSIONS—PEOPLE, PAST AND PRESENT—CARS AND DILIGENCES—BERNE AND ITS BEARS—PRISONERS—FEDERAL PALACE—PROMENADES—MOUNTAINS.

WE entered Switzerland by its northern gate; and as our German Guide-book says, "we have only crossed the border before we find ourselves in a different land, and among a different people," it will be thought no sin for us to say the same.

We did not read the Guide-book till long after we had made our observations, but our philosophy was instantly awake, wondering why those who had the same origin, and have spoken always the same language, should be found in paths diverging so widely in the journey through life.

We had thought that German Switzerland must be very much like Germany; but even the general features, as we glance superficially, offer scarcely any points of resemblance—in which remark we allude only to the people, their manners and customs; for now, as before, to these we are obliged to confine ourselves. The mountains, however grand, and the valleys, however lovely, must be passed by in silence; not because our eyes do not behold them, or our mind does not appreciate them, but because our "instructions" forbid us to dally among things beautiful, or our fancy to revel among things luxurious.

We wish to know what kind of people inhabit this wonderful land; and among the thousands—aye, hundreds of thousands—who have crossed its glaciers, and gone wild in its gorges, how few have thought it worth while to devote a page to the daily life of the shepherd and rover, though the imagination has woven a thousand tales of a people who do not really exist.

Yet the exclamations of surprise and discouragement are even more abundant when we say we are bound for Switzerland, than when our destiny was Germany. An " exhausted subject," says one. "Switzerland has been written to death," says another. "The people! Indeed, if you are to give us a book about the people, it will be more stupid still. They are no longer what they were in the days of chivalry and romance, but have degenerated into mercenary speculatists and plodding tillers of the soil. From being the most interesting, they have become the most humdrum of human beings."

To this we could answer nothing when on our way, because we knew nothing; and now shall leave our readers to prove whether those judge rightly who think a wilderness more pleasant to the eye than a fruitful field, and cottages smiling in the midst of plenty less idylish than the rude hut of the mountain.

Because they no longer wear the kilt and wield the sabre, it is not necessarily true that they have not inherited the proud spirit of their fathers; and songs of peace may indicate hearts as noble as the fierce war-whoop or the gay tambour.

This charge of degeneracy is something we hear so often, that we hope to prove its fallacy. The decision concerning the American Indian has been, that he could not be civilized; that he preferred the tomahawk and scalping-knife, the wigwam and the skins of beasts, to the arts and comforts of Christian people. Yet had whole nations of Indians voluntarily followed the plough and sowed the field, or in the course of centuries yielded to the subduing power of progress and settled in hamlets and in "white cottages with green blinds"—preferring cities and the hum of factories, what would have been said of them then? Exactly what people say of the descendants of Tell and the brave men who defended with him their birthright.

That foes without and traitors within, so long obliged them to wear the warrior's garb, and to be ever on the watch for those who left no defile of their mountains free from the tramp of conquering hosts, and allowed no valley to escape the ravages of the ruthless destroyer, has been the reason they have not taken a higher stand among the nations, and that their federal escutcheon has not earlier become a bright and shining light, shedding its beams over a continent. It is scarcely ten years since they were permitted to lay aside their armour. They have been the prey of every emperor, prince, and potentate from pole to pole and sea to sea ;* and to us it is ever marvellous, that in the days when their land was indeed a wilderness, and the most fruitful field *almost* a desert, they were able to march triumphant through disciplined legions, thronging from every point of the compass to defend their liberties and preserve their rights, remaining always a peculiar people, which no power could crush and no corruption entirely destroy. They have lived and fought till the nations are weary and give up the strife. They have at length agreed *to let them alone*, and, though the fact is but little known beyond their limits, it is yet true, that their present Government exhibits not less the wisdom which proves the

* In this general assertion, England is not included; and we might as well add, that in all cases where the term *European* is used, we refer only to *Continental people*.

superiority of their statesmen and legislators, than their success in battle proved the courage of their warriors and the skill of their generals.

Switzerland is the object of the envy, and malice, and vituperation of the despotisms which surround her. It is the policy, and it is the practice, of princes and their courtiers, to cause to be published continually the most slanderous falsehoods concerning the little republic, its government, its laws, and its people.*

Yet, in the heart of Europe, bounded on every side by empires and kingdoms, trying to annihilate them by force or seduce them by bribery, with emissaries, either open or disguised, for centuries throwing confusion into their councils, endeavouring to blind or corrupt them, they have survived and retained enough of strength and right principle to form a government, which, if not perfect, is in advance of most, and, in some respects, superior to all. God grant that no blow from without, and the wiles of no serpent within, may again endanger its foundations.

We came first upon Swiss soil in Basel, but cannot stop here to tell its glories—the grand old city that was the seat of councils, and entertained whole retinues of popes, and bishops, and cardinals, emperors, kings, and princes, with wise men from the East, long before America had a name. We will come again and assign it due place and importance among its sisters of the Confederacy. We must first give a few general impressions as we pass along.

It had been told us that the Swiss post allowed just forty pounds of baggage, and we therefore took just forty pounds, in

---

* We find this asserted by a German author, Dr. Kolb, of Speyer, who has lately published in Zurich a work on the political condition of Switzerland, including its financial, military, and commercial relations.

order to avoid all trouble of weights and measures, which we thus succeeded in doing, except on railways, where they allow none. But so much baggage every person may have without fear of the merciless Custom-house inspector ; and when it was set down on the platform in Basel *dépôt*, a man placed his hand respectfully upon it, and asked, " What have you in this ?" " The usual articles of a lady's wardrobe." " Nothing else ?" " Nothing." Upon which he respectfully bowed and departed. This is a pleasant beginning, and puts us in good humour, for nothing yet ever put us so thoroughly out, as to see our dresses and muslins, on which the laundress had left her best impression, overturned and crumpled by the rude assaults of an *employé*. Nothing ever obliterates so entirely every trace of more than one Christian virtue from our bosom as this barbarous infringement of the most sacred of human rights. That a lady cannot carry a comb and brush, and morning-dress, a few

"Pills, powders, patches, billet-doux,"

without having them submitted to the scrutiny of some solemn man of office, is indeed an evidence in any country that civilization has not done its perfect work. We are at last where one may have a little *sanctum* which profane eyes and hands cannot invade, and we must experience some very serious wrong to blot out the influence of this one incident on entering a strange land. So much for " first impressions " and " little things."

We are struck not the less pleasantly with these cars, constructed after the American model, with rows of seats on each side of a long carriage, the cushions of grey cloth, and the wood painted "curly-maple," all neat as wax. Here is a little room for *first-class passengers* at the end, also like those in every

American railway carriage, but here an extra price is demanded for those who occupy them. Not opening at the side, they are the thoroughfare through which every one must pass to reach places of lower rank, and offer therefore no privacy and no special advantage. But in a country so thronged with travellers of high and low degree, it would cause great complaint not to have some place set apart to give a nominal distinction and importance to those who claim to be of a superior order. We took a seat once among those exclusives, and found it the most uncomfortable we ever had in a railway carriage. It was a hot, dusty day, and the crowd was overwhelming. The room being small, one has continually the unpleasant sensation of short rapid drafts from constantly opened doors and always open windows. Two or three persons who could not find seats in the second class, took them without scruple in the first, the conductor making no objections and exacting no more money for the privilege. Those who had paid the extra price were thus incommoded, and had only the consolation of saying and exhibiting that they were first-class passengers, which we have often noticed was sufficient for some people, whatever the annoyance they might experience.

What a difference, too, in the officials, as they perform their several duties. Here is not the solemn look and heavy step of one who says in every motion: I am an officer of the Emperor, or King, or Grand Duke, as may be, with a cumbersome uniform to substantiate the assertion, all which made them, though uniformly courteous, as uniformly terrible. The first of this class whom we notice, answers to our idea of one who in boyhood sang Swiss songs on the mountains. We ask him a question for no other purpose than to see if his manners will correspond with his round red cheeks and merry black eyes.

Oh, yes; he has no idea that he is of any particular consequence, only that he takes all the tickets and keeps the accounts correctly. Now and then, as we pass through the villages, a nice looking peasant woman takes her seat by our side, and an ever varying costume is presented to our eyes, and also a respectable and self-respecting deportment, evidently the result of a consciousness that they are no man's servants. A German professor remarks that you see the same in the animals; the cows hold up their heads and look around with an air that shows their appreciation also of free atmosphere. Their heads are not oppressed with a yoke when they are in harness, but the burden comes upon their shoulders. That this is in any way the consequence of free institutions, we do not intend to imply; or that cows wear a yoke upon their heads in Germany, because they live under the government of a grand-duke; yet we could not help wondering how it should happen, that on one side of a small river it should be the custom for the animals to draw all weights in this way, and that on the other side of the same river, a few miles further south, they should be treated in an entirely different manner. We cannot stop here to speculate upon the matter, and pass on till we arrive at the capital of this famous republic, the seat of the Federal Government, the rallying point of the twenty-two independent States.

It strikes us as a pleasant city, with its quaint streets, built in arcades, its curious old towers, its ramparts converted into promenades, and its many new streets and buildings, sufficiently modern for beauty and comfort, without making a repulsive contrast with what is old. There is something about it which gives it an identity; with the individual features which every city must have, as a whole, it is unlike every other.

Its name of Berne was originally *Bären*, in German signifying bears; and from the reason, say the chronicles, that Berthold V., Duke of Zaeringen, its founder, slew on the spot one of these animals, and caused the first houses to be built of the oaks of the forest which then clothed the ground. This was in 1191. Whether history or legend, it is rooted very strongly in the faith of the people, and they have ever awarded peculiar honours to their redoubtable namesakes. On their municipal escutcheon the principal figure is a bear. High on each side of one of the principal gates are crouched two of these huge creatures cut in granite, with attitude and expression to make one realize all their fierceness; yet, grim though they are, one would not like to miss their familiar faces. In various other positions, on towers and pedestals, they are placed conspicuous; but more interesting still are the living ones, which have appropriated to their use spacious apartments in the most aristocratic quarters of the city. For many centuries, if not from the foundation of the walls, the people have entertained a certain number; and when in 1833 the race became extinct, new specimens were imported from Paris and St. Petersburg, and the last year two were born unto them, which was occasion for great rejoicing. Their sleeping rooms are caves in the side of a hill, walled and well carpeted with straw; their promenade and reception room, a deep square pit with walls and floor of granite, and bath rooms to correspond. The legacy of a wealthy citizen has secured them independence, and if they have any appreciation of the regard and admiration of their fellow-burghers, they must feel very rich.

How many of my readers know that the town of Newbern, in North Carolina, was settled by a colony from this old city of bears, two hundred having emigrated thither in 1710, under *Christopher Graffenried*? but whether they transplanted a menagerie we do not know.

We walk through the streets and meet a procession of strange, coarse-looking men in uniform, and learn that they are criminals, who, instead of being locked in dungeons, are made to toil. We have read that not fifty years ago they were marched through the streets in chains, to be the scorn of the populace. How great an improvement has taken place in their condition! Those who perform agricultural labour are accompanied to the field by a man, who carries a gun and sword. They are not allowed to speak to each other, and no one is allowed to speak to them. In the prison itself are workshops of every description, and each one is permitted to pursue the trade to which he has been accustomed, or to learn any he may choose, if he has none. If, in this way, one earns more than the expense of supporting him in the prison, half the sum is laid aside and given him when his term expires, so that many on leaving have no insignificant fund to enable them to commence some honourable calling in the world. Farmers in the neighbourhood often employ them as day labourers, paying them stipulated wages. We see them also employed in various occupations about the city, accompanied by an overseer, and in the coarse striped dress that makes it easy to identify them.

The prison discipline is thoroughly Christian and reformatory, and the institution so nearly self-supporting, that the average cost of each person does not exceed thirty-five dollars a year. Among those who think the old times better than the new, we certainly should not find the thieves and robbers of this establishment, to which the whole canton furnishes some five or six hundred. We cannot conceive how a prison can be conducted on better principles or come any nearer to perfection in its arrangements. We notice it particularly, as in some of the other cantons we are able to contrast the present with the past, in reference to the treatment of fallen humanity.

We inquire concerning the theatre, and learn that it is not a Government institution, but managed by a company, who keep it open only in the winter; from which we conclude, that the people cannot afford to amuse themselves, or that amusement is not so absolutely necessary to their existence as in some countries we have seen.

They have demolished the castles and built a *federal palace*. Our exclamation on beholding it is, "How exactly it corresponds with our idea of the little republic!" It is not magnificent or imposing, but there is a modest grandeur in its whole, and a modest beauty in its details, that comport with the pretensions of the people, though there could have been no parsimony in the council that voted about four hundred and thirty thousand dollars for such a purpose. It is more remarkable, perhaps, that the architect did not spend all the money they allowed him; though he answered their expectations in the results he produced. We walked through the rooms one afternoon just after the honourable members had ended their debates for the day; and supposing they had all departed, we took a seat in the presidential chair, in order to have a sense of the feelings of the President of the Swiss Republic. Our cicerone said, if we sat there, we must make a speech, upon which we replied, "Oh, yes;" and had just risen for that purpose, when the honourable gentleman whose particular office it was to harangue his "fellow citizens" from that desk, walked in. He bowed respectfully to one whom he must have considered an unscrupulous usurper, and we bowed as deferentially as possible, and resigned.

But we must not linger too long even in republican palaces.

A shady promenade attracts our attention, and following a narrow pathway we come upon a group of little girls, and learn that they belong to the orphan school near by. We sit down on a bench to watch them in their play. They are pinning leaves together with stems, and making wreaths and scarfs with which to adorn themselves, and then "go a visiting," as we have seen little girls do a thousand times. The conversation and the sports of children are the same in all languages and all lands.

We ascend an eminence, and find ourselves on what were in the olden times the ramparts for the defence of the town. Now it is a playground for children, and their merry voices make the same glad music, though it is not in one, but many strange tongues. We sit down on the roots of a tree, and a little boy not four years old looks a moment in our face, and without any more formal introduction climbs up and throws his arms around our neck. We teach him how to use his wooden shovel in the sand ; his tiny sister asks us to rock the cradle of her doll, and soon we are surrounded by a little train of wagons and hobbyhorses with their owners in amusing rivalry for our attention. How truthful are children ! How sad that they must be trained to all the deceptions of false politeness and the cold unchristian charities of the world !

We extend our walk, and without having been told, or thought, that from here could be seen the mountains, we look round indifferently, till by accident our eyes wander in a new direction, and rest on the distant horizon. "What are they?" was our first exclamation. The mountains? Yes, the mountains ! The clouds have suddenly broken and lifted their dark curtains ; the setting sun is tinging their tops with the soft tints of grey and purple, so that every line is traced as with a pencil against the sky, reflecting the snowy masses below in more brilliant whiteness. From no pen or pencil had we received the most shadowy conception of their grandeur. No pen or pencil can define the feeling, which seemed to fall like a weight upon our spirit as we gazed.

Their enchantment is like that of a beautiful face, changing with every varying emotion. Every hue of sunshine and shadow, every passing cloud, the seasons, morning, noon, and evening, the moon, the stars, every phase of the atmosphere—all these are influences which give them, every moment, a new charm.

One might expect to tire of those everlasting mountains, for ever and for ever there ; but they are never the same, even from the same point of observation. They are like a kaleidoscope with an endless succession of changes, a rainbow with its arch of gold and purple and scarlet spread out into immensity.

CHAPTER II.

URI.

TRAVELLERS AT FLUELEN—DESCRIPTION OF VILLAGES—HOUSES—ELECTIONS—
GRUTLI—COSTUMES—CALAMITIES.

IF our plan were to speak of the different cantons in the order of their rank, we should commence with Zurich, as to her is awarded the precedence in all things. But to suit our own convenience, we begin with those whose names are most familiar, and with which their history was first developed.

From the steamer we stepped upon the wharf at Fluelen, which is the port through which all must pass on their way over the St. Gotthard; and the arrival of every diligence presents in the great street fronting the water the usual scene of porters, valets, and coachmen—travellers who have passed in the night, where was to be seen the grandest scenery in the world, and will go home to say "they have been in Switzerland"—troops of young men with their long Alpine stocks, wreaths of evergreen on their hats, and their pockets full of "specimens;" and ladies in the height of the fashion, with so many grievances that one cannot help wondering why they do not travel in cavalcade, bringing their own mirrors, dressing-maids, and tapestry carpets. They are on their way to Ragatz, to Zurich, or the Rhigi, and in half an hour the village is as quiet as if they had never fluttered and whirled in our midst.

When the boat arrives, it is the same, with a little variation; they wish a coach to Altdorf, to Burglen and Attinghausen; and, with "Murray" in their hands, set off to see where Tell was born, and the men of Grûtli lived, and then hurry on to Como and Lago Maggiore, and before the snow is on the hills are back to Paris. They have travelled! Our mission compels us to stop by the way, and our astonishment is to see how little influence all these throngs from the great world seem to have on the people.

We set out alone one morning to explore the village. It is not very large, and only a few rods from the largest and very comfortable hotel led us into a narrow, dingy street, where the houses looked as old as their history. Sitting on a stone we saw a little girl very busily engaged with some netting, and, in accordance with our rule and inclination, we stopped to ask her a question. She was at first very shy and not disposed to be communicative, but, convinced of our friendliness, she became also friendly, and we asked her to walk with us a little way up the hill. She readily assented, her fingers never pausing an instant, however quickly she talked or ran. Before we had gone very far, all constraint had vanished between us, and she was henceforth our companion in the churchyard and by the lake, in garden and on the hillside, wherever we wished to stroll. We thought her at first about nine or ten years old, but when we asked her, she said she was sixteen; yet there was no deformity about her, and her face was bright and intelligent.

We went to the school-house, which was in the upper room

of a dwelling, and reached by a dark, miserable stairway. The village priest was also the village schoolmaster, which is often the case in Catholic Switzerland. Reading and writing, with a little of arithmetic, was the extent of the pupils' acquirements, but the penmanship was very beautiful, and, so far as their knowledge extended, it was thorough. On examining a beautiful writing-book, we asked our little companion if she could write as well, and she said, "No, not quite, but she could read and write, and so could all the children in the village."

In the churchyard we saw a large iron kettle filled with water, hanging by a pole, and a brush of dry boughs resting on the surface. "What is it for?" She answered by taking it up and sprinkling some graves with water. It was "holy water" and she crossed herself by dipping her finger therein and drawing it across her forehead.

The people are wholly Catholic, and date their conversion to Christianity so far back as 630, by Bishop Martin, who is the patron saint of the canton. They have still no city, only four villages and fifteen parishes. For a long time they were in some measure subject to the Pope, but since the sixteenth century they have chosen their own pastors, and paid them as they pleased. In every village there is a school in winter, but in summer the youth are so scattered among the mountains that it is not possible to continue them.

The people of Uri are decidedly a pastoral people, and their habits in conformity to their life. With the exception of a few in the larger villages, the houses are built after the model of those described in the earliest allusions to their history, and though they look very pretty in pictures, have not this virtue in reality. In front are the dates of the year in which they were built, and while looking so fragile as if they could not endure the shocks of twenty years of time and tempest, they have already stood several centuries.

The roofs are of long shingles placed upon laths, with a board lying crosswise, on which are set heavy stones, to prevent them from being scattered to the four winds, as they certainly would be by the first gale from the north. The first story upon the ground floor is devoted to wood, wagons and trumpery, and the second story is entered by stairs outside. This is a very common construction of peasant houses everywhere in Switzerland. The sitting-room and sleeping-room for the elders of the family are over the basement in front, and adjoining them behind is the kitchen, which reaches to the roof. A dark stairway leads to the chambers, which correspond to the front rooms below. It looks very dismal without and within. The great stove is sometimes of potter's ware and sometimes of bricks. The rude benches, upon which the family gather round the fire in winter evenings, are entirely of home manufacture, and so are generally the table and the chest of drawers, which are everywhere the accompaniments. Under the benches are long rows of old and new shoes, and over the stove, on strings or poles, long rows of clothes and stockings "hanging up to dry." A clock, which we recognize to have originated in the Black Forest, is fastened to the wall, and the pendulum swings to and fro laden with dust, while the wheels are sometimes trammeled by the work of spiders, who are free to go out and in, and spread over all their warp and woof. Under this is perhaps the picture of a dove, as emblem of the Holy Spirit, and here and there on the walls representations from the Bible and Swiss history. Over the table is a wooden chain, to which in the evening is suspended a tallow candle, and in the corner a crucifix, under which are amulets and gifts they have received in their pilgrimages to cloisters and consecrated spots. There will be a bed in each room, and one or two cradles, perhaps a loom, and apparatus for all manner of useful purposes hanging on nails to the walls. Over the bed, lying on two pegs, is a gun, and since the French invasion in 1799 they have added to this a Russian sword and a French sabre; and it was in this war that they showed they had not forgotten the use of those things; and the misery into which they were plunged in consequence of the invasion, gave an opportunity of proving that sterling virtues were still the tenants of their bosoms.

In front of almost every house is to be seen a trough, hewn out of a tree, for water, with a rude carving of a saint or hero standing guard.

Altdorf was nearly destroyed by the French, who set it on fire in 1799, and therefore has a new look, the houses being stone and covered with tiles. Twice before it has experienced a similar disaster, and therefore has little of the ancient appearance of the other villages. The two principal wells are ornamented with statues of Tell and a former burgomaster; that of Tell standing where he stood to bend his bow, and the other where the boy was placed with the apple on his head.

In the village of Burglen, the birthplace of Tell, and half a mile distant from Altdorf, is also a chapel, on the walls of which are painted the principal scenes of his life. The Reuss passes by, in which he was drowned whilst attempting to save a child who had fallen into the stream. In life and death he remained a hero. In 1388 was consecrated the chapel, which stands by the sea, on the spot where he jumped on shore from the boat. A procession from all the neighbouring cantons assembled on the Wednesday after Ascension, and heard mass in the chapel. At this first consecration 114 persons were present who had known Tell in his life. A similar procession takes place every year now, on the first Sunday after Ascension, when a steamer sets out with the escutcheon of the four forest cantons painted on its side, the broad banner of the Confederacy waving from a tall flagstaff in the centre, and the colours of several cantons in gay contrast on different parts of the deck. Leaving Lucerne in the morning, and stopping at all the villages on its way to collect the devotees, who appear in the brightest of holiday costume, it looks like a flower-garden dancing on the waters, or some fairy land, with "fairylike music," paying a visit to our humdrum world. Many smaller boats are in its train, and the little skiffs, with their parti-coloured awnings, and paddles of all the hues of the rainbow, are not the less like elfin sprites as they skip so merrily along.

The *fête* is a religious one, as are all in Catholic Switzerland, and the ceremonies at the chapel are those usual in the Catholic Church. The capuchins in their long brown mantles, and the monks in their cowls, bishops in gold and scarlet, and priests in their sable robes, are not the least conspicuous among the strange crowd.

They stop at the Grütli and the Tellenplatte, and then proceed to Fluelen, where they disembark, and form a grand procession to Altdorf, where the whole village is in waiting. Banners and streamers with mottoes are waving from the housetops, the streets are arched with wreaths and flowers, and young men and maidens stand here and there in groups, singing hymns and patriotic songs. It is thus they commemorate the past and enjoy the present. Modern events have taken no root in their soil or in their hearts. And, indeed, one may call the *Tellenplatte* the Mecca of the whole civilized world, and a proof that deeds of virtuous heroism find a response in every human heart.

During the last year the *Grütli* has been purchased by the contribution of a mite from all the school-children of Switzerland. The sum required was nearly eleven thousand dollars; but with scarcely any effort it amounts to more than half as much again, because the parents, fearing a deficiency, aided in the work. The sums collected from the children having been kept separate, it is found they alone have effected the purchase, and each little patriot is to receive a picture of the three men in the attitude of making the solemn oath on the spot. This same year Mount Vernon has become the common property of the country of which Washington was the father, evincing that republics are not always to be lawfully accused of indifference and ingratitude.*

* It was on the 10th of November, the one hundredth birthday of Schiller, that the writings were finished, signed and sealed, which conveyed the memorable spot from Mr. Truttman, the owner, to the possession of the whole confederate people. And on the day when the whole civilized world celebrated the birth of the great poet, he was not forgotten by the people whose glory he sang. The men of Uri, as in the drama, were the "first on the ground," and the others crossed the lake in a great yacht, singing as they came in sight of the mountain:

> "We heartily hail thee in distance,
> Still mountain that liftest thine head.
> Where the wavelet, that melts as it glistens,
> From snows everlasting is fed.
>
> "We praise thee, most peaceful of regions,
> We hail thee, thou holiest land,
> Where our fathers, with valorous legions,
> For ever burst slavery's band."

Arrived at the opposite shore, they were greeted by their waiting countrymen, and all ascended together to stand on the sacred spot where the patriot league was sworn. Here they formed a circle, hand in hand, and renewed the solemn covenant, singing afterwards some thrilling songs of freedom. Many liberty speeches were also made, and a resolution passed to place there a single shaft of stone, bearing the inscription:

> "To Tell's poet,
> On his hundredth birthday,
> The original cantons."

The annual election of state officers is the grand festival of each year in every canton, and yet is held always on the Sabbath. It is a religious and solemn occasion in their eyes, and Sunday the most fitting time for its responsible duties. Before *the act of mediation,* in 1816, the period of majority for every youth in Canton Uri was fourteen years of age, but it being held that he could not be a citizen before he was a man, the youth now waits till he is twenty before he can exercise the right of suffrage.

The place for holding the popular assembly in this canton is three miles from Altdorf, at the foot of a mountain in Botzlingen, within sight of the ruins of Attinghausen. On the 15th of April, fourteen days before they are to hold the election and transact the business of the canton, a formal notice is published,

During the dinners which celebrated the same occasion in Berne, a German finished his toast by wishing for Switzerland a Schiller. A Swiss voice quickly responded, "And we wish for Germany a Tell."

In Basle, the ladies, thinking they were unduly neglected, by not being invited to participate in festivities so proper to be graced by their presence, and the importance of which they so fully appreciated, resolved to institute a *fête* by themselves. Silently and softly, as was meet, they made the arrangements, secured the elegant *salon* of the Three Kings Hotel for the purpose, decorated it with a bust of Schiller, engravings, works of art, and wreaths of flowers, and at nine o'clock in the evening, while their lords were convened around the festive board in a distant quarter of the city, these fair conspirators assembled, but not with murderous intent. They were pleasantly surprised to find they had been remembered, and their plan approved by those who at first ignored their existence. Vases of flowers, with significant mottoes, were upon the table, placed, if not by fair, yet by skilful hands, and a bouquet of rare flowers adorned each plate, tied in graceful knots of white ribbons. The ladies exclaimed, "Better late than never," and evidently entered upon their festivities with more buoyant spirits. They read aloud portions of Schiller's poem, sang songs of freedom, and danced. They were not the less pleasantly surprised, in the midst of their mirth, by "Fireworks on the Rhine," which formed no part of their programme. At supper they gave toasts, indulged again in wit and song, and at twelve returned to their homes, not a little triumphant at the success of their plot, and their genuine enjoyment of an occasion where gentlemen had implied they were incapable of participating in the "feast of reason and the flow of soul."

specifying the time, which is the first Sunday in May, and the object of the meeting, from which no person is excluded except criminals ; and no one, however poor or ill-clothed, fails to be present.

After morning service in the church, the people form a grand procession. At the head are the musicians, and the drummers, and a company of military, who surround the national banner. Then follow two men clothed in the ancient costume of the heroes of Switzerland, carrying upon their shoulders enormous buffalo horns, ornamented with silver. Close behind them are what they term the *Land Weibel*, men who answer to the valets of kings, only they are valets to that invisible but important personage, the Republic. They are clothed with the cantonal colours—long loose robes, half black and half yellow, falling to the feet, and a large round hat, with points running out at the side. In England they might call them beadles, but it is difficult to find an exactly corresponding office, and we have therefore no appropriate appellation.

These important and very serious-looking personages carry the official seals, the keys of the archives, the sword of justice, and a staff surmounted by a globe, upon which is an apple upon the point of an arrow. Then follow the chief magistrates on horseback in their black silk mantles, and bearing a sword ; and lastly, counsellors and other citizens.

The seats for the assembly are arranged in a semicircle, and a large concourse being already seated, at the approach of the imposing *cortége* they rise and uncover their heads. On a table in front are the statute-books, and there the Land Weibel deposit the seals and keys, which are enclosed in a bag, also bearing the cantonal colours. Beside them is the ancient knife or sword used by the venerated heroes, and now the emblem of peace.

The officials take their places upon a platform, and the musicians play an air known as the "*Old Song of Tell.*"

The session is opened by the chief magistrate, who is denominated *Landamman*, with a speech recalling the principal events of their history, the blessings they at present enjoy, and, reviewing the past year, finishes with an allusion to their obligations to God as their divine benefactor, and the necessity of imploring his aid for the future; when all kneel down for a few moments in silent prayer. This is a most affecting and beautiful sight, so evident is the sincerity and depth of their devotion; and not the least attractive feature of the occasion are the children, who are placed in front of the platform within the circle, in order to be early impressed with the importance of republican virtue, and who are during the whole ceremony profoundly attentive. Women are allowed to be present, but not within, among their lords; they stand at a respectful distance without, but where they see and hear all that passes.

A month before the meeting, seven honorable citizens, each of a different family, are commissioned to prepare any resolutions, or propose any new measures of government. The first act of business for the day is for the Landamman to place these, if furnished, in order before the people. Every one is allowed to speak upon their merits, and to make any new propositions, and the discussions are often loud and stormy. When the vote is called, those who are for the affirmative hold up their hands, and when the negatives are counted, and there seems still a doubt, each party marches in single file before the table separately and the numbers are counted. A majority of one is sufficient to establish a law.

When all business is finished, the reigning Landamman renders an account of his magistracy, and asks if the people are satisfied with his administration. Being assured of this by loud applause, he steps forward and lays down his seal of office. All the other officials follow his example, and take their seats in the midst of the assembly. For a little time there is a profound silence, intended to be emblematic of the power of the people to govern themselves, when there is no visible government, no hand holding the reins. Then follows a little farce of mock licence, because they have no rulers and can do what they please, which speedily subsides into order, and the election of new officers commences.

The oldest person who has held the office of Landamman is invited to name a successor to him who has just retired, and often one of the most obscure among the citizens is nominated for this office and elected. The same person may be re-elected any number of times, if they choose, but it is not often done without an interval. In honour to Walter Furst they chose the chief magistrate from the family of Attinghausen for nearly a century.

When all the officers are elected, of whom the principal are twelve in number, they resume the places of those who resigned, and take the keys and seals in the order in which they were laid down. The oaths of office are then administered, in which they swear to respect the laws and the independence of the country, and the assembly disperses. It is very seldom that this solemnity and order are in the least infringed. A portion of the people indulge in games and songs, but there is a proverb, that "Uri is the conscience of Switzerland," and crimes and misdemeanours occur more seldom here than elsewhere.

They are superstitious, and have a thousand legends concerning the "genii" who inhabit the mountains, and who, they believe, dispel the storms and rule the tempests, watch over the fountains and render fruitful the fields. Their language is exceedingly poetic in relating these stories, and the flowers of rhetoric abound in the speeches of their magistrates, and even in the records of their statute books.

It is not known that they were originally the same people as the neighbouring cantons. Their traditions date to the time of the Emperor Theodosius, and a document in their archives, granting them peculiar privileges, bears the seal of Charlemagne. They were originally called *Taurisci*, probably from *taurus*, the Latin for bull, and the Romans may have found the formidable horns already on their armour. The men are still called the finest in Switzerland; yet, in many places, deformity and sickness appear as the consequence of bad food and unhealthy air. Meat is very rare; the various preparations of milk and cheese being the principal sustenance of the poor; and there live many who see nothing all winter but porridge, and all summer but goat's milk.

The dress was formerly blue small clothes and long white stockings, fastened together by leather cords and buttons, red vest and a leathern girdle, with the date of the year upon it when it was made, in colours wrought with a needle. Some wear a broad-brimmed hat ornamented with peacock's feathers. But now they have universally adopted the dress of men in all lands. Among the women, as usual, the ancient costume is preserved longer, though much modified. Still one may see now and then the red petticoat and red stockings of the olden times, the low bodice and full chemisette, with crimped cap-frill standing up on the head like the shell of the nautilus, and the little square collars and silver chains which form part of almost every costume in Switzerland. The collar is usually of velvet, wrought in silver flowers, or, among the poor, with coloured threads, square on the shoulder, and the chain of silver among the rich, and of steel among the poor, fastens to each corner behind, and is brought under the arm, hanging loosely, and meets a broad clasp on the corner in front. When the whole dress is neat and corresponds, it has a very pretty effect. We heard one day a loud clatter, clatter, through the street, and on looking closely saw a group of girls with sandals on their feet. They are made of maple wood, very large, and, slipping at every step, are like so many blows upon the pavement.

The people are subject to all sorts of casualties, which must be a continual drain upon their means. We were passing from village to village one afternoon, and as we were riding leisurely along, several men called out *halt !* at the top of their voices ; and upon *halting*, we learned that the road was stopped up by a *land-slide*, which had occurred only a few hours before, and which could have buried us beneath its mass of stone and mud if we had been happening to pass at the time. All travellers must go far round another way till it was mended, and this would require several days. These land-slides are frequent after a rain, and avalanches are of daily occurrence during the season of snow.

The pass of the St. Gotthard belongs to Uri and Tessin on the south side of the Alps. The first person who ever crossed it was an English mineralogist, July 25th, 1725. The second person was another Englishman, in 1773, who required the aid of four horses and eight men ; and the expense of going from Altdorf to Giornico was one hundred and thirty dollars. The path was improved, and became a great route for transport by means of mules, and yielded an annual revenue of more than eight thousand five hundred dollars to Uri alone. When the Simplon was finished in 1806, the St. Gotthard was abandoned, and the people saw their only source of industry cut off, unless they could build a similar road, which they resolved to do. It was a marvellous undertaking for Napoleon, and still more marvellous for the little Canton Uri to construct a carriage-way to Italy. But in 1820 in was commenced, and ten years later, in 1830, it was opened; other cantons having contributed to the work, and a native of Altdorf being the engineer. In 1837, nearly one third of it was swept away by a terrible storm, and in 1839 it experienced again a similar calamity. It leads the travellers through some of the finest scenery in Switzerland, and passes scenes of the most interesting historical associations, but the village of Andermatt, on the meadows, is the only one of importance for many miles, and the old hospice at the foot of the mountain was for centuries the only place of entertainment. Now there are hotels, but we cannot call them good.

The meadow must have been once a lake, and the grass is still nourished by a moisture that gives it a peculiar brightness. The butter which it produces is also of a peculiar golden hue, and the cheese of unequalled richness.

The snows last till April, and they have a proverb which says "No April so good that each hedge has not its hat." It is melted usually by the *faun*, a hot wind which blows from the south, and causes the drifted masses to disappear more in twenty-four hours, than the sun in eight days. It often continues in one current for a week without cessation, and sometimes with such violence that houses are unroofed and trees torn up by the roots. But at the same time it is so warm that the buds open into flowers in a few days, and are afterwards chilled by a wind from the west, thus blighting the hopes of the husbandman. Nine tenths of the storms come from the west. The *faun* is felt as far north as Zurich, and the rules of wind and weather baffle the wisest prophets concerning their freaks. The changes from cold to heat are almost instantaneous, and the barometer and thermometer run a race, but in opposite directions. It is scarcely possible to keep a fire while it lasts, as the flames are so suddenly increased as to endanger the buildings, and there is no certainty when it will appear.

But the " brave men of Uri" rise superior to all calamities, and where there is so high an appreciation of noble deeds there must be still the capacity to perform them. They have not many great names upon the scrolls which record the works of art in the quiet days of peace, though the sculptor Inrihof, long known at Rome, was a native of Uri ; and a poet, a historian, and a painter, have originated in three of their most secluded villages. The war-trumpet would be sure to call out their energies, but we hope it will be long ere its notes fall on their ears, and that ambition will be awakened to rivalry in not less honourable but more useful paths.

CHAPTER III.

SCHWYTZ.

ORIGIN OF PEOPLE—BRUNNEN—DILIGENCE—HOTELS—COSTUMES—IMPROVEMENTS—EINSIEDELN—PILGRIMS—LEGENDS.

IN Schwytz the people have a legend concerning their origin, which says, "Long ago, a colony from Sweden left their country because they had become too many, and there was no more room in the land. Their destination was Rome, but a wild storm which swept down the St. Gotthard prevented their crossing, and being also overtaken by robbers, and though victorious, much weakened by the combat, they resolved to settle farther north. Brunnen seemed to them a pleasant valley, and they found there good springs of water. It reminded them of the home they had left, and they built their huts by the sea. The question arose, what name they should give the new land, and two brothers wishing to baptize it, each with his own, had a fearful dispute, and at length concluded to settle the matter by single combat, the one who should be victorious acquiring the right to the coveted honour. *Schioit* and *Scheiz* were the competitors, and the first being crowned victor, with a little variation, his name has become that of a whole people."

There must be some foundation for the story, as it is commemorated by art as well as by song, and the two men of "giant form" and "giant mould" engaged in deadly strife are painted on the stuccoed walls of a warehouse on the shore of the lake, and its authenticity admits not a doubt in the minds of the narrators. The legend proceeds to state that Louis the German being emperor, they sent deputies to ask permission to settle in the land, which he granted, and also accorded to them many privileges; requiring no tribute, and promising that no foreign bailiffs should be sent to rule over them. The history recognizes their existence, and speaks of a similar deputation which took place in the ninth century. These privileges were confirmed by successive emperors, till they were looked upon as rights. They had enjoyed freedom so long that bondage was not endurable; and when the attempt was made by Albert, son of Rudolph of Hapsburg, to subdue them as an inheritance for his son, they revolted, and with their sister cantons of the lake formed the alliance which resulted in the "Helvetian Confederacy." This treaty was renewed in 1315, and those who formed it are also represented in full-length frescoes upon the walls of the same house by the sea. In 1815, was celebrated at Schwytz, the five hundredth anniversary of this union, when the people from every mountain and valley came with their banners and their songs to hold a glad festival together in the cradle of their liberties.

Brunnen seemed to us also a "pleasant valley," and we tarried there many days. We rose early to see the sun shed his golden light upon the waters, and sat long into the night to watch the moonbeams gild the ripples, and once saw them lashed into fury by a storm which sent them dashing and foaming against the rocks as if some mad spirit moved them with a living rage. And whether in sunshine or in storm, our thoughts wandered back to the little boat which darted over its surface impelled by the strong arm of the hero, in whose breast was a storm as wild, as he swore revenge and death to the hated oppressor. Now there are a hundred boats with their oars dipping leisurely as they glide along, and gay, laughing maidens are the rowers.

Four times a day steamers pass by, on one of which are painted the arms of the four cantons which border the lake, and over which waves the flag of the Confederacy. They are gay with many colours, like a fair maiden in holiday costume, and their decks thronged with pleasure-seeking travellers. Brunnen is the *dépôt* for the merchandise which is to pass the St. Gotthard, or which is brought over and destined for the north. Travellers from the north and east come also this way to embark for Lucerne, or to cross the mountains, so that all summer the wharf presents one scene of bustle and hum of business and pleasure.

In no other canton have we so pleasant remembrances of the kindness of the people. We now and then took a fancy to pass *incognito*, not understanding why we should not avail ourselves of this privilege as well as any princess or duchess, though it might not be for the same reason. We converted our name into a German one, by the addition of a syllable, and spoke the language of the people among whom we happened to be as well as we could. If Germans did not understand us, they concluded it was because we were Swiss, and if the Swiss did not understand us, they concluded it was because we were German, or from some outlandish corner, the dialect of which they had never heard ; and we allowed them to think what they pleased, never asserting that we were from one country or another, though we are quite certain they took us now and then to be fugitives from some rebellious colony, or emissaries from Austrian or Napoleonic head-quarters, these personages being at that time sufficiently abundant in many lands. The true nature of our embassy it would never occur to them to imagine ; but our adventures were many and amusing, though neither duchess nor spy. The obliging and lady-like hostess of the "*Post*" could not have treated us with more attention had we been empress, and without manifesting the least inquisitiveness concerning our "name and station, age, or race." No book was presented us, in which to record whence we came and whither we were going; every favour was granted that we asked, and many that we did not ask ; and the bill contained no long list of extras, and was in all things just and reasonable. She was a lady in her dress and manners, everywhere present in the sphere of her duties, attentive without being obsequious, generous in what she furnished, and without exaction in what she required. Guidebooks, which are no guide at all in these matters, do not mention it as among the "first-rate hotels," but it was among the best we found, and we therefore commend it, though they did not know, and probably never will, that we could thus reward them.*

---

* It was after this that we spent some weeks at the *Pension Jaggi* near Berne, and should be guilty of injustice not to record the sterling integrity of the old lady who has been for so many years its presiding genius. Her fault was always to forget the *items*, and we have heard those who had known her in the capacity of landlady nearly twenty years, assert that not the most captious traveller ever accused her of injustice or exaction to the amount of a centime.

"One good price, and done with it," is her rule, and she abides by it. She pays her servants, and they attend to her guests not less kindly than those who demand a fee

"Hotel keeping" is a peculiar institution in Switzerland, and cannot be passed by in silence. The charges are, as elsewhere on the Continent, so much for every item, however large or small it may be ; but in most places one may stay a few days or weeks as a boarder, paying so much per day, a sum expected to be less than when reckoned by the piece. As a general rule, it may be said of these hotels and boarding houses that they are good and reasonable. But the system of charging by the piece can never be just, and the custom of demanding "Trinkgeld," in addition to the bill, is a fraud, especially when most of the travellers belong to nations who do not understand the language and habits of the people.

One can never know with any degree of precision what the expense in any place may be. When the first sum is mentioned, in answer to the inquiry, "How much must I pay?" it seems small ; but when you have paid all the just and unjust *extras*, it is larger than in an ordinary hotel, where the whole sum is given directly and sounds enormous. Besides, it affords opportunities of making false accounts, which are abundantly improved. English people seldom read a bill, and in a great proportion of cases could not if they would. What the long string of items may be which they find presented for payment, they do not know ; and travelling for pleasure, and being in a hurry, they do not care. Yet now and then one takes the trouble to decipher the hieroglyphics, and often finds an enumeration of comforts and luxuries of which he has had no actual experience. One is always sure to be a candle charged three times its cost, when only an inch or two has been burned. They are thus able to

for every step. In this way there is no misunderstanding, and no petty disputes about a few pennyworths, which many people will dispute about, not for the value of a penny, but because they will not submit to injustice.

sell it over and over, and must find tallow, soap and spermaceti among the most profitable of their investments. We have seen travellers, who, having paid for the candle and soap, put it in their bags, and at the next place "found themselves," till they were obliged to purchase more in the same way. Another item is "*service*," being twenty, and often forty cents for merely the ordinary preparations in your sleeping-room, and which is no substitute for the "trinkgeld," which is as much more, and which if you refuse, your baggage is seized, and twenty servants stand in array to *fight it out*. They know you must yield, because it is a trifle compared to being delayed on a journey, and few people care to expose themselves to a public quarrel, the rights of which cannot be explained.

On the summit of the Righi, one may arrive at midnight and leave at sunrise, not seeing a servant, or having the least attention, yet the "service" is just the same. The hotel is good, and the arrangements marvellous to behold, when one considers that every article of food and furniture must be carried up on the shoulders of men; and during the season, the saloon and dining-hall present a scene like that of Baden-Baden. No reasonable person would be disposed to complain of a generous price in such a place. But why not have a uniform one, that allows every one to know what the expense may be of spending a night or a week on the Righi?

The deceptions concerning guides are the same. You are told that for a guide and horse you must pay four dollars; and having had no experience in this system of fraud, you suppose this the whole sum. When you descend, nearly a dollar more is demanded for "*Trinkgeld.*" At the foot of the Reghi we saw this disputed, and a quarrel was the consequence. The party were detained too late for the boat, and had to pay it in the end.

The law fixes the *tariff* for guides and horses, which is placed in a conspicuous place for all to read, but there is no mention of the " *Trinkgeld* " which is often demanded by the hotel keeper, and never a cent of it given to the guide. In our case,* the hotel keeper kept only half, and knowing that we were to leave in a hurry, the boat being in sight, he contrived to delay presenting the bill till the last moment, and looking only at the items, without adding them, we did not observe till the next day that several extra francs were set down without even the pretence of an item. The same thing is often done, and so successfully, that they have no fear of detection.

Another principle, both in hotel and shop-keeping, is, to charge all who speak English, a third more than any other people. A Swiss lady, who had married an Englishman, said she was no longer in favour in her native city among the tradespeople, because they could not cheat her husband as they had been doing for many years. But this is the practice over the whole Continent. We have seen the experiment tried very often of asking prices, within the same hour concerning the same articles, by a native and an Englishman, and the difference would be always a third, and sometimes one half. Every year brings a new throng, and they are all in the same hurry. Forty thousand is the average number annually in the public conveyances of Switzerland, and the season scarcely three months in duration. They wish, therefore, to make as much as possible, and are tempted to all unlawful as well as lawful means. But these are the sins of an individual, or a class, and not of the whole people ; and lately there have been formed associations among hotel keepers to prevent fraud and exaction. There is nothing demanded by the government for passports ; and postage and

* Lion d'or—Weggis.

telegrams are cheaper than in any other country of Europe. Neither in diligence nor railroad is any one allowed to smoke without the consent of the whole company, and the facilities for travelling with speed and comfort are carried to the greatest possible perfection.

"First come, first served," is the rule in the great coach, which still goes rattling over the hills and through the valleys, and the best seat is in the *coupé* in front, as there is nothing to obstruct the view, and there is room for only three persons. People who are only desirous of seeing the most wonderful scenery, can reach the important points in Canton Schwytz by steamboat and railway, and thus avoid the diligence. But our object being the reverse, we took the diligence and avoided the railway. It was only by this means that we could see the villages and their inhabitants.

The people being Catholic, and the life pastoral, they are very similar, in many respects, to their sisters Uri and Unterwald. "In the times that tried men's souls," they were not less brave; and in peace, they were as content with their rural retirements and simplicity.

Innovations march slowly among the mountains; yet Paris fashion plates have found their way into almost every hut and hamlet. The original dress of the men was similar to that in Unterwald, consisting of black leather small clothes, white stockings, scarlet vest, and blue or brown jacket reaching to the knee, and open in front. In olden times, the government officers wore scarlet mantles and perrucks, small clothes, with red coat, having many folds, reaching to the knee, and four sleeves, two of them hanging very loose, like those of Roman lictors. But now this is the dress of the standard-bearers and *Landweibel*, the officials appearing in black like other burghers, with only the addition of mantles of the same colour for state occasions.

The red petticoat and variegated apron have almost entirely disappeared ; but the jaunty straw hat, with bouquets of flowers and knots of ribbons, may sometimes be seen, with the long braids of hair interwoven with red, and brought down on each side of the neck in front. The bodice is usually of black, instead of blue, with scarlet lacings ; and the velvet collar has taken the place of the parti-coloured neckkerchief. Among a great portion, there is no remnant of the former costume ; and in some places it has all disappeared except the cap, which is always the last to be given up. It consists of two wings, like a butterfly, spread out each side, and the hair brought up between in braids, and fastened with a silver or gilt hair-pin in the form of a full-blown rose, and called *rose hair-pin*. Others wear the lace comb, elsewhere described, standing up so high, that in church or public assembly there is such a forest of caps that the speaker is entirely concealed from those behind. The nuns wear black and white veils, so thick that a pretty face is entirely concealed by them.

We have never passed through a Swiss village without seeing a carpenter at work on the houses ; and here and there some clapboards, some new shingles or window-frames, a new portico, or something that indicated a little improvement or the spirit of progress. In almost every village there are all grades from rich to poor, and the *striving to rise* which it is always pleasant to observe among human beings.

One of their authors says, six hundred years ago, Gessler was jealous of a peasant because he had a fine house. A little later it was the peasants who were jealous of each other ; but now a new or fine house is no object of wonder or envy, they have become so common. Among the poorest they are still old and old-fashioned, with the great overhanging roofs, without chimneys and without paint—not an object for envy even in their best days. The kitchen is dark, the great stove occupies a third of its space, and around it coo with the same familiarity a family of children and a family of doves. The great sofa, when it is clean, is the only comfortable-looking article, and is duly appreciated. There rest the elders from their labours, and tumble the little ones in their play. It is the throne whence issue all orders—the council-chamber where plans are made and politics discussed. But the new houses are pretty, often white, with green blinds. There are not many very rich, and there are many very poor in the land. The canton is forty square leagues in extent, and has 44,000 inhabitants, with no city, and in the largest village only 3,000 people. They are so proud of the past that they do not think enough of the present and the future.

Nearly everywhere we were almost the only passenger in the diligence, and occupied the *coupé* with the postilions. We saw at once that they had no faith in our *incognito*, but did not feel bound to remove their doubts, though if we had they might possibly have been more communicative. As it was, they were evidently afraid of betraying their country.

It was here that we first saw the pilgrims on their way to Einsiedeln. The first group we noticed had come all the way from the Tyrol. How poor and miserable, careworn and travel-stained they looked! What a strange infatuation that prompts them to seek comfort for this life and salvation for the future in the mummeries of a few monks in an old cloister! We were also on our way thither, though for a different purpose. It is the saddest of all the scenes in this pleasant land, yet we cannot pass it by.

Einsiedeln is the most renowned resort of pilgrims, not only in Switzerland, but for all middle Europe. The throng every year is still 150,000, and last year it was said to reach a higher number than ever before, though in 1700 it is stated to have been 202,000, and in 1710, the incredible number of 260,000.

The legend of the abbey, as given by the monks and credited by the pilgrims, is, that in the days of Charlemagne, a hermit of the noble family of Hohenzollern repaired to this remote wilderness, then called "Finsterwald," to end his days in solitude and prayer, devoting himself to the care of a small black image of the Virgin, which had been given him by St. Hildegarde, then Abbess of Zurich. In 803 he was murdered; but two pet ravens which he had reared, pursued the murderers as far as Zurich, and by croaking and flapping their wings attracted attention to them, thus causing their arrest. Afterwards they were executed on a spot where now stands the Raven Inn.

Meinrad, the hermit, had lived in a cell, but the renown of his sanctity prompted Erberard, another count of the same noble family, to found a convent upon the place; and he obtained from the emperor the grant of large tracts of waste land as an endowment. On the 14th of September, 948, the Bishop of Constance was to consecrate the church, but the night previous he was awakened by angelic minstrelsy, and in the morning received a message from heaven, that the consecration had already been performed by the Saviour and powers of heaven. Pope Leon VIII. pronounced it a true miracle, and in consideration of it granted plenary indulgence to all pilgrims who should wend their way to the shrine of *Our Lady of the Hermit!* He probably expected his command to take effect only for a few years, or during his lifetime, but the most ambitious of popes never dreamed that for nine centuries these worthless words would preserve their charm, and millions of people really believe they could blot out their sins by obeying his false and sacrilegious mandate. It is no slander to say, that a great proportion of those who come now have not even so good an object as this.

The 14th of September is still the day for the largest assembly, and presents the strangest concourse to be seen in any time, or season, or country; all languages and all manners, all costumes and all colours, being blended in the most inharmonious confusion. There are tents for pilgrims and booths for trade; devotees at their shrines, and jockeys at their stalls; the prayers of the pious and the curses of the profane; revelry, drunkenness, and debauchery; the gaudy trappings of the rich, and the beggarly rags of the poor, the grey old monks in their cowls, and the lisping children at their feet, all coming and going to fall on their knees before a little black image enshrined within the church, called the "Virgin and Child." There is never an hour in the year, perhaps, that some one is not muttering *Ave Marias* on the cold stones before this senseless object; and at many seasons there are hundreds, and sometimes thousands, prostrate together, all really believing when they rise that their sins have been pardoned. What a power in faith! Unless God has taken pity upon their ignorance and superstition, no influence from without has been exerted on their souls, yet they feel no longer the burden of transgression; but if sin really weighs upon their consciences, they must in many cases be more heavily laden when they go than when they came, but being rid of one load they are better able, perhaps, to carry another.

Zwinglius was curate in Einsiedeln from 1516 to 1519, and commenced preaching the reformatory doctrines to the pilgrims, and had the pleasure of seeing many adopt the true faith who had come there trusting to the efficacy of popish indulgences.

But the pilgrim shrines and the gory plains of Italy are almost enough to stagger one's faith in the efficacy of any means for spreading the pure principles of the Gospel of peace and righteousness.

The personal influence of the priesthood is much greater in Catholic Switzerland than in Germany at the present time, and the difference in those of the two faiths is far greater. Yet the people have never allowed pope and Church to trammel their political freedom. When fairly convinced that their cause was right, they defied all *bans* and prohibitions, till the politic holy father learned to go " so far and no farther " if he would retain a remnant among them as his loyal worshippers—his subjects they have never been.

In the canton there are six convents, three of which are for women, and thirty parishes. There is a school in every commune, and the priests are in many instances the schoolmasters; but instruction is not gratuitous in all, and except in the larger towns there is no attempt to keep the children together in the winter, and those who are on the hills in summer have of course very little opportunity for study. There is still among the people of the rural districts, isolated from the travelling world, much of the simplicity and confidence of the olden time, when, if a neighbour wanted anything in the storehouse or pantry of another, he took it and paid when it became convenient. The cellar and milkroom had no locks, and if some one needed milk or cream in the night, he entered and helped himself and left the money under the pan.

We can never forget the bright merry face of a maiden we met one day in our walks. We had acted in the spirit of primeval confidence, whether it would be approved now or not, and seated ourselves in a rustic arbour overlooking a beautiful landscape, knowing very well that if it belonged to a prince or nobleman we were committing an unpardonable offence. In a few moments two young girls passed by, and one looked in, and with most respectful manner said, "Good evening," according to the custom of her people, whether they meet friend or stranger. According to our custom we answered still more cordially, and she walked in and seated herself, saying, "It was very pleasant." There was neither embarrassment nor familiarity. We talked an hour together and then took a walk. She chattered all the time like a magpie, not seeming once to have the feeling that we were strangers, and her face was like the reflection of sunbeams on the water, so radiant that it had the power of a charm, riveting our eyes at the time and riveting our thoughts ever since. She was seventeen years old, she said, but appeared two years younger. She could not read, because she had been sick all her life, and knew nothing beyond the affairs of her native village. Her ease and naturalness were in consequence of her ignorance, like that of a child who has never learned the *art* of politeness. If she were not talking she laughed in the same careless way; was earnest if she spoke of anything serious; and we could not help thinking, if the village were full of such maidens, no wonder the shepherds are content. She belonged to the Muottothal, where we afterwards learned that this nobility and brightness of the face was characteristic of the people, where they are never sad, whatever may happen and however great their misfortunes, and say they are descended from the Goths, who were expelled from Italy in the sixth century. We would go very far to look again on such a countenance.

The chapel of *Our Lady of the Snow* upon the Righi is also the resort of pilgrims, who still trust to the indulgence promised in 1700 to all who should ascend and assist at a *fête* in honor of the Virgin. On the 8th of September, the day of the Nativity, every path to the mountain is thronged, and for more than half a century pilgrims were the only worshippers who climbed the dizzy heights. Now there are ten thousand every year, worshippers of nature; and the imagination cannot conceive anything more lovely than the view presented from the *Righi Culm*, when "the sun goes into gold," as they express it, or rises on a cloudless morning.

This and the neighbouring mountains are covered with a network of legends connected with their religion or their history; and we have heard stories of *pigmies* which were word for word like those to which we have listened in Indian wigwams.* They are represented as *little folk* with long silver beard and hair reaching to the earth, and wearing green coats and little caps. They were the special protectors of the chamois of the hills and the fish of the sea, and all who trespassed upon their dominions were sure to experience their revenge. They lived in subterranean dwellings, and came forth like apparitions and vanished as quickly.

---

* In this or any similar remark we do not intend to compare the people to Indians, here or in Germany, though, as far as our own opinions are concerned, we could not pay them a greater compliment than by so doing. But it would be an unpardonable negligence not to state a resemblance like this where intercommunication could never have existed, and when there is no proof or suspicion of a similar origin.

CHAPTER IV.

UNTERWALD.

ALPINE PASTURES—SENNHUTTEN—CHEESE-MAKING—COWS AND THEIR BELLS
—ALPINE FESTIVALS—AGRICULTURE—FETES.

"The pious Unterwalders." This is not only an appellation by which they are well known, but one by which it pleases them to be designated. Nowhere else in Switzerland are the emblems of their faith so thickly strewn on mountain and in valley. The cross reminds one at almost every step of Him who bore it, and here and there in every valley are little niches cut in the trunks of trees, with some image of saint or virgin imbedded gracefully in foliage, and often women kneeling before them with a chaplet in their hands. High up on the Alps are seen the little chapels for the use of the shepherds, for, like the people of Schwytz and Uri, they too are a pastoral people.

So early as 1308, they date their present laws concerning the Alpine pastures, and know that so long before this time that there is concerning it no record or tradition, here the shepherds fed their flocks. One can scarcely believe that those almost inaccessible heights and frightful gorges are measured and allotted with the exactness of a field or garden, and yet every cow has her appointed hill-top, and a goat may, at his peril, go browsing beyond his neighbour's limits. In different cantons the Alps are subject to different laws ; in some, as in Uri and Schwytz, belonging to the whole land, or as in Unterwald to communes and individuals, and the different pastures have names according to their respective merits.

The term Alps is not applied in Switzerland to all the mountains as we see it in books and hear it from strangers. Here it is used to designate the pastures, and they are divided into *Forealps* and *Highalps*. The high Alps are the loftiest verdure-clad mountains, where the cows can remain only six or seven weeks in the middle of summer, and in some places only three or four. These are considered the best for milk cows. The fore Alps are the pastures lying along the base of the mountain, and in which the cows remain for some weeks before and after their sojourn in their summer residence.

Individuals who own Alps either use them exclusively for their own cattle or rent them to those who have none, receiving for each cow a certain amount of money, or a certain quantity of milk, butter, and cheese. The pastures owned by communes are exactly measured and rented to so many cattle as can be nourished within the prescribed limits. For instance, so many square rods are considered necessary for a cow, and so many for an ox, a goat, a sheep, a horse or colt. The value of the land and animals is estimated, and a fixed interest paid for each. According to the amount of interest are the agreements concerning the building of the huts, furnishing the apparatus for making cheese, etc. If the interest demanded is small, the shepherd is expected to provide these himself; but if he pays only a small interest, the owner of the pasture furnishes at least a portion of the conveniences.

The persons who take care of the herds have names for which there is no equivalent in other languages. The principal person is denominated a *Senn*. He remains always by the hut, and takes the whole care of the milk. The *Vice-Senn* is next in rank and honour, and attends to transporting the products of the dairy, to supplying the establishment with fuel, and all that they need extra in the way of food. The third person is a sort of *Valet*, who waits upon them, and runs here and there, goes to the valleys, if necessary, and does all the cleaning outdoors and within the hut. Besides there is a cow-boy, who runs for the cows, and drives them to pasture; and if there are sheep, a shepherd is added to the company, who is in some parts called also a *Watcher*.

The hut of the Alpine shepherd cannot have changed in a thousand years, for no time, however primitive, can have seen it more simple than it is now. *Sennhütten* is the German word, and *Châlets* the French, for all those which are occupied by cheese-makers, whether they are large or small. Those which we see on the mountain heights are of logs, notched at the ends to fit together, with a roof of the same, or of shingles, kept in their places by stones. They are accessible to both wind and rain, and having no chimney, they are black with smoke, and make no pretensions to cleanliness. The milk-room is partly underground, and very dark, and so constructed, that, if possible, it may be kept cool by rills of running water. In the principal room a fireplace is made by digging a cavity in the earth and paving it with stones, and through a hole in the roof the smoke makes its exit, unless, driven by a contrary wind or its own evil propensities, it chooses to spread itself through the room, which is generally the case. Over the fire is a great copper cauldron, in which the milk is always warmed before it is converted into Swiss cheese. They put in the rennet, and stir it continually for half an hour, till it is curdled. One end of a cheese strainer is held over the edge of the cauldron, and with the other the senn dips up the curds, drains them a little, and puts them immediately in the press. It is no such long process as we have seen in other countries, where the "*milk is set over night*," and perhaps does not appear in the form of curds till the middle of the next day. The hurried process, and warming of the milk, makes the cheese hard, and give it a taste which our palate utterly refused to call good. By no possible training could we learn to eat cheese in Switzerland, notwithstanding their great renown. In the same smoky room with the great kettle, stands a tub for whey and a butter-tub ; on two poles hang the milk-pails, and on a bench stands a pail for the whey they drink instead of water. They wash the milk apparatus in whey, and often even their own clothes. Dippers spoons, and ladles lie upon a table, and there is still another tub to receive the milk, till the foam is settled.

There is a third apartment for a few pigs, which are fattened on the refuse of the milk-room, and over this a floor for a sleeping-room, where all throw themselves upon hay, and can, if they are sufficiently sentimental, contemplate the stars through the crevices in the roof.

One senn can take care of forty or fifty cows, yet there are many who have only ten or twenty. They must rise with the first ray of dawn, and with the utmost diligence cannot finish the morning's labour till nearly noon ; and after the second milking, late in the afternoon, all is again to be repeated. The assistants and cow-boy must be out in all weathers ; and from the day they ascend till they are fairly down in the valleys again, there is no rest.

The cheeses are everywhere of two kinds, *fat* and *meagre*. Into the fat ones they put all the cream, and the meagre are made of skimmed milk, or that from which part of the cream has been removed. In the whole Canton of Unterwald are made more than twenty thousand hundredweights of cheese every year, each cheese weighing from twenty-two to thirty-two pounds, and the average price being from seven to nine dollars a hundredweight.

Besides butter and cheese they have five or six preparations from milk and whey, made by different processes of boiling and curdling, and which they denominate Zieger, Suffi, Schotte, Siste, etc., and with these, many of them make all the variations of breakfast, dinner, and supper, which they know.

It is no slight labour to turn the great cheeses every day; and the salt, instead of being put in the milk or curds, is sprinkled on the outside and rubbed in with a stiff brush. "The cheese tastes much better," they say, "when the salt penetrates it from without." As it seems to us to taste horribly as it is, we cannot tell how much worse it would be if the salt penetrated it from within, though we are well aware that in our opinion we are differing from epicures in all the civilized world.

In Unterwald the Alps are known by their names, and the number belonging to individuals which can be specified in this way are nearly two hundred, and those belonging to communes, one hundred and seventy.

Besides these are the *Allmenden*, or meadows where those pasture cows who do not use the Alps, and who sell the milk in villages, or which are perhaps used by sennen who remain in the valleys. Still another kind are the *Rieder*, or marshy lands, which are worth very little; the hay which is cut on them selling for fifty cents a hundredweight. They are beginning to make them more profitable by draining.

We see the people everywhere on the mountains gathering *wild hay*, which grows in places utterly inaccessible to cows and goats, and which women and children reach at the risk of their lives. They make it into large bundles, and toss it down into the valley, and then carry it on their backs to the little stalls or barns, which are scattered over the hills for the purpose of storing it. There are often severe storms even in summer, when the cattle cannot feed in the pastures, but must be housed and fed ; and often an early snow comes, which obliges them to keep under shelter many days.

We have enumerated the general features of shepherd life, but shall now and then allude to slight variations in the different cantons.

In all the Alps of Unterwald one hears at early morning and evening the call of the shepherd to prayers. He on whom the office devolves, stands always in the same place, and by means of his Alpine horn, a sort of tunnel-shaped tube of wood, rings a peculiar series of changes, which echo far and wide, with a shrillness which only the mountain air can give. The moment it is heard, all commence their evening orisons, which sometimes consist of a few verses from the fourteenth chapter of St. John, or " Our Father who art in heaven," or " Praise God the Lord." If they are near a chapel, they enter ; if not, they kneel upon the rocks.

The *Ranz des Vaches* echo from every Alpine height ; but no idea can be conveyed in words of the peculiarity of these mountain choruses. They are not tunes or melodies, and are not governed by the ordinary rules of music ; yet they have rules, and in their native air are thrilling beyond description. There is very little motion of the lips or mouth, and the breathing is scarcely perceptible. Their character varies in different parts of Switzerland, and corresponds to the character of the people, and also of individuals, being gay and lively, or sad and melancholy, with the temperament of the singer and the occasion which calls them forth. Sometimes two or three sing together, and keep time and tune, but it is not usual. It is the song of the solitary shepherd on the hills, and invented not for communication with men, but with the animals, who are his life-companions. The literal translation of the French and German word is *cow rows*, and evidently refers to the manner in which the cows arrange themselves when coming at its call. Those who are in the habit of marching farthest have bells, and the moment they hear the *kuhreih* they wend their steps homewards, and are followed by all in a row.

When they ascend the mountains in the spring, or descend in the fall, it is the occasion of a grand *fête*, and they connect with it all that is possible of pomp, and show, and ceremony. For the largest and handsomest cow they have a large bell, which is selected with peculiar reference to its tone, and the two cows next to her in beauty are honoured with those a little smaller in size, but the tones of which are sure to chime with the larger one. They will sometimes pay from twenty-five to thirty dollars for a set of these bells, which is more than they would think they could spend for any article for their own adorning. These they are to wear only on *fête* occasions. They are hung upon an embroidered leathern band, and the cow whose neck receives the largest, immediately exhibits her consciousness of her rank and importance ; and though it is removed whilst she roams in the pastures, the honour it has conferred on her of *leading the row*, when they are called morning and evening, she never forgets, and should another attempt to assume this precedence, a regular battle follows, which the shepherd is often obliged to settle by placing the bell on her neck, that all may see that she is to be queen. She selects the best pastures, and beckons all to follow her steps. Yet it happens sometimes, that one, or two, or three cows remain during the whole summer rebellious, and are seen straying alone, in a way to show that they are jealous and dissatisfied, and acknowledge not the constituted authority.

When the morning arrives for going to the Alps, the senn, in his festival dress, and a milk-dipper slung over his shoulder, takes the lead, singing the *kuhreih* and followed by three or four beautiful goats. In striking contrast comes the queenly cow, with her proud, conscious air, making with the two who follow her a series of chimes with their clear-ringing bells, which they evidently appreciate and endeavour to regulate by their measured steps. Reversing the order of nature, the lord of the troop follows the ladies, but the milk-stool sitting high upon his horns gives him a distinguished air, with which he seems satisfied ; a sled, with all the cheese and butter-making apparatus, brings up the rear, and the young men and maidens, with wreaths and gay ribbons, dance, and eat whey and curds together, till setting day reminds them to descend to their homes in the valley.

In the autumn a similar *fête*, with additional ceremonies, takes place, when the whole troop returns for the winter.

The rivalry of the cows will seem a fiction to those who have not witnessed it, but it is mentioned by those who wrote hundreds of years ago, and will be confirmed by every shepherd of the Alps. If they remove the bell from the queen after having once placed it upon her neck, she is dispirited, and will not eat. If they give it to another, she hooks her and persecutes her till it is restored. When they have all been milked, no one ventures to move till she has marched forward; and when they return, she is first to receive the caress of their master, who pats her and talks to her as if she were human and could understand his words. That she appreciates his love is certain, for she will cross any chasm and encounter any danger to answer his call.

There is still, in the whole canton, no humming factory—no sound of hammer or loom. The products of their dairies are their only articles of commerce. In the winter they are employed in felling the trees and preparing them for firewood, and sell every year to the amount of fifteen to twenty-five thousand dollars' worth.

The cultivated land presents a curious appearance, being divided into regular patches in the neighbourhood of the villages, and rented to individuals. It may remain in the same family for centuries, who pay an annual tax for the privilege. There are fields of wheat, and the usual variety of oats, peas, beans, and cabbage. If one dies, or moves away, his *lot* falls to the commune, and is rented to another. The grass-land is rented in the same way, but the lots are often many acres in extent. Since their introduction, potatoes have become the principal food, instead of the porridge which formerly appeared morning and evening upon the peasant's table. Bread is improved by spreading upon it cheese, toasted until it is soft; but its digestion is considered so doubtful, even among themselves, that they call it *stomach plaister*, and in a song, its merits are wittily satirized as an invention to "hold body and soul together."

The people are entirely Catholic, and the little kettle of holy water hangs, not only by every chapel and at every churchyard gate, but in every house, for the purpose of crossing themselves; the people, however, are remarkably intelligent concerning their own history and government, and none are received to the communion who cannot read and write. The law requires all to attend school till they are twelve years of age ; and in the highschool at Engelberg are taught the usual branches of an accomplished education.

Religion enters into all their *fêtes*, and these are very many. The election takes place on the last Sunday in April, and with nearly the same ceremonies as in Uri ; the cantonal colours being white and red. They employ *runners* to carry into all parts of the canton the results of the election.

Their penalties for crimes and misdemeanors retain the simplicity of the olden time. Printed statute-books have yet no place in their judiciary system. They have no houses of correction for their own citizens, and say they are not rich enough to support foreign criminals who may fall among them. All who are considered incorrigible are banished, which is well for their own land, but not exactly "doing as they would be done by" for their neighbours. Sometimes the punishment is reversed, and persons are forbidden to leave the country or their own village for a certain number of years. Parents who do not "train their children in the way they should go," are placed upon a stone in a conspicuous place, with a rod in the right hand ; and formerly, every one who passed by was at liberty to use it upon their backs. So late as 1855, a father and mother were obliged to sit on this stone, with a paper fastened to them in front, on which was written, "Duty-forgetting Parents."

A person who stole a lamp was obliged to remain during service in church, under the lamp. Two children who had been guilty of stealing, were placed in close confinement every night, and for three years obliged to kneel in the same place during service on Sunday morning.

In 1855, a young girl who had been guilty of immorality, was obliged to kneel in church during three years in a certain place, and forbidden to leave the village on any occasion.

In 1851, a man who had with his wife been guilty of incendiarism, was condemned to solitary confinement eight years. Thinking it unjust and too severe, he ran away to Berne, to complain of his judges. The government of Berne reproved him for slandering his countrymen, and obliged him to stand on a stone in a public place a quarter of an hour with a *gag* in his mouth, and then to go home. The wife and accomplice was condemned to sit a quarter of an hour on the criminal stone, whilst the bells rang and the accusation was read against her, and to kneel, during Sunday service, in a conspicuous place, whilst the sermon was upon the sin of incendiarism; to spend two years in solitary confinement, and the next four years to attend divine service morning and afternoon on Sunday and every other festival day, and not allowed to participate in any of the duties and pleasures of honourable citizens. Often the punishment is merely to be publicly proclaimed "unworthy of respect." Whether it is owing to the nature of the punishments or the nature of the people, cannot be determined, but the crimes are few, and one can scarcely imagine anything more humiliating than these simple penalties.

In 1150, before the destruction of the feudal castles, the canton was divided into *Obwald* and *Nidwald*, and each had its peculiar customs. The cantonal arms (as the reader has seen at the head of this chapter) are *keys*—in Obwàld a simple one and in Nidwald a double one; but in their early history they were always united against the common enemy. In 1798, Nidwald was left to struggle almost alone, and stood 2,000 against 15,000 French. Being attacked at several points, and the victory becoming doubtful, old men, women and children marched forth, when the enemy became exasperated and delivered the land to fire and pillage. Among those who fell in battle were one hundred and two women and twenty-five children; and the loss of property, from all causes, was fifteen millions of dollars. What a destruction in a country only twelve square leagues in extent! A sixth part of the people were reduced to beggary. They were aided generally by their brethen in Obwald, and even by France herself after the war was over, to recover from their misfortunes. And it was at this time that the renowned *Pestalozzi* established a school in Stanz, the capital of the canton, beginning at first with eighty of these orphan children. Here he first tested his original method of teaching, which soon spread over Europe.

The guilds are retained merely as fraternal associations, and in Obwald one unites the members of all trades, holding only one annual festival. In Nidwald, the tailors and shoemakers recognize for their patron saint the Holy St. Crispin, and call themselves *Crispinians*. The patron saints of locksmiths and weavers, and all trades that "hammer and thump," are Holy Francis Xavier and Johann of Nepomuk. The Holy St. Joseph is the patron of silversmiths and goldbeaters; and all have their special days of celebration, usually in autumn or at the time of carnival.

St. Wendelin and St. Antoine are the protectors of shepherds, and their *fête*, as we have said, is on the return of the troops to the valleys. On Sunday, they place an image of their patron upon the altar; a sermon is preached in praise of pastoral life, and they march through the streets with music and colours, and bearing prodigious artificial bouquets. Three persons, disguised as "*genii of the mountains*," sweep the streets in advance of the procession with great branches of pine. The origin of these *wild men*, as they call them, is not known, but they probably date from the time when good and evil spirits were supposed to people earth and air and water. They all meet at an inn for a dinner, when speeches are made interweaving events of their history, and the *wild men* make a formal present to the Capuchins, who are always present, of two little cheeses, weighing about two pounds, and so dry and hard that they cannot be eaten, and receive gifts in return. After dinner, the procession forms again, and a distribution of valuable gifts is made to the poor. The second day are dances and other sports. The festival is called the "*Alperkilwi*."

The wrestling matches, which have become so famous, originated in Unterwald, and are still their especial national *fête*. On the 26th of July and the 10th of August, they assemble upon different heights of the Alps, and in the midst of a concourse of spectators perform various feats of wrestling, which require much skill and practice. There are ten methods of throwing an adversary. Each is allowed three trials, and he who brings his adversary upon his back twice in the three times, is victor. Their costume is but a slight addition to that of nature, as their limbs must be allowed the freest play. On meeting, they shake hands, and exchange congratulations and wishes of success. In one village of Berne and one of Luzerne are held similar *fêtes*, when wrestlers from the three cantons enter the lists as rivals.

There exist associations of women, who endeavor to understand the spiritual and mystical, called "Götti," and innumerable "brotherhoods," for all manner of study and pleasure, besides pilgrimages to Einsiedeln, with banners and crosses, and the ordinary festivals of the Catholic Church.

Some legend or superstition is linked with every village, valley, and chapel; and the land, not being so extensively rummaged by travellers, retains more of its primitive simplicity. Engelberg, they say, was formerly inhabited by evil spirits, who were driven forth by the angels, and thus received its name.

Drachenried, near Stanz, was once the abode of a monstrous serpent, which became so formidable that the inhabitants abandoned the valley and gave it the name of *Oedwyl*, a wilderness or desolate place. There had lived in the land a valiant man, who had distinguished himself in the wars and had been made chevalier, but having the misfortune to kill another in a duel, he was banished, as this was then a crime, because it deprived the state of a brave man. In his exile he heard of the ravages of the serpent, and begged permission to return upon condition that he should slay the monster. It was granted. He entered the valley, attacked the serpent, and finally destroyed him by thrusting a lance armed with thorns down his throat. But in the combat he received a wound which terminated his own life. A chapel was erected to his memory, and on its walls we read, To STRUTH VON WINKELRIED.

At certain times in the year, the names of all those who have fallen in battle or the service of their country are mentioned in church, that the youth may grow up with a knowledge of the sacrifices which purchased them their present blessings.

In Unterwald, one misses the milestones and sign-posts which in other parts of Switzerland stand by every high road and mountain path. When we ask, "Why is this?" they say, "It was the ancient law, that travellers should be guided on their way by the people free of charge." Whether it is the law now or not, it is the custom, and one they seem to enjoy rather than to consider a burden.

It is a continual source of wonder, why the people in the different cantons should be so unlike in some respects and in others so nearly resemble each other. There will appear now and then a custom common to the whole country, and another confined to one little valley or district.

In the story of the destruction of the castles, we read that the surprise was effected by a young girl admitting her lover to her room by a ladder, and an English guide-book remarks, that this is still the fashion of receiving lovers in Switzerland. Reference is had to the manner of wooing, which in some cantons is called "*Lichtgetren,*" in others "*Dorfen*" and "*Stubetegetren,*" and answers to the old-fashioned *going a courting* in England. The customs connected with it vary in different cantons, but exist in some form in all except two or three, which will be noticed elsewhere.

CHAPTER V.

LUCERNE.

ANCIENT LAWS AND CUSTOMS—CITY OF LUCERNE—SOCIAL LIFE—ASCENT OF THE RIGHI—ANCIENT PROCESSION—WEDDINGS.

LUCERNE is the fourth of the forest cantons lying on the sea, and so early as 768 was known as a city.

In no country are the chronicles so abundant as in Switzerland. Centuries before the art of printing was known, they were in the habit of preserving a record of events, not only to be placed in archives, but as heirlooms for the family. They present a most curious compendium of the history of the social development of the people. We read not only the acts of government concerning "state and diplomatic affairs," but its attention to the most minute of social duties, the details of dress, and the preparation of dinners.

The city of Lucerne has now a population of more than ten thousand, but the canton is much larger than during the days of its early history. The name is said to be derived from the Latin word *lucerna*, meaning a lantern, which was hung by the water for the boatmen who went up and down in the night. It remained in possession of the monks, to whom it was secured by

France, till the thirteenth century, when they sold twenty castles and bailifdoms, "with all rights and privileges pertaining thereto," to Rudolph of Hapsburg. When the three cantons were at war with Austria, Lucerne was continually involved in their quarrels, till at length, weary of the tyranny of the bailiffs, it formed an alliance with Uri, Schywtz, and Unterwald, making the four forest cantons, which henceforth stood side by side in their struggles for independence.

It has been the custom from the earliest times to preserve all trophies of victories, and to repeat the names of those who have deserved their country's gratitude, in order to be sure that the children grow up with a knowledge of these things. Among them is an old stove, which stood in the guild-room of the Butchers in 1332, when some patricians planned to deliver the city to the Austrians. A little boy had heard their plot accidentally, but was made to swear that he would not reveal it; yet, determined to save his country, he escaped and ran to the guild-room, where several butchers were assembled, and without speaking to any one made the following address to the stove: "O stove, I say to thee, that there are armed men, who plot to massacre all who counselled alliance with the three cantons. I have sworn to tell no person, so I make thee my confidant, O stove !" The alarm was immediately given, and the city saved.

The battle of Sempach was on their soil, and never a year has failed to see it celebrated with all due pomp and ceremony.

The whole canton is Catholic, and some eight or ten monasteries still exist, though many have from time to time been secularized by the government.

Lucerne took the lead in the war of the *Sonderbund* in 1847, in opposition to the Federal Government; and was for many years governed herself by an oligarchy, composed of patricians, who oppressed the people and kept the country subject to the city. But in 1848 they submitted to the new Federal Government, and revised their own constitution after the most democratic model.

The Jesuits endeavoured to obtain possession of the schools, but were expelled by a majority of the people; and the state has ever kept the priesthood in subjection, in defiance of all the thunders of the Vatican. In 1370, in order that the clergy should not be controlled by any foreign power, a law was enacted requiring every clergyman to swear "to consult no foreign judge, either spiritual or worldly, on penalty of losing all protection of the law and all the enjoyments and privileges of society." In 1609, a tax was levied on all ecclesiastical property, against which the Pope, priests and cloisters protested; yet the government remained firm, and so late as the eighteenth century, we read of the clergy being publicly reproved and punished by law, in spite of a bull from Rome. Yet the people are not less devotedly attached to their religion than their freedom, and would defend both with their lives.

There is a school in every commune, and in the city various institutions for pursuing the study of the higher branches of education. The fine arts are more cultivated than in any other canton, and music and painting diffused more generally among all classes of society.

There is more affability in Lucerne among the people, and pleasant reunions for sociality are more common than in the other cities. They are said to have originated in 1690 by a family who had three sons in France in military service, and who, when they returned, introduced Parisian habits. They had every week little unceremonious parties, and dinners upon the same principle, where eating and drinking were not the one grand consideration, but conversation and innocent amusement. We read in their chronicles, that before the year 1700 they began to have curtains to the beds and windows—to have mirrors and pictures in the parlours, and the chairs cushioned and painted.

Specimens of the old houses without chimneys, and roofs with shingles and great stones, and little panes of glass a few inches in circumference, are still to be seen ; but the new ones are large, with good fireplaces and windows, which make the rooms light and pleasant. Everywhere in these four cantons the walls and ceiling overhead have panels instead of plaister, and are painted white, or pink, or yellow, according to the taste of the owners. The paint is often of the most beautiful brilliancy, shining like glass, and gives a remarkably neat appearance, as it is more easily kept clean than paper or stucco.

Meat is not yet common among the country people, except on Sundays and festival days. Oatmeal porridge was formerly a great dish, and the usual breakfast and dinner of the peasantry; now they add roast potatoes and milk, and among those in comfortable circumstances, coffee is drank three times a day. For dinner they have potatoes, fruit, pear or apple sauce, bread and milk, and sometimes in the evening bread and cider.

It was a Spanish minister who introduced coffee in the seventeenth century, and sugar was known immediately afterwards. Tea is not mentioned till 1666, but beer so early as 1590, and is now very common everywhere. In 1687 it is recorded they began to *drink* tobacco, as it was then universally denominated, instead of smoking, and the peasantry are always to be seen with a pipe in their mouths, the same as in Germany.

They are not an entirely pastoral people, but a portion of them are devoted to agriculture ; and great enterprise has been displayed in draining marshes and bringing water to irrigate

4*

sandy soil. In 1806 the Lake of Sempach was dug many feet deeper, to win land upon its shores; and since then two or three others have been brought into narrow limits in the same way.

The canton is twelve leagues in length and ten in breadth, and the cattle within its limits are estimated at about fifteen hundred thousand, and the cheese at five hundred thousand, dollars. These cantons, on an average, are not so large as the counties in the different States of America, yet what a population of men and animals is concentrated within their boarders! Everywhere are to be seen great fields of rye and great orchards of fruit, and the modern improvements in agriculture are very generally adopted.

There are more manufactures than in the other forest cantons, though not so many as in Zurich, but several for gloves and paper, and in the country the leisure is devoted to braiding straw.

The first printing-press in Switzerland was established in Lucerne in 1410, and from here one was transferred to Paris by a Swiss, in whose honour the French hold a *fête* every year at Sarbonne. The guilds no longer exist in the canton except as associations for improvement and the convenience of festivals, every person being allowed to make shoes or print books, sell tape or dispense "apothecary stuff," according to his taste or interest; and the forests are also free to all who wish to hunt.

We ascended the Righi from the village of Weggis, which belongs to Lucerne, though from its position one would think it should belong to Schwytz, as do all the other points from which paths lead, culminating at the top. Our guide was the personification of good nature, and had a bright intelligent face, so that we chatted with him for very pleasure. Those were his father's cows in the pastures through which we passed, and the merry chime of their bells inspired him to sing for us the *Ranz des Vaches*, and the echoes rang far and wide among the hills. They did not make cheese, but sold the milk, as the number of cows they owned was not enough to make it the most profitable. He owned two horses, on one of which we were being jolted and jagged; and did scarcely anything else in the summer but accompany travellers on the mountain. "And what do you do in the winter?" we asked, "I cut wood to sell."—"Do you own a wood-lot?" "Yes; several."—"Have you a wife?" "Yes, eine Frau und drei Kinder" (a wife and three children). —"And what do they?" "My wife spins cotton sometimes and combs silk." This we afterwards heard was the employment of many in this village, where there are pretty cottages with green blinds; a three-story schoolhouse, also painted white; and blooming gardens, in which flourish chestnuts, almonds and figs, because they are sheltered from all winds in a little niche of the mountain. The silk is brought from Italy, and distributed in all the forest cantons to be prepared for the weavers of Zurich and Bale. We seé people with great packs of it on their shoulders, or hanging by the windows in *hanks*, threads and *snarls* of it lying on the floor, as we have been accustomed to see tow, and this we may also see in Lucerne.

About half a mile from the top of the mountain is the Chapel of Maria, of the *Kalt-bad*, derived from a cold spring, which bursts from the earth near by, called the *Sister's Born*, and concerning which the legend says, that in the time of William Tell, three sisters fled from the tyranny of the Austrian bailiff, and hid in a cave on the Righi. Not even the shepherds knew of their concealment. They lived on roots and berries, and drank water. In the valley they were quite forgotten, and believed to be dead. But one day three stars appeared over this place and stood still, filling the heavens with their brightness. They visited the spot, and found the bodies of the sisters.

A peasant once saw a dragon flying from the Righi to the Pilatus, and something monstrous fell from under his wings. He went to the spot and found a large stone, which to this day has wonderful healing powers.

The Pilatus is still higher than the Righi, and more wonderful in its history and traditions. By the people it is believed to derive its name from Pontius Pilate, whose remorse drove him to this solitary place, whence he plunged into the lake. It is the special abode of pigmies, dragons, and evil spirits.

At one time there lived on one of its heights a rich man, named Klaus. He had a poor cousin, whose daughter, Magdalen, came to him one day, saying her mother was sick, and wanted a piece of cheese. He refused, and sent her away. She had a lover, named Alois, who kept his herds on a neighbouring hill. She went to him, and he gave her all he had; but as she descended a steep, she made a false step, and her cheese went rolling to the bottom of the valley. She sat down and wept bitterly; but a slight pull at her sleeve caused her to look up, and she saw a little man in a green coat and long beard, with a piece of cheese on his shoulder, and some mountain-weed in his hand. It was the hour of twilight, and he spoke softly to her, and said : " I know what has happened to you ; take this cheese, and make of this weed a tea for your sick mother, and she will be well. Be patient, and you will have your cheese again." He vanished, and Magdalen hurried home to her mother, for whom she made the tea, and saw her immediately restored to health. When they cut the cheese, they found it gold. With this, they purchased large Alpine pastures. Magdalen became the wife of Alois, and they lived to see the old miser as poor as they had been.

The stories are innumerable of the revenge of the pigmies upon those who hurt chamois and catch fish in the lake. A bailiff of Lucerne, in 1592, swore on his conscience that he had always longed to see a pigmy; and one day, when he was fishing for trout at the foot of the Pilatus, something jumped upon his neck and pushed him in the water, saying, "You also destroy and drive away my animals." He succeeded in reaching the shore again, but was always lame.

The steamers which ply on the lake belong also to a company in Lucerne. They are very pretty and neatly finished. The captain of one of them told us that they take on an average above five hundred dollars every summer from passengers alone. To go through from one extreme of the lake to the other, making the usual stops by the way, requires five hours, and there are four daily boats. In winter, there is only one, for the mail. The captain said his salary was equal to four hundred and thirty dollars a year.

We experienced here one of those instances of exaction for which the people have become so famous, and which impartiality requires us to record, though those instances were few, as far as we are concerned.

Having walked about the city, we arrived at the boat before some other members of our party, and wishing to be sure to see them the instant they appeared, we seated ourselves on the portion of the deck devoted to second-class passengers. Very soon we were rudely ordered to rise, and the bench was taken away. We moved to another quarter, and soon received the same command in the rudest accents, accompanied by the rudest manner.

They pretended to need all the deck for some horses, which were being transported also over the St. Gotthard. At length we took a movable chair, and made ourselves comfortable in a little nook by the stairs. From this we were almost pushed overboard, and at the same time informed that only first-class passengers were allowed those seats. We now for the first time understood the motive of so much insolence. From strangers they expected the first-class price, and determined to have it by obliging us to go to the first-class deck. This was proved soon afterwards by some peasants taking the same seats and retaining them unmolested. We had not thought of remaining among the horses, cows, and *Bauersleute*, any longer than till our friends should arrive; but not liking compulsion in a matter which should leave each person free, we determined to remain, and demanded a seat. It was granted; but when the fare was collected, we were presented a *first-class ticket*, and only just before we were to land, so that there was no time for parley or proof. Besides, no person would think of resisting a second time in Switzerland, whatever injustice he might experience, unless he was willing to stay for a regular court trial, which, we have no doubt, would decide justly even to the uttermost farthing. But the people have lost none of their warlike propensities, and in all their quarrels, with one another or with strangers, their first impulse is, to "knock everybody down." In one of the Zurich journals we saw a remonstrance against the company who manage the Berne and Thun Railroad, which forms a line with the boats to Interlaken and through the Lake Brienz. The custom was to give return-tickets to persons making excursions, and these had been refused. In the course of the discussion it came out that they had made a mistake. Their usual discrimination had failed, and they had denied to some of their own countrymen an accommodation they intended only to deny to strangers.

While our fairylike boat is dancing on the waters, we are reminded of a grand nautical procession which took place on this same little lake more than two centuries ago, when a deputation was sent from Lucerne to meet the representatives from Uri, Schwytz, and Unterwald, who were to have also in their company the deputies from Valais, to form or to cement their federal alliance. It was the grandest affair for those times of which we find any record, and the remembrance of it is still honoured among their festivals.

In two large boats embarked the honourable members of the council and servants of the government. In twelve smaller ones, bearing the names of the twelve months of the year, were other distinguished persons; and as a guard of the little flotilla, two hunting ships. The officers on board each wore the federal colours, and upon the ships of honour were twelve little boys in the oldest costume of the country, and long plumes waving from their little black caps. Flags were flying upon every tower and pinnacle of the city, and six hundred soldiers stood upon the bridges and wharves to fire salutes upon their departure. In the midst of great rejoicings they set sail, the two hunting ships in front, followed by the first ship of honour, and six of the second rank. Then the second ship of honour, with the remaining six in its rear. So they sailed to the little town of Altstadt, where they met their guests, who immediately came on board, and they returned, having the large ships in the centre, with the six smaller ones forming a half moon on each side.

On arriving again on shore a procession was formed with banners and music, conducting them through all the streets, the little boys always in front. For supper they were disposed in two hotels with six members of the council in each party. The next morning, at six o'clock, all were again in grand procession, with trumpets, and drums, and music, on their way to the collegiate church, to consecrate their alliance by solemn religious ceremonies. The banners of seven states were arranged round the altar, which was also beautifully decorated. The music was performed by eight instruments and a choir of voices, and twelve pieces of artillery announced the commencement of service. A sermon was preached by the high priest, and then the oath administered to the deputies with their hands on the holy book. When this is finished the bells peal forth, the artillery is again fired, and a *Te Deum* sung, and the procession again moves forth to the Council House, where the long mantles of the magistrates are removed by servants, and they descend to the *cornhouse* underneath to partake of the grand dinner given on the occasion. Here in a great hall are sixteen tables set wholly with silver. Nothing can be more curious than the details of such a dinner, but we have rooms for only a few. The servants were some of them merely to occupy posts of honour in different parts of the room, and others to wait and tend. In all, they numbered *twelve hundred and seventeen!*

The guests remained three days, and the dinner was every day equally sumptuous. The several courses are chronicled with all the minutiæ of venison, fish, and poultry. The items of one dinner will give an idea of an entertainment of this kind in those economical times when people did not spend their money foolishly, but lived in beautiful simplicity!

First dinner—first course.

Twenty-two principal dishes ; side dishes, two peacocks, twelve Welsh hens, eight English pies, twenty-four boiled capons with sausages, twenty-four dove-soups, twenty-four tongues with sausages, twenty-four marrow tarts, twenty-four mixed dishes of veal, twenty-four of venison, twenty-four of fowl, and twenty-four of beef.

Second course. Six Welsh pies, twelve large stuffed stag-joints, eight joints of venison, twenty-four roast capons, twenty-four dishes of roast fowl, twenty-four of game, seventy-two dishes of something of which we can by no inquiry or study learn the name or composition, twenty-four dishes of salad, twenty-four of plums.

Third course. Six plates of sugar-work, consisting of two castles, two triumphal arches, and two wall-fish; eight cold game-pies, eight fancy puff-cakes, twenty-four almond tarts, twenty-four of crabs, twenty-four of sugar-bread, twenty-four of candy-confectionery, seventy-two of different sugar-work cakes.

To each course were two hundred and fourteen dishes, besides the wine and beer, and each day saw an equal number. When the "gracious Herren" had been feasted three days after this fashion, and the whole city had been put in requisition to do them honour, they returned home, no doubt highly gratified with the attention paid them; if not, they must have been very difficult to please.

The number of festivals in modern times has somewhat diminished, but there are still very many.

The *Kirchweih* or church consecration, which is still celebrated in some form in all Catholic communities in Germany and Switzerland, we find to have been of much more consequence in the early times, and to have cost the city every year eight hundred dollars. Now it is reduced to a simple procession and dance.

The shooting festivals originated in 1452 and continued till the seventeenth century, when they were allowed to fall into disuse ; but in the eighteenth century they are again revived in more than their original consequence.

New Year's day is scarcely noticed. Christmas, which is everywhere else celebrated on the 25th of December, is solemnized in Lucerne on the 6th, Michaelmas Day—for what reason we cannot learn. Those who go from house to house to inquire concerning the behaviour of children, are a procession of boys, one of whom is arrayed as a bishop, accompanied by two angels, followed by a person dressed in black with his face painted of the same colour. He carries also a black bag, and threatens all naughty children to tie them up and carry them off. But this is being superseded by the simple custom of placing gifts upon a table to surprise the little folks in the morning.

The harvest, threshing, raising and taking possession of a new house, are marked by some festal scene.

Nearly all the peasant-marriages take place at carnival, and most of them also on Monday. If they come from a neighbouring village to church, the bells announce the arrival of the procession, and a curious spectacle of old and new-fashioned vehicles, with people in all manner of gala dresses, presents itself. The bride enters first with wreath and white apron ; an old woman follows her, who is mistress of ceremonies, and who is called *Gelbe*, or yellow woman. She has on her arm a basket, in order to take the bridal wreath after the ceremony. Next come the women of the party. Behind them is the bridegroom in a black mantle, his hat in his hand and a little knot of flowers on the top of his head ; then the men of the party. Mass is said, and music gives the signal for the bridal pair to stand before the altar. After being pronounced husband and wife, they return to an inn for merry-making, which is commenced by the bridegroom dancing three times with the bride, when the *yellow woman* takes the bridal wreath and bouquet of the bridegroom and throws them upon the fire, and derives from the manner in which they burn an omen of happiness or unhappiness for their future life. She then presents each guest with a pocket-handkerchief from the bride, and receives for her gifts in return. They each drink and are merry till night, when the immediate neighbours accompany the bride to her new home. She is then confided to the *yellow woman*, who remains a long time with her in secret council, and fulfils the office of *femme de chambre*.

The *Kiltgang* is the universal mode of wooing; the lover visiting his betrothed in the evening, to be pelted on the way by all mischievous urchins; or if he is seated quietly with her by the winter fire, they are sure to be serenaded by all manner of *cat voices* under the window, which are continued till he issues forth, perhaps at dawn in the morning; and however long may be a courtship, these *caterwaulings* are the invariable attendants, and not the most lamentable consequences of those nightly visits, recognized, however, as entirely respectable and conventional in every canton.

But there is one custom, which is peculiar to Lucerne, and which is mentioned in the oldest descriptions of the people. Like many another, it is also confined to one part of the canton, and distinguishes the people of Entlibuch in the southern limits, where they are said to be the liveliest, wittiest, and gayest of all the people in Switzerland. They indulge in a continued series of gymnastics, theatricals, masquerades, and poesies. They quarrel very often, but make peace again immediately, because they do not like the interference of courts and lawyers. Being given to amusing themselves at others' expense, they learn also to bear ridicule without anger.

After divine service on the last Monday of carnival, they assemble before the townhouse in each *commune* to listen to a poem, which is recited by some village wit, and the special object of which is to satirize the follies and foibles of any person who may have subjected himself to such reproof; and often it is many, instead of one, who see themselves thus portrayed. No names are called, and the whole may be a caricature, yet each one recognises himself, and is at the same time recognised by all. The poet arrives on horseback in some strange costume, and wearing a great hat ornamented with flowers and looking-glasses. The magistrates receive him and offer him wine as testimony of honour. He then descends from his horse, and, taking from his bosom a large paper bearing the seal of Entlibuch, begins his recital. However severely any one may be lashed, he makes no demonstration, but the orator is said to make sure of his way home before the sun has set; else he may experience tangible proof of the revenge of some luckless swain.

CHAPTER VI.

ZUG.

PLEASANT CUSTOM—CHURCHYARD—FIRST BATTLE FOR FREEDOM—HOME SICKNESS OF SWISS SOLDIERS—WITCHCRAFT—FORMS OF PUNISHMENT.

Zug is a "very little city," so small that one can scarcely believe it has the honour to be an "independent republic." On the map it is altogether an invisible power. One enters its territory, and, before he can think, is out of it, unless he decides to stop by the way. This almost any one would be tempted to do who should happen to be greeted in their friendly way, in some lone place, without knowing that it is the custom, and practised the same for all.

Wherever they meet a stranger they offer him the hand, and in so cordial a manner that one is troubled to know how to receive it. Our first experience of it was when walking in the street, as some little girls came running out of school, and one after the other each offered her hand, looking very playful and a little mischievous, as if they thought it were an old fashioned custom which we should not understand, and yet which they could not neglect. We did not understand, to be sure, but thought at first they were little beggars asking for pennies, but soon learned that they were little friends, who knew us at a glance to be strangers, and gave us this pleasant welcome. We returned it as cordially, and they ran skipping, and hopping, and laughing, away. But it is something to be treasured for ever in the memory, and disposes us so kindly to the people that we are in danger of shutting our eyes to all their faults.

There is a quiet cheerfulness in their manners, which is different from the gaiety of Entlibuch and the vivacity of the inhabitants of the Muottathal, but which is not less charming. They are Catholics, like their neighbours, but less superstitious, though not less devout. The cemetery testifies to the honour they pay the dead, and the taste which characterizes the living. Almost every grave is a flower-bed, kept always in the freshest bloom, and the gilt cross which marks its head is hung with wreaths. Each grave has also some testimonial to the honourable birth and condition of those who repose beneath. They have adopted for their government one which gives the utmost freedom, but have lost none of their respect for " old families." This is observable everywhere in Switzerland, and in some cases amounts to most ridiculous inconsistency and folly. There can be no sin and no harm in possessing a long line of noble ancestors, but, as Bulwer somewhere says, " It is the founder of a family who is most honoured," he who by some striking and noble deed first won renown ; and it is equally true, that it is often the last of a noble name who least deserves respect.

In this little churchyard armorial bearings are to be seen upon the humblest tomb. There is here no such rushing tide of human events to wash away the past with its memories as we see in the New World, and no such opportunity to acquire influence in a new way. They therefore cling to the old, and rest their pride on what their fathers did, instead of doing something for themselves.

It was the soil of this little canton which first received the baptismal blood of freedom at Morgarten; her sons have ever been among the bravest in every land, and she has gone hand in hand in all things with the forest cantons, yet, from some reason, she is far less known, and her name appears not so often in song and story.

There are still ruins of old castles on the mountain crests, but they have shown a utilitarian spirit we have not elsewhere observed, in transferring the stones of one to build a school-house in the city. It is composed almost entirely of the old walls of Hünenburg, and has stood in its present form and capacity since 1714. The story of the destruction of Waldenburg is related elsewhere, but there is another version of it among the traditions of the people, which shows equally the rudeness of the times and the hatred of those who ruled over them.

The servant was one day sent to market to buy meat. When a piece was cut for him, he said it was not such an one as would please his master. The butcher asked him to mark the place from which he should take a slice, and his hand was no sooner stretched forth in obedience to the request than it was severed by the axe and thrown with the meat into the basket. "Now, see if that suits your lord," was the injunction with which he went howling home. The Lord of Waldenburg swore vengeance against the city, but the time was past when his oaths caused the people to tremble. He was himself afraid, and fled to Zurich, taking care to conceal his way by having the shoes on his horse's feet turned backwards.

At the battle of Sempach the might of Austria was broken, and the family of Hünenburg, which was also that of Waldenburg, hung no more together. Many laid aside their family name and became burghers of the city, and others emigrated to distant lands. Having lost their importance, they preferred not to remain where they would be reminded of their lost power, and sold all that was left to them, to become exiles and strangers in the homes of their fathers.

In Zug, the people bought the land inch by inch. Every one who contributed became a member of the commune, and those who had no money gave a bed, a kettle, a little grain, some clothes, the most trifling objects they could part with, the smallest piece of coin, it was the price of their freedom; and the names of women and little children appear on the list of those who would thus purchase themselves for ever free from feudal tenure.

In 1435, a third part of the city was submerged in the sea. A slight shock from an earthquake had previously produced large fissures in the walls, and made the houses tremble, so that the people had left the shore of the lake; but, no further evil consequences ensuing, they returned one day, and the same night the water covered them. The superstitious said "fish had undermined the foundations," and the story is not yet quite obsolete. A cradle was found floating on the water the next morning with a little boy lying snugly in its pillows, unconscious of the calamities which had deprived him of home and friends, and equally so that he was not rocking for his own pleasure on the waves. He afterwards became mayor of the city.

War and pestilence have also swept over them, and from the battle of St. Jacob, to which two hundred had gone from Zug, not one returned. But nothing could wean them from the love of arms; and it has been often the case, that so many have been absent in foreign lands that not enough were left to till the soil and perform the necessary mechanical labour. Of the two thousand, eight hundred who went into the service of Venice against the Grand Turk in 1688, all but one hundred and seventy-eight died of pestilence and home-sickness. They were not allowed to form separate corps under their own colours, and it broke their hearts. Zurlauben, the leader of one brave company of two hundred men, came with nineteen and a soiled banner home.

The same custom obtains, as in the forest cantons, of repeating in church at certain periods the names of those who had fallen in battle, or on any field died gloriously.

The *home-sickness*, of which we read in the regiments of France, was not confined to them alone. In every country they pine for their mountains, and the *Ranz des Vaches*, when sung on the plains of Italy, or to the time of the "gondola's dipping oar," had the same influence as in the gardens of Paris. They would become emaciated, and in a few days exhibit all the effects of a long illness. It is a wonderful proof of the power of mind over body; for there could be no affectation in their case. It was a prostration which they could not control; but often the assurance that the next day they should have the money to go home, gave a man strength to rise and walk. The musical *Kuhreihen* has no words; but one who has seen the Alpine shepherds with their flocks can easily imagine the thoughts that would accompany the notes in a foreign land. An English poet has clothed them in the following rhymes:

I.

"Oh, when shall I visit the land of my birth,
The loveliest land on the face of the earth?

THE COTTAGES OF THE ALPS.

When shall I those scenes of affection explore,
    Our forests, our fountains,
    Our hamlets, our mountains,
With the pride of our mountains, the maid I adore!
O when shall I dance on the daisy-white mead,
In the shade of an elm, to the sound of the reed?

II.

"When shall I return to that lowly retreat,
Where all my fond objects of tenderness meet?
The lamb and the heifers that follow my call,
    My father, my mother,
    My sister, my brother,
And dear Isabella, the joy of them all?
O when shall I visit the land of my birth,
'Tis the loveliest land on the face of the earth?"

I.

"Ah, when shall I see once more
All the objects I adore!
    Our limpid *rills*,
    Our hills, our vills,
    Our mounts sublime!
    Pride of our clime,
    The so gentle *Isabeau!*
    Beside the Elm—beside its flow,
Again when shall I on the ground
Dance to the reeds' delightful sound?

II.

"Ah, when shall I see once more
All the objects I adore—
    My father, my mother,
    My sister, my brother—

> My lambkin's caress—
>   Spread over the mead,
>   My flocks at feed—
> My shepherdess!
> Ah, when shall I see once more
> All the objects I adore?"

The canton is but little more than ten square leagues in extent, and yet has a population greater than Uri, which is four times its size ; and they are nearly all a pastoral people. On many of the old houses are quaint inscriptions and hideous paintings, which contrast strangely with the modern life of the people. There are few traces of the ancient costume, except on *fête* days, when the maidens appear in their green petticoats and red stockings, with knots of ribbons and gay streamers, and the dance does not interfere with their religion, or jar with their devotions. Their festivals, and the principal features of life, are the same as in the forest cantons ; but in the days that are past, those dark days of superstition and ignorance, the little Zug was even more guilty than they, in accusing falsely and inventing tortures.

The belief in witches is the most marvellous of all human infatuation ; and the funeral pile of the Hindoo, and the crushing wheel of the Juggernaut, have no more revolting history than the dungeons and guillotines of every Christian land in the seventeenth century. It was not enough that they were cut off by the sword, by famine, and pestilence, they were murdered by hundreds on their own free soil. In the course of two months in the year 1660 more than two thousand were burnt for this imaginary crime in this one little canton.

In 1737, a weak-minded young girl, only seventeen years old, returned from a visit to Lucerne, where she was honoured by a conference with the Jesuits, and represented herself as a witch. This gave her the power to testify against others, and in consequence of her base assertion, ten persons were condemned to death ; eight of whom were women, one aged seventy years and another only eighteen. Six of them were burned or strangled after having their flesh torn with glowing tongs. Those who confessed themselves guilty, experienced sometimes an alleviation of their punishment. One old woman, who would not confess, was thrown into a dungeon little better than a grave, where she was also put to the torture, and where she finally died of cold and hunger.

Many of those instruments of torture are still to be seen, and it is not very many years since some of them were used, though not to punish witchcraft. The rooms are still in the darkness of night. No ray from without penetrated them when witches were their tenants, and neither the beams of day nor the light of Christian sympathy and knowledge have ameliorated the condition of those who are now condemned to punishment in the old "Kaiben tower." The cells are a sort of wooden chests, perfectly dark; and in order that the criminals who occupy them may preserve no knowledge of time, those who bring food, and who must necessarily have a lamp or candle in order to grope their way, are commanded to enter at irregular hours, but to come all seasons of day and night, till there is to the miserable victim no more morning, no sun nor moon, no brightness and no shadow, only one long dreary duration. One can almost imagine the wheel and the thumbscrew to be pleasant relief to such an existence.

These creditable inventions of the golden age of simplicity are still here ; and also a sort of basket called the "witches' tub," into which they were crowded and screwed to indescribable anguish. There are also the great timbers for crushing, the pulleys for adjusting the apparatus in the nicest manner, and three great stones, the largest two hundred pounds in weight, for suspending to the limbs as a last resort for those who would not confess themselves guilty of a crime of which they knew not the meaning. The bastinado is also here, but the wreath of iron spikes, and the boards for stretching the body, and the cramping-irons to fasten it, are considered unworthy the patronage of modern philanthropists. These punishments are for those guilty of ordinary misdemeanors; incorrigible criminals are sent to Zurich, and formerly many were transported to the galleys of Italy. Not long ago, a man was chained to the walls of his own house; and yet Zug is not a day's journey from Berne, where exists a prison so perfectly combining punishment with humanity and reform.

The cantonal colours of Lucerne, Zug, and Zurich are the same—blue and white—but differ in the arrangement. In Zug, a blue stripe passes through a field of white on their shield, and on the *Landweibel* the dress is blue around the shoulders, and below entirely white, with a blue stripe down behind. The election takes place on the first Sunday in May, and the Laudamman remains in office two years. The age of citzenship is nineteen years, and though entirely Catholic, they do not allow their monks any part in the affairs of the government. The principal articles of their constitution date to the fourteenth century; and in 1814 they were peremptory in demanding that it should be *written*, in order to feel secure, and their constitution is now one of the best in Switzerland.

There are nine parishes and four convents, in which are educated many priests for the rest of Switzerland. The girls in the Catholic cantons are said to be more universally educated than in the Protestant cantons; though this education is very limited. They are taught to read and write by the nuns, and many kinds of needlework, which is certainly better than nothing ; and we hear it very often asserted that they are also more moral. The reason of this may be, that the standard of housekeeping and *comfort* is not so high. They do not wait till they are rich, or are sure of a competence, before marrying; and this is true of every country, and especially of cities. Where society demands, of all who are *passable*, a certain style in order to move in a certain rank, those who cannot afford it preserve their rank and sacrifice their honour.

From Zug there is also a large emigration of young men to other cantons, who wish to engage in trade or industry for which opportunity is not furnished at home. They have always distinguished themselves as soldiers, and have furnished a creditable number to the ranks of authors and men of letters. There are not so many in the forest and central cantons as in the north and west, but yet none of them are without their artists, poets, and historians.* It was Louis Pfiffer, a Swiss general, native of Lucerne, who, with his six thousand soldiers, saved Catharine Medicis, her son, and all the royal household, and led them safely from Maux to Paris. It was a native of the same canton who made the first dictionary of Swiss dialects, and another who produced the first *bas-reliefs* of Swiss scenery, now so common. One of their musicians was master and composer to Prince Conti, and another, in 1720, was one of the best organists of Europe.

---

* A book has just been published in Zurich, " Lives of Distinguished Men, Natives of Switzerland," which we commend to those who think Switzerland has produced no great men. It is curious that so many pens should have set to work this last year to do justice to the little republic.

In Canton Schwytz, among their heroes the name of Reding is most conspicuous, and some one of the family distinguished himself in every Swiss battle. One of them also made a memorable address at the Council of Constance. The learning of Paraclese was nearly unparalleled; and the volumes of Raymaun are still invaluable to those who would write of ancient history and diplomacy. The poets and painters are also numerous. We find in the lives of nearly all these men remarkable and interesting incidents exhibiting their moral heroism in overcoming obstacles, their struggles with poverty, their sufferings and trials in painful positions, which are the surest proofs of the genius which inspired them. Our plan and limits do not admit of our relating these things, but so much we cannot help seeing and saying, that the air of republicanism is not the miasma it has been represented, blighting to every germ of talent, and covering with mildew all the fruits of genius. It cannot be true, because it is contrary to all the laws of God and nature, that freedom should not be a healthful sustenance for the soul of man.

CHAPTER VII.

VALAIS.

CROSSING THE FURKA—RHONE GLACIER—INN—MANUFACTURIES AND AGRICULTURE—LOVE OF LIBERTY—CRETINISM.

THE ancients used to say, the Rhone came " out of eternal night," but we know now that it comes from three little springs more than five thousand feet above the sea, but which unite and soon disappear under the great mass of snow and ice denominated the *Rhone Glacier*, which lies between the Getershorn and Galenstock, two towering peaks, which limit Valais in the northeast.

It was on one of the hottest of summer days that we crossed what is called the *Furka Pass*, and about three o'clock in the afternoon, on our way westward from Andermatt, in Canton Uri, that our guide said to us, " You can take a last look at this little village, for you will not see another till to-morrow night." We knew that we were to cross one of the longest and dreariest of the Alpine passes, and knew, of course, that there could be neither fruitful plains nor laughing valleys on the tops of the mountains, nor in the gorges between them; yet it sounded almost like a death-knell as we heard it, and looked around to say farewell to the little huts, among which nothing would have tempted us to stay, if we could never have the hope of reaching another of the dwelling-places of men. The hills were not yet bare; there was now and then a tuft of shrubbery, some trees looking as if it were a winter's instead of a summer's day; and grass, that was tall enough and green enough to tempt the mower's scythe; for it was being cut by men and transported on the backs of women from every knoll and crevice to their distant winter homes.

But even these pleasant oases soon disappeared; our horse was moving at the slowest possible pace to which four feet could measure their steps; the sun, which had been at midday fiercely hot, was beginning to look pale and dim; no living thing was to be seen to vary the monotony or break the stillness, except the little form of our young companion, who, with his long alpine stock, jumped over ledge and rock, and climbed the dizziest heights, while we were plodding along the one narrow, unvarying path; the mountains grew more grand and terrible in their height, and the gorges more fearful in their depth,—we could very easily have believed that we should *never* more reach human habitation.

"Are there any more difficult heights than these?" we ask of our machine-looking old guide, who says he has been this way with this same horse every week for ten years. "Och, ja wohl," he replies; "these are nothing; these are no mountains at all,"—upon which he stops and pats affectionately his good horse, sees if his shoes are fast and the saddle is right, asks us if we are weary, and jogs along. What is he thinking, we wonder; he does not look as if he ever had a thought; yet he knows every mountain by its name, every tradition and legend;

and this being his duty as guide, he stops at every point and repeats them. Now and then we must ford a mountain torrent, which comes foaming and dashing on the way to its bridal with the Rhone far away in some distant valley. We should demur and decline all such adventures, if it were longer of any use; but having put our "hand to the plough," there is no turning back, though the courage has every moment to receive a new spur, in order to be equal to the exertion.

Now and then we meet a lone traveller like ourselves, and it becomes a question who shall run the risk of rolling over into the gulf below, by turning out where there is scarcely room for the hoofs of one horse; or perhaps a merry party, reminding one of the caravans of the desert, where lords and ladies, tents and baggage, are being transported from city to city by sedans.

At length we reach the Furka height, some eight thousand feet above the sea, and scarcely feel that it is the middle of August, where the snow is lying in drifts and the frost is upon our eyelids. The red roof of the little inn looks cheery without, and the bright fire blazing within is genial, but for the sake of recording it in our note-book, we go out and enjoy a game at snowball, putting our cheeks in a glow, which the good wine of the innkeeper heightens, and also helps to increase our powers of endurance to the point of another three hours' ride, to which we are compelled before we can find lodging for the night.

We soon learn, that the mountains we left behind "were no mountains at all," and resort to the precaution of drawing our ample capuchin closely over our eyes, to shut out the dizzy depths, till at length the great glacier appears, and the Rhone flowing quietly out from some unfathomable vault beneath the massive arch. It is only a murmuring brook; but before it reaches the lake it is joined by eighty more, which swell it to a mighty stream, and during the melting of the snows cause it to overflow, to the destruction of whole villages, which are nevertheless immediately rebuilt on its banks, as neither landslide nor avalanche, flood, fire, nor famine, ever frighten the Swiss from their mountains or their villages.

It is the most gloomy vision imaginable to come in view of one of these *crevasses*, just as darkness is covering it with her sombre shadows. The snow is not the pure white of a winter drift, but as if a spring thaw had just spread her dingy mantle over it; there is not a tree or shrub or spire of grass on all the surrounding heights, the cold is that of blue November on one of her moodiest days, and we are chilled as if a March wind had penetrated every pore. It is grand, but it is also terrible, and we shut our eyes.

We cross a little bridge and find ourselves in the midst of a herd of shaggy goats, before the door of the little inn. Alas! they say there is no more room, and we say also, "We have no more strength, and it is already dark. If we sleep with the goats, you must find for us a lodging-place." When, indeed, did it ever happen that an inn, great or small, was filled to its utmost capacity? They succeeded in finding us "accommodation," if it deserves the name, where everything is the perfection of all that is dismal and forlorn.

We ascend by a ladder to the corner of the garret, where, by the help of *blanket-shawls* and other conveniences, we enjoy a "room to ourselves," and learn in the morning that three persons who came after us were also in the same way "accommodated." Next to an inn, there is nothing which can be expanded and compressed, moulded and twisted, into so many useful forms as a blanket-shawl. It is the *ne plus ultra* of inventions. Ours served as altogether the most impenetrable partition-wall to our apartment; for in the others, which were boards, were so many *imitation crevasses* that we were haunted all night by *Jack-o'-lanterns* and *Will-o'-the-wisps*. From our window, of four lilliputian panes, we looked down upon the snows which the summer suns of centuries had never melted, heard the rushing waters as they exultingly burst their icy bands, the bleating of the goats—who seemed to be disturbed in their midnight slumbers, or never to enjoy any—and the incessant creaking of the rickety house, and footsteps of those who are certainly night-walkers, if not somnambulists. The dust of the downy coverings performs for our nostrils the office of cayenne pepper or black snuff, and the cold could scarcely have been greater if we were lying upon, instead of at the foot of, the glacier. Yet we sleep, and wake "in the morning early," with a health of body and an exhilaration of spirits it was never our fortune to experience after a night upon "velvet couch with silken curtains gay."

We look forth, and now it is a sight worth all the trouble, and pain, and anxiety, we have been at to behold it. In Canton Valais alone there are one hundred and thirty glaciers, and this is said not only to be the most beautiful among them, but one of the most beautiful in Switzerland. The lower part has the form of a cataract suddenly frozen, while its crown is composed of Gothic arches, fanciful colonnades, peaks, spires, and stalactites, on which the sun is shedding a flood of golden light, reflecting, in myriad fantastic shapes and changing shadows, each glistening point and proud pilaster. Like some grand cathedral-dome, the Galenstock rears its head, and forms a dark and solemn relief, and the cloudless blue of the vault above casts over all the soft hues of peerless beauty. We walk out to stand by the cradle of the "little *Rhodanus*," fretting like an infant in its swaddling-clothes, and reflect, as we often do by the pillows where rests an immortal mind, " What a terrible power is slumbering there, unconscious of the glory and majesty it is to reveal—of the good or the evil it has the power to bring to a world teeming with human life !"

Very little indeed does the proud river know of the happiness it scatters in the valleys through which it winds, or the misery it causes when it rushes wildly over meadow and moor, tearing down forests and sweeping away villages in its course. But not only the Rhone itself, but many of the rivers which flow into it, also cause avalanches and floods, so that throughout the canton these are the occurrences of every year, destroying millions of property and hundreds of lives.

Three or four miles from the Rhone glacier is the village of Obergestein, which is the place of deposit for that portion of the Gruyère cheese which is destined for Italy, and also where the four little mountain paths meet which lead over the passes most dreaded by travellers. Here occurred, in 1720, an avalanche which enveloped eighty-eight persons in its snowy winding-sheet. Upon the tomb in which they were afterwards enclosed, is inscribed: *O Dieu! Quel deuil! 88 dans un seul sépulchre!*

Besides floods and avalanches, there are frequent earthquakes. In 1855, in a little village where the Wisp falls into the Rhone, they were rocked several months, till finally only seven houses were left habitable, and the damages extended hundreds of miles.

Even the Simplon does not escape the ravages of the mountain torrents, and in 1834 and 1839, nearly eight miles were destroyed, many bridges swept away, and in some places every trace of the beautiful structure effaced.

There is every variety of climate, from the torrid zone to Spitzbergen, and seven-eighths of the plants peculiar to the climate and soil of Switzerland are to be found within its limits. Yet the people are in many respects far behind those on the north side of the mountains, though it cannot be from the reason that their resources are insufficient, if rightly used. One reason they give themselves is, that the military service, which has drawn so many of their youth to Rome and Naples, has been the death-warrant of home industry. There is no capital for the commencement of enterprise, and they do nothing by associations themselves, and allow nothing to be done by others.

There is no department of manufactures in any flourishing condition, and even the braiding of straw, which the government introduced a few years since, found not sufficient favour in their eyes to spur their hands to diligence, and there was no convenient market for the sale of their wares.

In the summer, three thousand are employed in the Alpine pastures, and for all who remain, agriculture is the only labour. In this they have latterly made some advances. Lands long held in common, and free to cattle, have been divided and apportioned to those who would cultivate them. For many years the potatoes almost failed, and this led them to the cultivation of maize in the southern portions, where it is waving, if not in its pristine magnificence, at least in respectable size and proportions, the silver tassels peeping out from goodly ears that are afterwards converted, not into "Johnny cakes" and "brown loaves," but into something that might answer to "hasty pudding," or "mush."

There are also many sunny hill-sides clothed with vines, and they are beginning to cultivate the mulberry. Within a few years, specimens of beautiful glass have been produced, and in one village a paper factory has been established.

In some parts there is no deficiency of talent, as many painters and sculptors evince, and in others no deficiency of energy, as their marvellous little canals for the irrigation of their lands fully prove. One sees them everywhere in the valley of the Rhone, running across the hills, conducted over ravines, and passing through solid rocks for miles, till they reach some dry and parched plain, where little lakes are formed, from which sluices convey the water where it is needed. With them, as with others, " Where there is a will there is a way."

But their wants are few, and, like the people of Unterwald, their devotions many. There is a peculiar beauty in their rustic chapels; and one may meet in every path the pilgrim on his way to shrine or temple, or with folded hands kneeling before some image of saint or Virgin, with an air of sincerity and faith which is always beautiful, whether in pagan or Christian. But if our inquiries or philosophy follow them elsewhere, we cannot help wishing there were less zeal and more knowledge.

It is always a difficult matter in Catholic Switzerland to reconcile this apathy in their practical affairs—this trust in their religion—with the energy and defiance they manifest under the slightest political control. The Pope in his palmiest days was not allowed to meddle in their elections, and princely bishops have been dethroned for endeavouring to impose upon them a bailiff against their will, or to restrain them in the exercise of their right of free suffrage.

The expression, now common in all lands, "the people rose *en masse*," originated in Valais, from the curious manner they had of *rising* to redress any grievance which they considered as imposed upon them by those in authority. Whatever might be his position or office, the person who had become obnoxious was represented in effigy, by taking the trunk of a tree and fashioning a rude head at the top, and setting it in a public place, where it was christened by the name of *masse*, which in German, French, and English has the same signification—a heap or bulk of something. But the people treated it as if it had really human understanding, and either by some machinery, or by a person concealed within its huge proportions, it was made to show signs of intelligence. The secret of this, however, was known only to a few.

The populace assembled, and some person appointed addressed himself to the image, asking, "Of whom hast thou to complain? Is it Baron B. or Lord L.?"—always being sure to mention the name they were preparing to execrate. The *masse* bowed his head very low in assent, and the people uttered loud cries of rage and vengeance. They then drove a quantity of nails into the trunk, though we do not learn for what purpose, or what they were to signify, unless it was crucifixion, and bore it aloft, followed by a triumphant crowd, and placed it before the door of the person accused or hated. He understood, without further communication, that his fate was sealed, and took refuge in flight, thus renouncing all future pretensions to power or influence among them. If he attempted any resistance, his house would be destroyed, his property seized, and his partisans killed.

It is a curious fact, illustrative of the manners of the Middle Ages; and not less curious, that the phrase should have crept into every language, and the custom, in some modified form, have characterized the revolutionists of every period and nation, with a similar expression denoting their popular outbreaks.

In the German portion of the Canton Valais, they keep these old times in remembrance by dramatizing them, with the people for actors, and very likely the village curate for stage director.

The Reformation made some converts among them, but a popular assembly in 1603 decreed that the new doctrines should not be preached, and banished all who had adopted them. In 1607, the Jesuits were established as teachers in the colleges of Brigue and Sion, and continued there for more than three centuries. In 1847, after the war of the Sonderbund, they were banished from all Switzerland by the Federal Government. No Jesuitical school, college, or association, can exist within the limits of the twenty-two cantons. Against this measure there was much remonstrance and many rebellions, and, with the suppression of the convents of Argovie, caused great alarm to the Catholics, but they have finally subsided ; a new constitution, satisfactory to all, has been completed, and a new code of laws promulgated instead of that which had existed for centuries, and which was written in Latin.

Public instruction is now the care of the state. Every commune is obliged to support a school, and all children are compelled to attend till the age of fifteen, and a cantonal normal school educates the teachers. It is only ten years since this system went into operation, and there are already three hundred schools, and nearly fourteen thousand children attending them. There has not yet been time to educate a generation, but they are beginning fully to appreciate the benefits to be derived from schools, and make constant efforts to improve them. No canton has suffered more than Valais from the ravages of foreign arms, and when we take into account all the calamities which they are continually experiencing, we cannot marvel so much at their ignorance and poverty.

A lordly bishop still rules at Sion, and is the ninetieth who has sat in the same chair. His power is somewhat restricted in later years, as he is now the subject of the state, and elected by the Grand Council, but his influence is scarcely less over the people. There are, besides, seven convents of different orders. The one at St. Bernard is known to all travellers who cross the mountains at that place, and many do so on purpose to see the old monks and their dogs, who have charge of it. It was established in 962 by St. Bernard, of Menthon, archdeacon of Aoste, who endowed it and placed there monks of the order of St. Augustine. Those of the same order live there still, only about twenty residing constantly at the hospice, others, supported by the institution, exercising hospitality at St. Jou or Jovet, another mountain pass, and others at Simplon; when they are old and sick they resort to Mortigny, and some are curates in villages.

There can be no life more self-sacrificing and benevolent than that of the monks of St. Bernard, as most English tourists know.

Napoleon crossed by the Great St. Bernard, and it was the toils and losses he experienced which decided him to construct the Simplon, on which thirty thousand men were sometimes employed at once, and the expense of which was about twenty-seven thousand five hundred dollars per mile. It requires three days to traverse it from Montigny to Milan, and its breadth is, through the whole distance, from twenty-five to thirty feet. Yet the army of Napoleon III. strewed it with the sick and dying on their march to Italy in April, so intense was the cold, and so deep the snow, and the obstructions so many, though art had done all in her power to smooth the way. Thirty thousand persons pass over it every year, and as many over each of the others; and if the whole object of travellers is to see fine scenery, they can be sufficiently gratified on either of these great *chaussées*, and need not cross glaciers or climb precipices, at the peril every moment of sacrificing their lives. But there is a fascination about the mountains, or a spell in the atmosphere, which, when once experienced, seems irresistible, and to act like a magnet or charm. We have met persons who have spent every summer for years in pedestrian excursions in Switzerland, without having passed a week in exploring any other land. And there is certainly an exhilaration which one would gladly realize for ever, if it were possible. We doubt whether misfortune or evil tidings of any description would exert the slightest depressing influence on the spirits anywhere between five and eight thousand feet above the sea.

But the evils of sickness and deformity are nowhere more deplorable than among these same mountains and valleys. The victims of *Cretinism* and the *goître* are the most revolting objects our eyes ever rested upon, and they are to be met oftener in Valais than any other canton. But philosophers have discovered the causes in the unhealthy position of certain villages, from marshy lands or stagnant pools, where the mountains prevent a circulation of air, increased by want of nourishing food and ignorance of physical laws. But there is no mention of these unfortunate beings in the valley of Aoste when Cæsar conquered it and Augustus founded a colony there. Their beauty and their valour were a marvel to the Roman general.

Neither are these two frightful forms of disease peculiar to Switzerland, as some people imagine. We met a young lady who ran to the glass every morning the moment she awoke, to see if she could discover any enlargement of her throat, and another who measured her neck every night, to be sure and flee the moment there was any danger. But in England alone there are thirty thousand people in the different stages of idiocy; and in the village of Pelcham, on the Danube, there were found five hundred men not able to bear a sword.

Goitre seems to be only a physical calamity, a hideous roll of flesh protruding from the throat till it sometimes reaches the ground, and is so burdensome that the person afflicted with it cannot walk uprightly. Cases of it are frequent in some counties of England, South America, and some islands of the East Indies. Switzerland being the most travelled, is most exposed to observation and censure.

One of their physicians, in a treatise upon the subject, says, "Is it not a far higher proof of civilization to provide for the happiness of our lowest and worst people, than to decorate our streets with galleries, statues, and monumental trophies?" The institution established at Interlaken for the reception of Cretins has performed many wonderful cures, produced great amelioration in obstinate cases, and more than all, perhaps, led to inquiry in other lands, attracted the attention of physicians and physiologists to these and other maladies, and thus proved a beacon light to the world without, though within there seems only the blackness of darkness.

The history of the establishment is well known. It stands upon a high peak called "Abendberg," "mountain of the setting sun," and originated with a young professor in Zurich University, *Guggenbuhl*, who resolved to devote himself to the study of medicine with reference to the relief of this miserable class of human beings. They do not attempt a cure unless the patient is received before the age of seven years. The remedies are bathing, exercise, amusement, and especially the influence of personal kindness and interest. It must be the noblest mind and the purest heart that can devote a life to such labours;

there is something so repulsive in the idiotic stare and vacant smile, united with the deathlike pallor and the absence of all appreciation on the part of the recipient for weeks, for months, perhaps for ever ! We could not help exclaiming, " If there are angels in human form, here they are, ministering to these wretched creatures !"

We saw a cat painted by a Cretin, who had this one talent and taste, and executed his portraits to the life, without the slightest sense or understanding concerning any other earthly thing. Of course his malady was only partial ; but most of them have only the power of motion and the instinct which prompts to eat and drink ; and there must be a universal reformation in Valais in all their domestic habits before they can deserve to be called Christian or civilized, notwithstanding their churches and works of art, their political freedom, and their education. Many of the most distinguished generals in the French and Italian armies have been Vallasians, and not a few have attained eminence in science and *belles lettres*.

There is also in some valleys a remarkable type of beauty, both in men and women. But one wishes there could be a mission established for teaching housekeeping when the homes are exposed where these same people live. The contents of any respectable pigs' trough would be more palatable than what they concot, to say nothing of the utensils, where an old woman wears a leathern apron, and whilst wondering what is her profession with such a costume, looking as if flood and fire would be the best ordeals to which to subject it, we behold her gathering its stiff folds in one hand, whilst the other acts as egg-beater to a mass of yolks she has poured therein. We afterwards learn this is her common pan for all purposes of stirring, mixing, and beating for the various compounds they make in exercising the culinary art ; and certainly no invention could expect to provide for a greater economy of labour. Yet a pretty maiden, who is taught cooking in this way, wears a hat which costs perhaps from twelve to twenty dollars, the foundation being Italian straw, and the trimmings all manner of ribbons and flowers, crimped, and plaited, and folded in a way to use the greatest possible quantity of material. They look very jaunty and coquettish, and set off their pretty faces to perfection, which they seem to know very well. Whether knitting or netting, braiding straw or breaking flax, tending silkworms or spinning thread from little wheels, which they carry about, there is a grace and litheness about them quite different from the gayest and prettiest on the northern side of the mountains. Not the less conspicuous is it in the little beggars, who will kiss the hand to you in the most gracious manner before extending it for pennies, or they throw you a bouquet, or crown you with a garland, or sing a song, for which they expect a reward, and which you find it very difficult to refuse.

They have a curious custom in several places of amassing great stores of certain kinds of provisions, in order that when they die there may be sure to be enough for a feast for the mourners. And when they go far down in the plains and vineyards for the vintage or to gather fruits, if one dies they do not bury him in a strange land, but place him on a mule, and when it is night travel slowly homeward, stopping now and then to pray around the unconscious companion whom they escort.

CHAPTER VIII.

VAUD.

CHEESE SOCIETIES—UNION DAIRIES—WINE-PRESSES—BLACKSMITH'S SHOPS—LACE-MAKING—VINTAGE FESTIVAL OF VEVAY—SHEPHERD SONGS.

VAUD is the pattern canton in all that concerns agriculture and the interests of rural affairs. With her originated almost every improvement; and possessing a climate which exhibits every degree of heat and cold, her soil is also various, and prompts experiments. A half-century ago she did not produce one third grain enough for her 150,000 inhabitants, and now produces more than enough for nearly 200,000. Yet they continue the custom of allowing a portion of the land to lie fallow, not every third, but every sixth year, especially in the northern parts of the canton, but not as in the olden time, without exercising judgment, and departing from the rule at any time if it seems best.

The principle of association enters into all their operations, by which the poor are made rich, and the rich not impoverished. Not only the village cheese-press, but the threshing machine, the wine-press, the sheepfold, the bakery, and the blacksmith's shop are common property; and when a family is too poor to pay for the use of any machine, it is granted free, upon the principle that the prosperity of one is the prosperity of all ; and if one is allowed to suffer, the detriment extends directly or indirectly to each member of the community.

Union dairies were not formed till the nineteenth century, and now there are 433 in this one canton, and they exist more or less extensively in all. In New England, families which possess few cows have the custom of *exchanging milk*, in order to make larger and richer cheeses than could be made with the small quantity of one. Here, the custom was exactly the same, till by degrees the whole village, and sometimes cities, became partners of a cheese society.

They build a house, and furnish it with cauldron, cheese-tubs, pails, dippers, ladles, and all necessary apparatus, and hire a cheese-maker, paying him with a certain portion of cheese and whey. A committee is appointed to superintend the details, keep an account of all expenses, inspect the arrangements, to be sure they are neat, and to attend to all the interests of the association, each member contributing to the expense in proportion to the number of cows which he has. The milk is sent to the dairy twice each day, the average quantity of each family being ascertained, and the laws of the association not allowing any to be sold elsewhere. The quantity of cheese is of course apportioned according to the milk furnished, and the association attends to the selling and repayments.

If others wish to join, they pay a slight entrance fee, according to the capital of the association and the milk they send ; and if the society dissolves, everything is valued, and each one remunerated according to his portion of the expense at the beginning.

In the country of vineyards the wine-press belongs to the community, and the sum which each one pays is fixed either by law or custom, the rich paying generously and the poor nothing. A man whose wealth is in vineyards will perhaps have a press exclusively his own. We have seen such an one in a large building, the cellar of which was devoted to tuns and hogsheads of wine. The grapes were pressed in the mill, and the juice conducted to the lower regions by means of a pipe, thus saving the labour of transporting it.

The bakeries are the same as in Germany,* except that they are not government institutions. In some places the bread is kneaded at home, and merely baked in the common oven; and in others the meal is furnished and all the labour performed by the baker, who is paid according to agreement, often with dough, and sometimes depending entirely on the generosity of the *Frauen* for whom he moulds and bakes. As they look very doughty, and quite content with their position in life, we must conclude the dough is not dealt to them in mean proportions. The poor often pay nothing, and it is becoming more common to bake in families, thus allowing a greater variety, which is a want one feels sadly when a common oven furnishes all the bread. The difference is greater in Switzerland than in Germany in the quality produced in different places, perhaps because it is not all made by the same government receipt. There was scarcely any resemblance between the delicate little *brods* of Berne and the great loaves of Zurich, yet they were both good. In Glarus it was horrible, and in Graubünden still worse, yet in each village it would be different.

In districts where wheat is extensively cultivated, threshing

---

* We do not mean to imply that in Germany the government has any pecuniary partnership in the baking, but that it is licensed, protected, and cared for by the government, and the price of bread fixed by law. In Switzerland it is a voluntary association with which magistracy has nothing to do.

machines are common, are owned by the commune and rented, moved by water and sometimes by horse power, as the labour of men is needed in the other departments of agriculture at the time of threshing.

The *sheep-associations* employ a shepherd, usually a little boy, who has the care of so many sheep, the number depending upon the nature of the pasture. This belongs sometimes to a society, and sometimes to the commune, and is rented to as many sheep as it will nourish ; and if those who belong to the association have not enough, they *take a few to board;* and in this, as in everything else, there is the same beautiful care for the poor. Each association is sure to have room for a sheep or two of a widow or some unfortunate family who are depending upon the wool for their winter clothes, and yet own not a bit of land. The wool, flesh, and milk belong to the association ; and the shepherd is paid by contribution.

The village blacksmith is also common property, receiving a salary, and shoeing horses and mending ploughs according to prices fixed by law. In this way he is sure of a competence, and every village is sure of a blacksmith ; and being entirely a voluntary arrangement between the parties, must be entered into, because in this way they secure the greatest good with the least trouble and expense.

Not the least useful among these attempts to promote the common good are the life insurance companies for the cows. In some places horses are included, but the greatest number are for the *horned creatures.* The company is formed after the manner of those which insure the lives of people, and so much is paid for each cow according to the original capital, and an annual tax as may be required or agreed upon. The treasury is for the purpose of meeting exigencies, and in some communes amounts to so large a sum that the interest alone is sufficient to indemnify for all annual losses. If these are very great, from any special cause, a contribution or tax is assessed.

The rules of indemnification vary among different companies, but it is usual to pay two-thirds of the price of the animal if it is a cow; and if a horse, only one-half. A valuation is made twice a year, but sometimes so much is paid *a head*, without reference to the price of the animal. In communes where there is a forest, wood is often given in compensation for losses or a sum of money, or so much per cent. If a poor man loses a cow, the society makes him a present, which, with the sale of the skin and horns, shall equal the full value of the animal. Pecuniary aid is also granted in cases of misfortunes from other causes. If any difficulties occur, they are settled by arbiters.

Among some families there will be also a common plough, or they hire one for the little time they wish to use it.

The instances are not rare of poor families receiving a bit of land, enough for a house and garden, with timber to build, and assistance in making it habitable.

But they are not an agricultural people only. Their watches *keep time* with those of Geneva, and their laces rival those of Flanders. But nearly all who are engaged in mechanics are the descendants of the French refugees, of whom six thousand settled on Lake Geneva, after the Edict of Nantes, and brought with them their skill in various branches of industry. A single shop in Lausanne sends twenty thousand pairs of gloves to Paris, where ladies buy them for Parisian and think those by any other name cannot possibly *fit*. They are made by the skilful fingers of the peasant girls in the surrounding country.

In the valley of St. Croix are seven hundred kloppers, weaving the delicate meshes of *thread-lace*, which must also pass through a Parisian shop in order to become sufficiently *distingué* for a lady of quality. Dresses, shawls, and veils are also the work of their hands, and in all the varieties are employed nearly four thousand women. Their wages are nearly the same as those of the embroiderers in St. Gall and Appenzell. They weave into the braids of their hair a red ribbon, and draw over it a network, that softens the tints and adds to the charm; and in their dress and in their homes there is the neatness of those who have not only the means but the inclination to improve in all things.

Here are also manufactured pretty flower-baskets, and some fifty thousand music-boxes, every year. The tongues of the lace-makers move like their kloppers, and those who make music by machinery are disposed also to make it with their voices. Is it owing to their labour, or to the air and the sunshine, that they have become celebrated for their lightness of heart and blitheness of spirit? Some would answer, "To their French extraction;" yet in another village, not very far distant, those who had the same origin look like so many people in a galloping consumption. One would as soon expect a pearl as a *bon-mot* from their lips, and will certainly take a chill if he remain long in their midst. But a cold north wind sweeps down through the valley, which may be the principal cause of their cadaverous countenances; and another may be, that every house is a shoemaker's shop, which sends forth an equal number of "boots and shoes daily." Wages have increased a third in Canton Vaud in the last half century, and the quality and abundance of food improved in proportion. Black bread has almost entirely disappeared in the cot of the labourer and the Sennhut on the mountain. In the valley of the Joux, where fifty years ago there was scarcely a garden, and vegetables as rare as the wheaten loaf, may now be seen the flower-bed beneath every window, and the patches of peas, beans, and cabbages spreading far and wide.

It is a land of vineyards and rich pastures, and wine and cheese occupy a large space in the cellar of every prosperous household. The juice which is expressed from pears and other fruits, except apples, is called in Switzerland *Most*, and this and cider are also among the winter stores. Since it became the custom to furnish their own cellars, the inns are not so much frequented, though neither here nor elsewhere are they by any means deserted.

Fresh meat does not often appear on their tables, except on Sundays and festival days; but ham, with potatoes and other vegetables, almost every day for dinner. Among the peasantry, four meals a day are customary, and at two of them wine never fails. The lowest class of labourers are not content without at least a quart daily, besides a glass of brandy before going to work in the morning. Pancakes and waffles with wine are the evening repast, and cheese on all occasions.

The pride of the Senn is to see his hut lined with smoked meat; and in order to be sure and rival his neighbour on the opposite hill-side in this respect, he will live upon cheese and whey till his meat is spoiled. Hanging upon strings against the walls of the storehouse may also be seen slices of bread with a hole through the middle. When they are dried, he eats them with a bit of toasted cheese dipped in wine.

In alluding to the shepherd-life of these regions, Byron says: " The music of the cow-bells in the pastures, which reach to a height far above any mountains in Britain, and the shepherds shouting to us from crag to crag, and playing on their reeds where the steeps appeared almost inaccessible, with the surrounding scenery, realized all that I have ever heard or imagined of a pastoral existence—much more so than Greece or Asia Minor, for there we have a little too much of the sabre and musket order, and if there is a crook in one hand, you are sure to see a gun in the other; but this was pure, unmixed, solitary, savage and patriarchal. As we went away, they sang the *Ranz des Vaches* and other airs by way of farewell."

As we have elsewhere explained, the genuine *Ranz des Vaches* has no words, but we have found one or two simple shepherd-songs which are said to have a date more ancient than any man's knowledge, and which are yet to be heard every day among the hills, that sound so shepherd-like, we have transcribed them, making the translation literal, word for word, without any attempt to give them an English versification:

"THE SONG OF THE ORMONDS.

"The shepherds of the Colombette rise early,
Ho, ho, the cows to milk; ho, ho, the cows to milk.
Afterwards the milk must be set to curdle,
Before the cheese can be made; ho, ho, the cows to milk.
You are come to the ford and cannot cross,
   Ho, to the milking.
Poor brother, what shall we do? We must go to the priest,
   Ho, to the milking.
And what do you wish that we say to the priest?
   Ho, to the milking.
He must say an *Ave Maria*, that we the river may cross;
   Ho, to the milking.
Peter knocks on the door, and says to the priest,
Ho, ho, the cows to milk; ho, ho, the cows to milk.
'We are stopped at the ford, say an *Ave Maria*;
Send us your maiden, we will make her a fat cheese.'

'My maid is too pretty; I am afraid you would keep her;
Then God would be angry, and you must come to confession;
Go away, friend Peter, and I will say the *Ave Maria.*'
  Ho, to the milking; ho, to the milking."

"THE STORM.

"It rains, it rains; my fair one, put on your cloak and gather your sheep. Listen to the patter among the leaves: it rains without ceasing. The weather is black as ink, and it begins to lighten.

"Hear! the thunder begins to roll. It is nothing; fear not; keep close to me. I see already our cottage, and near it are my mother and Judith. Both hasten to meet us.

"Good evening, dear mother, and dear sister, good evening; here is a lodger I have brought for the night. Make a bright fire, she is cold and wet. I will in the meantime go for the sheep. We must take care, dear mother, of her beautiful flock. We need some fresh straw for the lambkins. It is well, dear mother; now let us go to the kitchen. Oh! how pretty she is, undressed and barefoot!

"Now we will have supper; here is your chair; sit near to me, and set the candle near your dish. Taste your porridge. Oh! you do not eat, my little one; you are too sad and shy.

"See, here is your bed; go and sleep sweetly. Yet from your pretty mouth I must have one kiss. Good night till we meet again. To-morrow my mother and I will go to your father and see what he says."

One can easily believe these to be the words of the simplest of shepherd boys, befriending a little maiden as simple, who also tends her flocks among the mountains.

The heights of the Jura have no peaks covered with eternal snow, but they are verdure-clad to the very tops, and furnish some of the richest pastures in Switzerland.

Here are to be seen Senn-huts which are like villas, and which are occupied by whole families during the summer, who receive guests and entertain them with milk and honey, wine and cheese. In one of them, on a mountain overlooking the plains of Grandson, Bertrand wrote his romance; and Monsieur Delessert has created an Elysium on Mount Tendre, from which one may overlook Canton Vaud, the chain of Alps, and nearly half Switzerland. Yet, they are Senn-huts still, because there the cows are milked and the cheese is made, though upon a grand and beautiful scale, from which all primitive simplicity has departed. The vineyards are like those of France, and the wines the delicate wines of Burgundy. On the vines of one kind are great clusters of the most beautiful amber colour, and on another, small, close, round bunches nearly black, so deep is their purple hue. The former need a fertile soil, while the latter are set in dry places, and often take root in beds of flint. Where new earth is needed, it is carried in baskets to the highest points, and old stocks grafted by making an opening five or six inches below the surface.

The vintage takes place usually about the first or second week in October, when the vineyards present the same scene as in Germany, and the whole land keeps festival. The white grapes are crushed in tubs and carried to the press immediately; but the black are kept in great vats, till fermentation commences. Both remain during winter in tuns; and in March the wine is poured from the *lees*, and the best quality bottled and sealed. The white wines are the lightest, are soonest fit to drink, and keep the longest, some of them thirty years. The juice of the purple grape is stronger, and in standing changes to an orange tint and becomes milder, but keeps only ten or twelve years. The lightness of the soil and the inclination of the hills affect their taste and quality.

The costume of the vintagers is very coquettish, varying somewhat in different places, but usually a skirt of blue bordered with lace, and bodice of black, with a gauze or crape kerchief over the bosom. The short, full chemise sleeves leave the arm mostly bare, and the hair is puffed beneath a wide-brimmed straw hat, the crown of which rises to a point like the neck of a bottle which has a glass stopper, the most curious of all head-gears.

In Echallen, in the heart of the canton, great preparations are made for every festival, whether it is the vintage, a village raising, or a shooting feast, by washing or whitewashing the houses, and all the marriageable girls appear in new dresses, never wearing the same a second time on festal days.

In Pailly, another village, all the maidens appear in black on similar occasions, with gold chains, standing before the doors to offer refreshments to those who pass, each family coveting the honour of showing hospitality.

But the grand festival of Canton Vaud is the *vintage fête of Vevay*. Its origin is not known, but from many of its features it is supposed to have originated in Greece, or to have been instituted here by Grecians, in honour of some person or occasion not now understood. Bacchus and Ceres have lost none of their importance in the ceremonies of the present day, and may have been the personages for whose benefit the festival was first given. Others think the monks of the early times wished to reward the diligent and encourage the culture of the vine, and therefore created the *fête*, distributing prizes at the same time that they diffused pleasure. One of the mottoes upon an ancient banner was " Prayer and labour ;" and whether the society was ancient or modern, it exists still. Those who have the best vineyards are reported by a committee, who visit all the neighbouring country to examine them, and on the day when *la fête des vignerons* is celebrated, their names are made known, and medals awarded.

There is a comical mingling of ancient and modern, sacred and profane, but without any intention of profanity. The principal actors know nothing of the heathen gods, or the mythology of the ancients, and very likely they do not know much more of Noah and the spies of Canaan.

The procession begins with the representatives of spring, crowned with garlands, who are followed by forty young men, laden with all the instruments used in wine culture, either new or made clean and beautiful for the occasion. Then come what are called the priests of sacrifice, leading the consecrated ram, and Oenophren bearing the altar. The high priest follows, with a troop of beautiful children singing sacred songs.

Why Silenus "riding on an ass" should be included in such a festival, we do not understand; yet there he is, followed by Bacchus in his car. Ceres and Pallas are attended by a train of priestesses with their emblems, sickles, and wreaths of wheat, while in a long train are arranged the shepherds with their crooks, the mowers with their scythes, hay-makers with their forks, and the Senns with their milk-pails and cauldrons, in costume to correspond with their labour, and singing the songs of their several professions.

At the head of the third division are the spies of Canaan, represented by four officers of the guard, bearing rich purple clusters, which could not have been excelled by any the land of Canaan ever produced. Cyclops actually working at his forge, and a wine-press in full operation, drawn by horses, are the next conspicuous objects, with many vintagers carrying baskets filled with grapes, and their shears in their hands; and last, but not least, father Noah in his ark, surrounded by his wine-drinking sons.

The songs are in all languages or dialects, the costumes of

every variety, and the banners displaying appropriate mottoes, while happy faces are not the least brilliant feature of the scene.

At the windows of the houses appear the spinning wheels, also in gala attire, various utensils of household economy, and cooking apparatus, as emblematical of industry.

A rustic wedding is always a part of the *fête*, when a fair maiden receives a dower, and is crowned queen of the day, and gentlemen and ladies honour them with their presence, and join in their dances, singing :

> "Each with his sweetheart, oho, oho.
> Since four summers have they loved one another;
> Let us honour them with song, and wine, and dance,
> Each with his sweetheart, oho, oho."

All is finished with a procession of old men in the costume of William Tell, who are followed by the multitude to the shade of the chestnuts on the bank of the sea, where the tables are spread, laden with all that can tempt the palate, while everything to gratify the eye is arranged in not less generous profusion. Grapes of every hue, fruit of every variety, all the implements of agriculture and many of art; baskets of all that the earth produces, the cheese of the mountain and the loaves of the valley; every invention of cookery, and all that fair hands can form, are displayed with a taste which lacks nothing, and an abundance which knows no limits, while every garden must have been robbed of its treasures, and every parterre despoiled of its beauties, to crown the whole with garlands; and the libations, not of new wine, but of old, are long and deep.*

It is a curious fact, that the quantity of soap used in the can-

---

* The reader will remember also that it is new wine, and not old, that intoxicates.

ton now is three times greater than thirty years ago. Here the great wash occurs twice a year, as in Germany, and the articles of a bride's wardrobe are counted by dozens, or ten and twelve dozen of each, not a rare dowry.

Among the rich every trace of the old life and customs has disappeared; and though in the seventeenth century a dancing-master was banished because he allowed persons of two sexes to remain together after ten o'clock, now they may dance all night, and till the dawn, without being molested by the government or any lesser authority.

The *Kiltgang*, or nightly wooings, are the universal custom with the universal consequences, but in general the wife is treated with marked respect, is made keeper of the treasury, and consulted as the oracle of the family. In harvest, women are seen in the fields following the mowers, receiving in their arms the grain as it falls, and placing it carefully on the ground. They also take care of the gardens, are seen in towns wheeling little hand-carts, "with light wares laden;" and here, as elsewhere, are the water-carriers on all occasions.

There are remnants still of the days of superstition, when the devil was supposed to understand and meddle in all human affairs, and was designated by some twenty different names, as "serpent," "sly one," "old one," etc., and believed to be cloven-footed and clawed.

Witches assembled at the rising of the moon, and their evil influence was charmed away by a verse of the Bible chanted by a priest. A beautiful neckband was placed upon a cow as a charm, and pigmies rode through the forest on pigs, using their tails for bridle and reins. Fairies with diamond eyes scattered riches, and in which the faith of the people never faltered, though they remained always poor. Whoever found at midnight a four-leaved clover would inherit wealth. Over every fountain was a protecting angel, and at every burial the death-wine was drunk.

When Canton Vaud was subject to Berne, the government endeavoured to compel them to economy by law, and we find the same ludicrous enactments as elsewhere.

Among the articles of the wardrobe of a noble lady of Vaud, in 1643, were a chain of 880 pearls, gold bracelets, a necklace of diamonds, and roses of rubies, and rings of all precious stones. The nobility alone were allowed to wear gold, silver, brocade and lace. Burghers were forbidden to wear caps which cost more than eight dollars, and their wives were allowed but one dress and one petticoat, and no false hair. The wives of the clergy were forbidden to appear in taffeta, satin, or velvet. Coffee, tea, and chocolate were proscribed to all except my *gracious Herren* of the aristocracy, and only the *Landvogt* was an exception in the prohibition of smoking tobacco and taking snuff. On one occasion, availing himself of this permission, he produced his box in church, and passed it around for all to take a pinch. The preacher paused, and looking seriously at his excellency, said, "In this house we *take* only the Word of God."

Now, the law commands that a pastor's house shall be built with six rooms for the family, besides storeroom, chambers for servants, cellar, and room for catechumen. The rich dwell mostly on the banks of the lake, and exhibit all the elegance and luxury of English country-houses, with the varied architecture of Greece and Rome, or the Gothic of the Middle Ages. For windows, pillars, and wherever ornament is required, they use a kind of soft sandstone, which they call *molassa*, and the bricks, made by a mixture of the sand they obtain from the sea, are a pale yellow, and are used for partitions, chimneys, and arches, with a very pretty effect. The roofs are covered with slate, which they bring from the Canton Valais.* When one wishes to build a house, he gives his idea to the designer, the size of the rooms and of the whole, and the material. The cubic feet are then taken, for which he pays so much each.

Formerly, the garden beds were all made by square rule, the trees set in straight rows, and the parterres like churchyards, surrounded by walls; but taste is beginning to diffuse itself with utility, and comfort to go hand-in-hand with beauty.

The law also prescribes, that the schoolhouse shall be provided with two rooms, kitchen, cellar, storeroom, dining-room, and woodhouse, as it is occupied by the family of the teacher; and the houses of the middle classes generally have a dining-room and guest-room, one for parents and one for children, besides pantries, storerooms, etc. There may not be any more room than formerly, but it is better used. The stairs are of stone with iron railings, the walls are papered, the roofs plastered and ventilation secured.

But remnants of the days of old are still to be found, or rather experienced, in curious old laws that were promulgated before the Roman conquest; and some pages of their statute-books still bear the sign and seal of king Goudebaud. They have at different times blotted out, revised, and added, but there is always something disagreeable in proclaiming ourselves wiser and better than our fathers were, which is, notwithstanding, a great stumbling-block to improvement.

The towns on the sea are the resort of strangers of all nations, especially of English people, who pay their taxes at home and

---

* Pebbles for the streets, they import from Savoy.

live abroad, it being impossible to do both, where taxes and expenses are both so great.

We saw a family brought into the same ludicrous predicament here as in Germany, where a father, mother, and five children came *abroad* without the marriage certificate, which alone could prove their respectability, or rather entitle any new comer into their midst to equal honour. Not till the little one was born, and its name taken to the registry office, did any one dream of the calamity which had befallen it, but though the parents, children, and others stood as witnesses, no petition could induce them to soil their pages with the record of a birth where there was no writing to prove the relationship of its parents. But as the laws concerning marriage are mostly to secure property rather than honour, no great evil will result to the little one, unless her prospects of inheritance should be increased far beyond what they were then.

We saw this summer a notice of a marriage between parties, one of which was from Zurich, the other from Friburg, and they were to live in Soleure. The marriage took place in Berne, and fifteen testimonials and special documents were necessary to make it lawful; upon which the editor of the journal indulges in witty speculations, that all who are looking forward to matrimony will be for consolidating the confederacy and generalizing its powers.

Another case occurred, when Americans, for some reason, were called upon to prove their marriage, and though the minister asserted that he knew the parties, and could not doubt their word, nothing less than seven witnesses standing in a row could satisfy the cantonal law. If citizens of another country wish to marry and settle in their midst, they must bring a certificate from their own government that they shall be provided for in case of misfortune ; or if the husband and father die, that his family shall not become a burden to their adopted country.

We were one day overwhelmed with reproaches because many of the emigrants to America were disappointed or deceived, or not properly provided for, by the government. But when we asked in return, what does any government in Europe do for strangers who may land on their shores ? they were obliged to answer, " Nothing, but to ordain that only those who have passports and plenty of money shall be allowed to stay an hour in their midst." What would they do, indeed, were fifty, or twenty, or even ten, to be thrown suddenly upon their charities, as are thousands every week upon the benevolence of Americans?

In Canton Vaud there are nine hundred and sixty societies of various kinds for the promotion of the general welfare. Five hundred and thirty of these are agricultural, fifty religious, and fifty benevolent.

The cantonal colours are green and white, in equal proportions, the words "*Liberty and Country*" appearing upon the white ground of their escutcheon. The inhabitants are Protestant in greater proportion even than in Geneva ; and in no other canton has equality a more genuine reality, or are the comforts of material life more universally distributed. This is a testimony we like to render as a proof that a proper attention to health and personal comfort does not interfere with the flights of fancy, the designs of art, or the investigations of philosophy. We have counted more than sixty celebrities among their authors and artists, some twenty of whom were poets, novelists, and painters.

We need not tell Americans that Agassiz was born on the banks of Lake Leman, nor enumerate his titles to the honours his own country and ours have bestowed upon him ; and we do not know which is the most proud—the little canton to have given him birth, or America to have adopted him.*

* In the village of Yverdon, at the foot of Lake Neuchâtel, Pestalozzi established one of his schools. The English guide-book says it was broken up, and he was obliged to flee, and that however good his theories and system of teaching, he succeeded miserably himself in putting them in practice. On what authority they make the statement they do not say, but there is no truth in it. Troubles which had nothing to do with his system or practice of teaching obliged him to leave Yverdon, from which place he went to the father of Fellenberg, who received him with open arms, and offered him apartments in his castle to open a school. He was not very prepossessing in his appearance, and Emanuel Fellenberg, being then a child, thought as he saw him coming that he was a beggar, but the narrative his father gave him of the noble life and sacrifices of his friend, made an impression upon his character which influenced his whole life. The following extract from one of his private letters will show the spirit in which he taught, and with such a spirit he could not help being a good teacher:

"I was from morning till evening in their midst; all that could happen to them in soul and love they received from me. My hand rested in their hand, and my eye rested on theirs. My laugh accompanied theirs, and my tears flowed with theirs. They were excluded from the world; they were by me and I by them. I had nothing—no household, no friend, no servant around me; I had only them."

Like all those who originate something new, and great, and good, he was derided, and had enemies. He struggled, too, with adversity and many obstacles; but if, as John Müller said, "He who founds a school is greater than he who conquers a province," Pestalozzi is greater than a hundred princes and generals, for he is the real founder of hundreds and thousands of schools.

CHAPTER IX.

GENEVA.

CALVIN—JEWS—LAKE LEMAN—WATCH-MAKING—SOCIAL LIFE—SWIMMING SCHOOLS FOR GIRLS.

THERE is perhaps no city in Switzerland which exhibits so great a degree of intellectual activity as Geneva, though it still partakes something of the severity of Calvin and the reformers of his age. Not only the social life, but the legislative and judicial proceedings, still bear the impress of his sternness and rigidity.

When they threw off the yoke of the bishops in 1535, and declared themselves independent, they adopted the new religion, and Calvin became their judge and legislator. He made the laws, organized the Church, and founded the schools. His active mind was everywhere, and the traces of it exist still in every institution. Many of his measures seem very rude and barbarous now, but he thought them necessary in the turbulent times in which he lived. His doctrine was not considered exactly democratic at the time he preached it, and there are more perhaps in these days than then in his native city who are of a similar opinion. They are not a remarkably devout people, or their devotions are performed somewhere besides at the foot of the altar.

They passed through all the gradations of spiritual and political emancipation common to the nations struggling against foreign and domestic tyranny, ignorance, bigotry, and prejudice, and their statute-books exhibit the same inconsistencies we have found in their sister cities. While they offered refuge to all who fled to them from persecution on account of difference of belief in certain dogmas, they imprisoned and tortured by hundreds those who were accused of being "possessed of devils," or having intercourse with familiar spirits. Towards the end of the sixteenth century, five hundred were condemned for witchcraft in the course of three months, and suffered the various penalties invented for such criminals in those days of darkness and superstition.

They were not really one of the members of the Swiss Confederacy till 1814, though they became the allies of Berne in 1526, and of Zurich in 1584. Rousseau and Voltaire pronounced their freedom and happiness without alloy, and sung of them as possessing almost an Utopia; but they have since made many changes, and if they deserved then to be called a liberal and liberty-enjoying people, they deserve it still more at the present time.

In Geneva, the Jew is not subject to a single restriction from law, custom, or manners; yet there are not two hundred within their limits. In some of the restrictive cantons the plea is made that, if they admit them at all, "they shall be flooded with low Jews;" but it seems to be proved, that where they are treated like other people, they are not inferior in ambition or self-respect. In Alsatia, one of the southern provinces of France, there are forty thousand, and their children all attend school, and their employments are the same as those of so many people of any other nation. They are driven to peddling and mean offices by the narrow-minded policy of Christians; and where allowed to pursue honourable callings, the proportion is not greater than among others of the mean, exacting, and dishonest.

The laws concerning Jews, in Switzerland, do not seem to be connected at all with the peculiar faith of the cantons; as in one, which is entirely Protestant, they are free; and in another, like Bâle, the policy is most illiberal and restrictive.

Tessino is the most thoroughly Catholic canton, and the Jew has there every privilege of other citizens; and also in the Catholic cantons, Friburg and Valais; while in Schwytz and Zug they are not allowed to come even within their borders. In Zurich they do not allow a Jew to live, trade, or own land, without the consent of the commune where they wish to settle, and Lucerne does not grant naturalization to Jew or Christian either, as a right, but will sometimes bestow it as a favour. In Unterwald, the law prohibits them to reside, but they say no Jew ever asked the privilege! In Protestant Glarus, they are liberal; and in Protestant Appenzell, they are again restrictive.

It is impossible to reconcile these inconsistencies, otherwise than by the influence of families and local prejudice; and these do not seem sufficient to account for differences on this subject, or any other within so small a circle as the limits of Switzerland. Yet, in some cantons lying contiguous, there is scarcely any more resemblance in character, laws, or customs, than in people separated by seas.

Geneva is little more than twelve leagues in extent, and is surrounded by Catholics; and, except the part lying on the lake, and one little almost invisible corner which touches Canton Vaud, is entirely bordered by empires and monarchies. In succession, Rome, Germany, France, and Savoy have quarrelled with her and about her, the one rending her in twain, and the other appropriating her *in totum*, century after century ; and yet she stands there, the proud little canton ; never losing her nationality, or allowing others to mistake her identity. She is Geneva through all time and all changes.

Lake Leman is first mentioned by Cæsar, who found it already bearing this name, or Liman, the *Lake of the Desert*. It is a pity it should not have retained one so poetical, and one which would admit the other cantons bordering on the sea to an equal participation, which would be no more than right, when she waters a larger portion of their territory than the one which shares her cognomen. It will seem very prosy to pass it by without some rhapsody, but nearly two hundred poems and romances have been written on its shores since Rousseau sung of " Clarens, sweet Clarens," * and among the authors are Byron, Lamartine, and Victor Hugo. Their " beauties" are in every guide book, and neither Mont Blanc, the Jura, or " sweet, placid Leman," could receive any additional honour from our pen ; but let no one presume that our heart has failed in its homage.

Zeneva was the original word for Geneva, and in the middle ages the city was known as ·Gehenna. Her escutcheon is emblematical of her history, not having been changed since a century before her independence. A perpendicular line divides it into two equal parts, exhibiting on one side a field of gold with the half of a black eagle, and another side red, with a key turned wrongside up. The *Landweibel* appear also in yellow and red on election-day, the red being predominant. The arms were borrowed from the empire and Church, and signify the double rule to which the city was subjected in the middle ages.

* Byron's words.

The rural population * occupy only one third of the canton, and on an average every two families own real estate. The manufacture of watches is the great industry of city and country, and busy fingers are at work upon the curious and almost invisible machinery, not only in the shops of the city, but in families as they have leisure, and in the cottages scattered here and there in the country.

The history and process of watchmaking are familiar to readers of all countries. In Germany it dates to the middle of the fourteenth century. We read of a watch presented to Charles V., in 1350, not larger than an almond. A goldbeater of Italy sent one to Duke Urbin, in 1542, small enough to be set in a ring. Parker, Archbishop of Canterbury, left one to his brother, Bishop Ely, mounted on the head of an Indian gold-headed cane.

The society or corporation of watchmakers in France received their first regulations or laws from Louis XI., in 1483 ; and as an art, watchmaking was introduced into Switzerland in 1587, but did not become a science till the seventeenth century.

After the discovery of the oscillation of the pendulum by Galileo, other discoveries and improvements followed each other in quick succession, and clocks began to strike in every kitchen, and watches to tick in every pocket. Here they are within the means of the cook and the chambermaid, who do not seem to look upon them as any special ornament, but as useful only in telling when the meat is sufficiently roasted, or *Monsieur* will return to his lunch.

In Geneva the first laws concerning this industry are dated in the year 1600 ; and in 1685 there were one hundred master watchmakers, finishing five thousand watches.

* The rural life is nearly the same as in Canton Vaud.

Towards the end of the seventeenth century clocks were applied to the determination of longitudes, and the mainspring and regulator perfected by scientific Englishmen, repeaters invented, and weights employed in marine clocks.

Two distinguished Frenchmen, Romilly and Le Roy, whose names are familiar wherever a pendulum swings, invented the best methods of measuring time at sea; and these inventions have been perfected till there seems nothing more to be done, but to make clocks and watches after the most approved patterns. Those who manufacture them now in greatest abundance know very little of the scientific principle upon which they go; and machines have been constructed which fashion by means of steam and water power many of the most difficult parts. Those which are still the work of hands are scattered in different places, one making all the pointers and another all the wheels, a third produces a spring, and a fourth the pendulums, neither having the least idea of the use of the several parts, and no more idea of the really wonderful little watch as a whole, than he who makes ploughs or polishes curling irons. But they cannot be put together or kept in order without comprehending the principle upon which they are constructed, as well as the mechanism by which they are kept in operation.

The watchmaking industry attained its greatest height in 1789, when the city of Geneva alone employed four thousand workmen, besides two or three thousand in the country and in Savoy. In the year 1819, seventy thousand were finished, but now not more than half this number annually, though there are forty-seven factories for making the cases alone. They produce, besides, a million of dollars' worth of jewellery, employing between one and two thousand persons, of whom several hundred are women.

Geneva gold is considered the finest, and her ornaments the most beautiful. Some people profess to be able to distinguish them in the midst of any crowd. In order to prevent fraud, the government appoints a committee of surveillance, who inspect every workshop and all the articles made in it, to be sure no unlawful weights or measures are used and no false alloy. The amount of gold used annually is seventy-five thousand ounces, besides five thousand marks of silver, and five hundred and fifty thousand dollars worth of precious stones.

The French custom-house allows each person to carry two Geneva watches across the border free, but for each one extra a duty of one dollar is demanded, which is very little compared to the ancient tariff, but perhaps the profit is not less to them, as smuggling has proportionally decreased.

The first steamboat was placed upon the lake by an American in 1843, and was named the *William Tell;* now there are three or four in summer, and two in winter. All do not pass through the lake who visit the city, as many go directly through Savoy to Italy. The number of passports *viséed* in Geneva in a year is between twenty and thirty thousand ; and in one year the number who travelled by the different public conveyances in all Switzerland was within six weeks five hundred thousand.

Four hundred emigrants from Geneva and Canton Vaud founded the Geneva of the New World in 1803, and a colony from Vevay in 1801, at the other end of the lake, founded New Vevay and Monterey in Indiana, where they planted the first vines. Several hundred went in 1833 from Bernese Oberland to Canada, and there is an Alpina in New York, a Glarus in Wisconsin, a Highland in St. Louis, and a settlement from Basle and Appenzell in Kentucky, all baptising their homes in the New World with some appellation which reminded them of those they had left in the Old.

The English guide-book, upon the authority of some writer not mentioned, in alluding to the influence of Calvin in Geneva, remarks, that "He was chosen member of the consistory; and that this was scarcely inferior to an inquisition, claiming the right to examine people's private affairs and those of their families, making laws concerning dress, and punishing all offenders with the greatest severity." As a specimen of these enactments they give the following, "that a dinner for ten persons shall be limited to five dishes; that no one should be allowed to wear plush breeches; violations of the Sabbath were to be publicly reproved, adultery punished with death, and the gamester to be obliged to stand in the pillory with a pack of cards tied round his neck."

They might have found far more ridiculous ones than these; but we have sufficiently shown in the extracts we have given from the statute-books of other cantons that this peculiar and excessive legislation did not originate with Calvin, and was not confined to Geneva alone. In Catholic Lucerne at the same time the laws were of the same character; and the scrutiny of the Government in all private affairs was not less severe, though the Church was subject to the state, and the clergy had nothing to do with the temporal power. It was the fault of the times, and among all nations the same. It is not many years since it was the law of England that no Roman Catholic should possess a horse that cost more than five pounds; and we saw the other day, that a magistrate had been fined in an American city for a violation of the Sabbath, though his sin was merely driving in a carriage, and what nobody now considers a sin, only that the law made a half century ago still remained on the statute-book, and some enemy availed himself of the opportunity to make the accusation.

In Germany and Austria this legislation concerning all these minutiæ still exist, just as it did in England and America two hundred years ago; the Government exercising a constant supervision and interference in the petty daily routine of individual life. No laws of Calvin were more ridiculous than those now enforced every day in these imperial and princely dominions; and those who will examine the early provisions of the Puritans, will see that they began by taking the same care, meddling continually with what should be left to every person's private judgment.

In Switzerland there was scarcely any attempt to revise the law codes till within fifty years, and some stood in all their pristine barbarity till 1848, and a few are not changed yet. But Geneva is not of this number. The government of Calvin was austere, and his measures rigorous in the extreme; but what was particularly evil in his legislation ceased long ago, while the schools he founded and the systems of improvement he instituted still exist. He was a misanthrope, not from his religion, but from his physical temperament. Zwinglius, with equal zeal in the same cause, was a social, genial man, not censorious even in those cold, harsh times, but tempering the truth he preached with a love and sympathy that made it all the more welcome.

All manner of benevolent and reformatory institutions are as numerous in Geneva as in Basle; and though it is not yet much to boast of, their affability and hospitality are a little more Christian and modern than in some other places.

In some respects the customs of society are the same in Switzerland as in Germany; in others, they are as different as if there were no relationship between them in language or contiguity. It is one of the unaccountable things to the solution of which we can never find any clue, how there should spring up here and there a point of etiquette, a peculiarity of dress, a manner of cooking, to distinguish a few who are in all other respects alike.

One sees, immediately on entering Switzerland, that women are much more free than in Germany. They are everywhere alone, walking, riding, visiting; and one feels instantly in any of their towns or villages that there is no such scrutiny or gossip about a lady who may be travelling or residing among them for any purpose, either secret or revealed. They are altogether more given to minding their own affairs, for the reason, perhaps, that they would have very little time for anything else, if they undertook to look after those of people who pass through or stop a little while among them.

The most peculiar of their customs in social life is the formal arrangement of children into circles of friendship called *Sociétés de Dimanche*, which continue through life. The parents select ten or twelve in the families of their acquaintances of the same age as their own, and they meet every week on Sunday, when children, to play, and as they grow older, to talk and dance, each child of the family having a circle of its own, the brothers and sisters not belonging to the same. When very young, the parents or guardians are present at their meetings; but as they grow older they are left to themselves, and the bonds of friendship and the promises of matrimony are formed with indissoluble ties, almost without the knowledge of others.

Chaperoning and matronizing are not at all the necessities they are in England, France, or Germany. Young ladies and gentlemen have pic-nics, rides, and excursions by themselves; and from all we can learn, conduct themselves as properly, and remain through life as worthy, as the ladies of any other nation. But these circles to which they are confined tend to make them exclusive, narrow-minded, and awkward. Being accustomed from childhood to associate with a few in so intimate a manner, they are not at ease in the presence of others; they have no general topics of conversation, know nothing of the world, and, the society thus furnished them being sufficient, they take no interest in any one beyond it, for the purpose of pleasure or benevolence. We do not know how general this custom may be, but find it in the principal towns from the extreme north, Basle and Schaffhausen, to the extreme south. We never heard of anything of the kind in Germany, yet at a ball or party the supper and other ceremonies are nearly the same in both countries. Among the eight or ten thus bound together by the most intimate ties of friendship, each is also the *confidante* of some one in particular, to whom are confided all her secrets, to whom she goes for counsel, and whom she prefers in all things to any member of her own family. Sisters are often strangers to each other, and often, too, estranged by these very means. The members of the circle to which each belongs may not have the benefit of ordinary acquaintance. They are not necessary to each other, because their sympathies are enlisted elsewhere. Between parents and children it is the same. It is strange a mother can be thus willing to renounce the affection and confidence of a daughter. The arrangement is with special reference to keeping them in what they deem "first society," and preserving them from plebeian associations. The boys of the circle are selected from families which render them proper matches for the girls, and with the hope that a mutual attachment will be formed. This is often the case, and an engagement made before the parents know anything of the matter. If anything so fortunate does not happen they look around among those outside the circle for a suitable connexion, and with those whom the parents think proper the daughter must be satisfied.

When acquainted with the details of such an institution, one no longer wonders at the unsociality and exclusiveness of the Swiss. We almost wonder that they possess even a remnant of human sympathy; and many people who dwell among them for years really believe they do not. But, as we have elsewhere shown, it is not among the lowly that we find these things, and we have seen them when enjoying the liberty and benefits of another institution, where we have obtained a much more agreeable impression.

The swimming schools of Switzerland and Germany are more worthy of imitation. These are now universal; and along the banks of lakes and rivers are to be seen everywhere the little temples for the exercise of these graces. We have seen twenty or thirty at a time floating on the blue waves of Lake Leman, and sporting in Zurich's bright waters, and never saw a merrier sight. The art of swimming is now considered an accomplishment, like that of dancing or drawing, and we think may very reasonably rank above both. It conduces far more to health, and quite as much to elegance and grace.

The arrangements are temporary in most places, being removed in winter, and consist of rows of rooms along the shore for dressing, from which they descend by stairs to the water, where a large inclosure is formed of boards, and, if the water is deep, a floor made of planks, but all so loosely that the current of water is not suspended, but kept constantly fresh. A lady is the teacher, and for those who are not expert, cords are stretched from side to side to be ready in case of accident, and for convenience in walking about; and around the waist a band, which connects with one held by the teacher, who leaves it loose until danger requires it to be called to their aid. They are first taught to balance themselves on the water, then to use the limbs, and when thoroughly at ease, all supports are thrown off and they glide about like dolphins, and splash like so many porpoises, turning somersets, swimming upon their backs, and performing all manner of gymnastics, with no more fear than the natives of the watery element. No exercise can be so healthful, as it calls into play every muscle, is exhilarating, and, with so many together, a diverting amusement, as it admits of the utmost *abandon* without possibility of danger to morals or delicacy. They have a uniform of red, or white, or grey, according to their taste, so loose as not to interfere with free motion, and black oil silk caps for the hair. Often they pass the limits of their little domain, and sail far out into the open water, a phalanx of mermaids, and would certainly not be the timid creatures women usually are if wrecked on the ocean. We should like to know that every sea and river in America could exhibit a similar scene.

The list of *savans* in Geneva would equal that of Zurich in length, and no words of ours could add to their renown. It was not the birth-place of Calvin, but was the theatre of his labours, and of many of the scarcely less bright and shining lights of his time. His house is still the Mecca of Protestant pilgrims. Rousseau was born in Geneva, and she gave Solone to England, Le Clerc to Holland, Lefort to Russia, and Neckar to France. Here, too, was the home of Vernet, of De Luc, Provost, Baulacre, Romilly, Le Sage, Diodati, Mallet, Pictet, Berenger, D'Ivernois, and Jalabert. Voltaire did not live in the city, but it was the scenery around her waters that tempted him to form his little paradise at Ferner, and that has tempted from time to time nearly all the *beaux esprits* of Paris; and her lake has been the nucleus around which have gathered those of all the world, especially the unfortunate who must fly from oppression, or who sought a solace for their misfortunes. The history of these alone would form an interesting volume, without including what they have themselves written. Byron found it "beautiful as a dream ;" and one can almost rejoice at the affliction which sent him forth a lonely wanderer when he reads the "Prisoner of Chillon," "Manfred," and "Childe Harold," the songs which he sang on Geneva's banks. Madame de Staël, surrounded by her brilliant coterie, lived at *Coppet*. The new castle was owned first by Count Dolina, and next fell into the hands of a rich banker of St. Gall, not a millionaire merely, but the lord of many millions. In the reign and through the injustice of Louis XIV. he was despoiled, and died in the miserable hut of a poor woman of Versailles. It then became the possession of the minister of this king, the father of Madame de Staël. She was the magnet which attracted all the sages, philosophers, and literati of the then known world—a constellation perhaps the most brilliant which has ever shone upon it. Napoleon scattered them to the four winds, though he could not put out their light —alas! that he should have learned afterwards so bitterly what it was to be a fugitive and exile. There is scarcely a sod of the republic which has not been pressed by the foot of the unfortunate. When will despots learn to make their own so free that they may walk it over without fear, and meet their own subjects without trembling?

We need not mention D'Aubigné, whose "History of the Reformation," enchanting as romance, is read in every village of America. There are still wise men in her university, and literati, both men and women, whose names will be recorded by future historians as worthy to stand side by side with those of the past.

CHAPTER X.

FRIBURG.

GRUYÈRE CHEESE—GESSENAY SHEPHERDS—CHEESE ARISTOCRACY—SWISS SONG—INFLUENCE OF AMUSEMENTS—LEGENDS.

IF one mentions having been in Friburg, he is immediately asked, "Did you hear the organ, and did you taste of Gruyère cheese?" The organ is in the church of St. Nicholas, and called the first in the world. Its size is that of a small church, and its music that of all the spheres, and, of course, indescribeable. The cheese we tasted on shipboard, while crossing the Atlantic, and have never ventured to do so since, even when in their midst. They are made among the mountains which occupy the southern part of Friburg, the northern part of Valais, and the western part of Berne; all bearing the name of Gruyère, one of the oldest, quaintest, and most curious of all the old towns in Switzerland.

Among these Alpine pastures may be seen all the grades of shepherd life, and every variety of mountain scenery. On the heights of Gessenay one may go to sleep in Lapland and awake in Sicily, if he spends the night in almost any of its huts, which the rocks cover so completely that not a ray of the sun penetrates the atmosphere till in all its midday splendour it bursts upon the view, and for a little while the heat is so intense that the same rocks are sought for shelter which a few hours before seemed like icebergs.

The whole region is one vast pasture-land; and the people, father, mother, and children, are shepherds. They have no permanent residences in summer, but, literally, not only take up their beds, but their houses, and walk. The same is true of the Simmenthal. Each hill is covered thickly with houses, not with a proprietor in every one, but many being the property of an individual, those for the cattle having nearly the same appearance as those for a family.

They are all built of wood, the upper story consisting of long timbers of pine, so arranged as to give free course to the air, and the roof kept in place by great stones. Each beam and rafter is numbered and called by name, so that if "the winds blow, and the floods come to beat upon the house," the fall thereof may be great, but the misfortune can be easily remedied. It does not take long to rebuild; and though it is upon a rock, and not upon sand, they are very often carried away. Like the Arab, they travel with their tents, though they are of wood and stone instead of cloth; and they cross ravines and ford streams instead of wading through the sands of the desert.

There is scarcely an acre of cultivated ground to be seen; now and then a little hemp or flax, or patch of potatoes; but it is only within the last half century that they have thought of eating bread, and when wheat was introduced it created almost a revolution. It was one of those dangerous innovations, which must first be mentioned cautiously, lest the State should be placed in peril, and extravagance corrupt the people! They used to bake little barley cakes, which, like sea-biscuit, were affected by no changes, and enough were made in spring to last through all their migrations.

Their wealth is cheese, and their heirlooms are also cheese. Whoever enters the right storehouse, may see one bearing the date of 1643. By some they are asserted to improve by keeping, and others declare them to be no better than sawdust when past a *certain age!* For ourselves, they seem the same whether old or young, and to have in them no good thing ; yet they go as luxuries beyond the Mississippi and the Ganges, to America, India, and the islands of the seas. These tufted knolls afford nourishment, not only to the tenants of the cot, but to the proudest prince and nabob in his palace.

But, not only is cheese their wealth and heirlooms, but the basis of their aristocracy. The shepherds of Gessenay and the surrounding Alps are also magistrates and other officials, and yet do not disdain to drive their own cows to pasture, and superintend the operations of the dairy. They are the simplest of herdsmen, and have no higher ambition.

But a little lower are the dwellers in the ample and picturesque *châlets*, with servants to whom they say, " Go, and he goeth ; come, and he cometh." They neither drive cows themselves, nor milk them ; they are a few feet below their neighbours, and feel many degrees above them. We descend yet a little, and find those who only buy and sell the cheese after it is deposited in the storehouse : they are financiers ; neither manufacturers nor petty dealers, but wholesale and commission merchants, not at all to be classed with the people at the middle or top of the mountain.

The size of the cheese has also something to do with defining this aristocracy. Great proprietors with large pastures make larger cheeses, and sell them at greater advantage. Like all other people who have the means, they indulge in luxuries, and assume something of state, though dwelling in a *châlet*. Others imitate them as they become able, and thus follow all ranks, till the owner of a few cows in a single Sennhut among the rock ends the train.

But cheese are also subject to the fluctuations of the market; and, in these cases, those " of giant mould " are the first to feel the effects. Then the little cheeses begin to look up, and aristocracy bows its head; the levelling principle applied to the next of rank is *upwards* and not *downwards;* and so the little world is balanced among those solitudes in the same way as in the city among millionaires.

With the shepherds of Gessenay, every move is a *fête;* and when they have only to cross a stream, or exchange one side hill for another, or mount to the top of the next ledge, the procession is arranged in the same order; the cow with the silver bell taking the lead, the master of the troop with his shrill horn, and the young men and maidens, crowned with flowers, following according to their rank, singing songs and filling the air with merry music. The picture of pastoral life is far pleasanter when whole families dwell also in huts on the mountain, as it relieves the dreary solitude, which one cannot help thinking is neither pleasant nor healthful.

We are almost ready to say with the proverbial line, " Where ignorance is bliss, 'tis folly to be wise." Here there is evidently the happiness which consists in ignorance and carelessness of all the world beside. No prince looks with more complacency upon his subjects than he who sits upon some great boulder and watches his herds, one group descending a steep, another coming out of a wood, a third traversing a prairie, till all are collected around him; not less proud or tenacious of their rank than the "Geheimräthe" and "Obergerichtsräthe" of Deutschland around the throne. The songs of the milkers are not from cowboys alone, though theirs are sufficiently merry.

"THE SWISS BOY.

I.

"Come, arouse thee, arouse thee, my brave Swiss boy!
  Take thy pail, and to labour away.
Come, arouse thee, arouse thee, my brave Swiss boy!
  Take thy pail, and to labour away.
The sun is up with ruddy beam,
  The kine are thronging to the stream,
Come, arouse thee, arouse thee, my brave Swiss boy!
  Take thy pail, and to labour away.

II.

"Am not I, am not I, say, a merry Swiss boy,
  When I hie to the mountains away?
For then a shepherd maiden dear
  Awaits my song with listening ear,
Am not I, am not I, then, a merry Swiss boy,
  When I hie to the mountains away?

III.

"Then at night, then at night, oh! a gay Swiss boy!
  I'm away, to my comrades away.
The cup we fill, the wine is passed
  In friendship round, until at last,
With good night, and good night, goes the happy Swiss boy
  To his home and his slumbers away!"

Because "a maiden dear, may await his song with listening ear," it follows, that loves and marriages both take place whilst they are watching the herds and tending the flocks, but they are usually deferred to be solemnized on festal days in the village during the winter.

The well-meant but ill-directed zeal of the reformers led them to forbid the dance and song and festive mirth, not knowing that, unless they substituted something in their place, they only produced an aching void, which drove the revellers to darker deeds. The human mind cannot live on vacancy, and it must be one of marvellous construction that can support itself on solitude. Statistics prove, that excitement does not cause so much insanity as meditation ; and not so many cases of madness occur in great cities as in rural solitudes. The first case of suicide among these simple Alpine people was known when they were condemned to practice the forms of a new religion without understanding anything of its spirit. Neither their minds nor hearts had received any cultivation that fitted them for a serious and earnest life. What were they to do or think about, suddenly condemned to idleness, with no food for thought, and no idea of even the meaning of meditation ?

Statistics also prove that there are not so many cases of insanity among Catholics generally, as among Protestants. One reason may be that the assurances which they continually receive of pardon, and their credulity with regard to the efficacy of the means they use for salvation, preserve them from disturbing doubts and fears, and the amusements which they are allowed divert them from speculations which avail nothing even with strong and healthy intellects, and must surely destroy weak ones, if they do not utterly distract them.

We do not give this as an argument in favour of Catholicism, but only as a fact. There is no reason why Protestants should not be as happy as Catholics. Those who are ignorant, or those who need it for any reason, whether of one faith or another, should be furnished with healthful amusement ; and those who are content with intellectual cultivation and resources, should endeavour for an hour to conceive what they would do without them.

A lady sits in her pleasant parlour, surrounded by every comfort, and reads, in the columns of a newspaper, that "there is to be a ball on Sunday evening, for servants and apprentices." She exclaims in great horror against such a desecration of the Sabbath, and wonders how people can indulge in such low amusements. We do not say so to her, but we are very sure, had these people possessed her advantages for cultivation, and had they a beautiful house like hers in which to receive company, and could they purchase as many books and pictures, be entertained with music, and surround themselves with every luxury to minister to their senses or their souls, they would never once think of a dance in a miserable inn. To give them her pleasures till they are capable of enjoying them, would be no kindness; but how many of them would she be willing to deny herself, in order that they might be elevated and purified to enjoy what she does?

It is the testimony of every traveller, that the difference between Catholic and Protestant Switzerland is observed instantaneously when the line is crossed which divides them. The Catholics are not so intelligent, not so well clothed, and live not in so good houses. They usually occupy the regions most cold and rugged. Among the shepherds they form the greatest proportion. Their life is simple, their amusements many, and their religious ceremonies performed with a grandeur which attracts and wins them. They are happy on earth, and believe they are fitted for heaven. They do not see the need of anything more.

A Frenchman soliloquizes concerning them in the following manner: "Protestants spread in the valleys and cities, and are industrious and rich. They have manufactories and gazettes—they *calculate* rather than *live.* Their lives are passed between the comptoir and manufactory. They give to the service of God only the time when they can do nothing else. Sober, cold, and quiet—they are rich. It is not the fault of the politicians of Basle that they do not set a printing-press or factory on every pinnacle of the Alps; but when they have made the shepherds as wise as journalists, of Capuchins philanthropists, of the herdsmen as many weavers as at St. Gall, or *beaux esprits* as at Lausanne, what will they gain? With all the effort and goodwill in the world, could they make finer men than at Appenzell, or more beautiful women than at Engleberg? All science could not make the pastures produce anything but grass, or the milk anything but cheese! Should they live in palaces, could they breathe a better air than on the Alps, or repose on bank-notes, could they sleep more sweetly than in their cots? Would they be more happy, when with more wealth they had acquired more care? And should it ever happen, that another revolution swept over Switzerland, would not the men of Uri or Valais defend their country as bravely as a gazetteer of Aargau, a rhetorician of Lausanne, or a banker of Basle?"

This reasoning sounds very well, but it is sophistry, nevertheless. They might defend their country as bravely, to be sure, but no more so; and when there is calamity from fire, or sword, or pestilence, whose bank-notes build again the cottages, give food and clothing to the poor, and bid peace and plenty smile again in the desolate land? For centuries, the monks and their establishments were supported by collections from every part of Switzerland; and the poor who crossed the mountains in their pilgrimages, or to sell their cattle and produce, were entertained free, and if they were sick, had every care "without money and without price."

It is not the whole of religion to attend church or make long and many prayers. That this proves a very pleasant and profitable diversion to those who have no other way of spending their time we doubt not; but there is a higher faith and better charity than this. It requires far more grace to perform well the active duties of life than it does to listen to fine music, good sermons, or beautiful prayers. A man may be a better Christian in a counting-house than in a cathedral, because it depends entirely on the motive with which he performs the duties of both places whether he is a Christian at all. The herdsmen of Uri and Valais may be as good and happy as the merchants of Basle, Zurich, and St. Gall, but this is no reason for leaving them in ignorance and superstition. Neither is it of any use to make laws forbidding them, or any other class of people, to dance or make merry, so long as they are not educated for a higher life. Those who preach to them from the pulpit should also do more; and those who sit in pleasant parlours and call them heathen, should ask, "What has made the difference between me and thee?" Christ not only preached "the sermon on the mount," but he walked about among the people, attended their weddings and their feasts, entered their cottages, and partook of their humble fare. Who does not see that the presence of superior refinement and intelligence on any of these occasions would soften the merriment and refine the character? Alas! from whom shall we expect such an effort and such a sacrifice, among all those who deplore the degeneracy and ignorance of the people—among those who profess to be the disciples and followers of Him who "went about doing good?"

The law again allowed the peasants of Gessenay first to dance on week-days and at certain annual festivals; but now there is no restriction—they may dance all the year. It was found they would resort to the woods and ravines at midnight, and the evil consequences became more, and had a more frightful fatality, than when they were permitted to assemble at proper times and in proper places.

They have a curious custom of assembling at little inns called cabarets, after morning service in church at New Year's Eve, every unmarried youth conducting a maiden, whom he has chosen for the occasion. They spend two or three days there together, and when they leave are betrothed. The marriages are performed at the Feast of Annunciation, when they go in pairs to church, powdered to correspond with their mountains, and the bridegroom carrying a long sword. If it is a widow who marries, they choose a king, and bear him on their shoulders around the village, with great noise and shouting, finishing with theatricals, representing various scenes in their history.

A traveller relates, that one day, when climbing the mountains, he met a young girl who had sole charge of the flocks and herds, no other person being within miles of her. He asked her to give him a cup of milk. She answered, "The milk belongs to my mother." "But I am very thirsty," said the wanderer. She looked down a moment in deep thought, and then ran quickly away, and soon returned with a foaming tankard. He offered her money, and she said with serious surprise, "You told me you were thirsty, and I gave you milk ; what would my mother say if I *sold* her milk ?"

Similar instances of patriarchal unworldliness are still to be met everywhere among the shepherds, and still a thousand years may leave them unchanged. So long as their life is so simple, their hearts and minds must retain a corresponding childish simplicity.

Their superstitions have the same character, and their mythology is fashioned according to their mountain domains and their daily labours. Any calamity in their dairies is ascribed to evil spirits, and fortunately the countercharm is not less convenient than the instruments of evil. By striking upon the cauldron of cheese, insupportable torments are inflicted upon the invisible inhabitants of the air, and put an end to their machinations.

A young shepherd was tempted to leave his herds and follow the chamois, but no success attended him. He wandered far and wide, and at length lost his way and sank to the earth from weariness and exhaustion. Then appeared one of the spirits of the mountain, and said, " The chamois which you hunt are mine, why do you make war upon them ? Arise and return to your flocks, and if you trespass no more upon my domains, you will again prosper." He was then guided by the spirit to his cabin, and deserted not again his troops.

Long ago there lived, in a fertile valley of the Senetsch, an old woman, so rich that she could cover with her cheese all the way from the village to the mountain, but she was also miserly, and so avaricious that she would not give a morsel to the poor or the hungry. One day she met a woman very old and destitute, who begged her for a bit of cheese. She refused, leaving her to famish by the wayside. But it was an angel in human form, who immediately arose and shook the mountains, so that their foundations gave way, and the valley was devastated with ruins. To this day it is called "*Mont Perdu*," as a warning to all against inhospitality and avarice.

The inhabitants of Friburg are divided into three distinct classes—German, Burgundian, and Roman. In the region of Gruyère they belong to the last division, having a peculiar language, a peculiar dress, and a peculiar beauty. They wear little felt hats, with many flowers, ribbons, and laces. The hair is drawn back from the forehead, so tight that it leaves the top of the head soon bald, being braided and tied with a velvet ribbon. The scarlet bodice is laced, and very stiff, giving them an ungraceful air, especially when old. Among the German population, the dress is like that of Berne, with the exception of little black caps crimped up at both sides. In other villages, on the borders of Vaud, the head is weighed down with great crushing braids of hair, matted with oil, and surrounded with a broad-brimmed straw hat. But on festival days scarlet is the universal costume, with a black silk apron, a white kerchief on the neck, and silver chain, to which is attached a round box, which they carry as a charm.

Bulle, some fifteen miles from Friburg, and near Gruyère, is the great *dépôt* for the cheeses as they come down from the mountains, for the wood which is cut in the forest, and the straw which is braided in the valleys. It is here, therefore, that the great fairs are held, and droves of fatted cattle come in autumn to find purchasers, and where the hats are gathered together by hundreds and thousands ; and a little further down, at Romont and St. Dennis, the beautiful horses are prancing and neighing which have been trained in the little republic to form the cavalry legions of kings and emperors.

Friburg is not less interesting in its history and development than the other cantons ; but we have dwelt so long upon the present, that we have no room for the past. The people are mostly Catholic, and the influence of the priesthood, with that of the government, was against culture. Before 1798, there was not a school in the country ; and every one who could read and write was considered a marvel. But in 1807, the famous Peter Girard * commenced a system of instruction which spread his renown as a pedagogue throughout Europe, and in 1830 the

* Girard was a monk.

government assumed the care of public education. To send their children to school from the age of six to fifteen is obligatory upon all parents; and the State supports a normal school for the preparation of teachers, who have a fund, which the government also aids, for the assistance of the sick and infirm.

The cantonal colours are black and white, in equal proportions, and the votes at elections given still by the simple mode of raising the hands.

The modern methods of agriculture have been universally adopted, and every village has its union dairy, as in Canton Vaud, the number of cows having increased many thousands in a few years, and the value of each cow also many per cent.

Straw-braiding, as we have said, is the principal industry, besides cheese, and there must be nearly a hundred thousand square rods of land devoted to raising rye and wheat to obtain the material. Upon this same land, between four and five thousand quarters of grain would be reaped if it were allowed to ripen, thus taking, it might seem, so much from the amount of bread in all countries where straw is braided. But, of course, without the demand for straw, no such quantities of rye or wheat would be sown; the people know whether it is more profitable to make hats or loaves, and would not do the one if the other yielded the greater benefit in any way.

Hunting is a privilege granted by the State, but upon the voices of the singing birds there is no price, and they seem to be more in number than in any other forests, and sing in sweeter strains. The flowers, too, are of marvellous beauty.

The ladies of the city have the gifts of grace in manner and conversation; but the city itself is so old that its age cannot be told, and its beauties are all of the dilapidated order. The bridge across the river Saane is, like their organ, one of the wonders of the world, and built by natives of the canton, who had never seen a suspension-bridge before. The architect was a Frenchman. It looks, at a distance, like a thread stretched across ; but when it was finished, in 1834, the bishop of the town, the members of the government, and two thousand persons marched over it twice in procession, preceded by a military band. It was one of the grandest gala days in the experience of the canton, though popes and cardinals have marched through her streets. This was a great triumph of art, and a noble monument of their public spirit.

The architect of their organ was born on their soil, and they have produced a painter second only to Holbein. A naturalist from Friburg is attached to the royal gardens of Paris, and they boast of many historians and military men.

CHAPTER XI.

NEUCHATEL.

QUEEN BERTHA—TROUBLE WITH PRUSSIA—MILITARY SYSTEM—WATCH-MAKING—LANGUAGE.

THE history of Neuchâtel has been the most intricate, and her life the most turbulent of any of the cantons, and only since two years has she been quite settled in full membership with the Confederacy. At the time of her alliance, and ever afterwards, she was a sort of princedom or landgravate, belonging first to one ducal house and then to another, who, either by conquest or inheritance, claimed a right to rule over her.

The country was first held *in fief* by one of the princes of the house of Burgundy ; and in the tenth century, Queen Bertha, wife of Rudolph II., ruled, who was beloved in her life, and mourned in her death, and whose memory is still precious among the people.

She was called *Bertha the Spinner*, and in Neuchâtel and Canton Vaud the anecdotes and legends concerning her are the winter tales and summer visions of every household. She is said to have founded the Collegiate Church of Neuchâtel, in 938, and there to have had her principal castle, though it was then but a small *bourg*, with a few dwellers in huts for its inhabitants. But she went from village to village, stopping a little time with one prince, and then with another; and as she rode along she was an example to all women, for she held the distaff before her, "spinning as she went."* Her husband was long absent in Italy, and she ruled his subjects as a loving mother rules her children. In a little church in one village, where she is represented as having set the example of spinning, is a picture of her, under which is written, "*Bertha, the humble Queen.*"

She established in every cloister a school for youth, a hospital for the sick, and provision for travellers. She caused many fortresses to be built for protection, and her husband also regarded the rights of the people; so that everywhere now, those who respect industry, economy, and piety, mention their names with the same honour and love as that of the fatherland.

After a wet winter, the peasants still believe she appears and scatters a sackful of treasures over the land. It was she who caused the vines to be planted; and once she saw afar off a maiden spinning while she tended her sheep, and bestowed upon her gifts to encourage industry. She knew how many eggs were laid in her *hennery*, and attended to her maidens at the wheel, and the labourers in the field.

It is not strange that the descendants of one whose memory was so cherished should have also found favour in the eyes of the people, though they were far from inheriting her virtues. In the course of centuries, the claimants to the little princedom became very numerous, so that, in the commencement of the thirteenth century, there were thirteen who professed to inherit sole right and title to the succession. Their power was not very

---

* It is said also that she rode after the fashion of men, otherwise she could not have spun.

great, to be sure, as the people guarded jealously their rights
and privileges ; yet, whoever lived in the castle was called
"*Prince of Neuchâtel.*" In 1707 the heirs of one line became
extinct, and it was necessary to choose another. Frederic I. of
Prussia was one of the pretenders ; and, because he was a Protestant, and they were just then very jealous of France and
Catholicism, they gave the preference to him, exacting, at the
same time, a promise that he would confirm them in their rights
and privileges, and not disturb their alliance with the Swiss.
Thus they remained a century, when, in the wars and treaties
with Napoleon, France again acquired possession of Neuchâtel ;
and when her fortunes changed once more, it fell back to Prussia.

In the meantime there had risen a strong party, who wished
to make the canton a republic and ally on equal terms with the
other states of the Confederacy ; and the Congress of Vienna,
in 1815, whilst acknowledging Prussia as nominal chief in Neuchâtel, incorporated it also as one of the cantons of the Swiss
Confederation. So it remained till 1830, with a republican
party striving to get entirely free from Prussia, and a royalist
party striving as earnestly to effect a separation from the Swiss.
The majority of the people wished to belong to Switzerland ;
and, from its position and relationship, this seemed the most natural appropriation.

The French revolution disturbed them again, and it was soon
found that the half-way connexion was a hindrance, rather than
a help, to the Confederation. In trouble, Neuchâtel could be
of no service, because she was not free to act her pleasure ; and
when the new constitution was formed, in 1848, the Confederacy
refused to admit her on the old terms, and a Prussian army was
soon on her borders.

It was evident to both parties that there could be no more

peace without war, yet diplomacy, and the interference of the "great powers," deferred an open rupture several years still.

The royalist party, however, were not idle, and, on the night of September 2d, 1856, the people were surprised by a party taking possession of the castle, imprisoning the members of the Government, and proclaiming the King of Prussia.

The republicans flew to arms, and their friends in the neighbouring cantons came quickly to their aid. Seven hundred royalists were taken prisoners, and the old Government restored. Prussia felt bound, of course, "to maintain her honour," and succeeded in winning France to join her in threatening all manner of evils to Switzerland if the rebels in Neuchâtel were not subdued.

The Federal Government had not hitherto meddled in the matter, as the little canton did not belong to them, but when France stood defiant on one side, and Germany offered free passage to a Prussian army to march to their destruction, it was time for the Government to awake. It was a good opportunity of proving their union and their strength ; and there was great rejoicing among the crowned heads and the advocates of the "right divine," as they were sure an end was now to be made for ever of the troublesome republic.

It was not ten days before the Christmas of 1857 that the decree was issued setting forth the danger, and when the festal morning arrived it found 16,000 homes deprived of husband, son, or brother, who had voluntarily shouldered the gun and knapsack, and in an hour transformed themselves into soldiers for the defence of the fatherland, and by each Christmas fire were the arms of those who remained, to be ready at a moment's warning. The forest cantons, who were themselves the rebels in the war of the *Sonderbund*, had already forgotten their private feuds, and rallied to a man around the common standard. Many, too, in other lands, when the intelligence reached them, hastened home, never thinking a moment of private interests when there was a common danger.

This was an unexpected demonstration, and the armies of kings and empires resolved to pause before engaging in such a strife. Diplomacy was again invoked, and Prussia at length resigned her claim to what she had no power to hold, and Neuchâtel became a member of the Swiss Confederacy. But the lovers of court titles and liveries are still many within her limits, and their pretensions, if not their hopes, are far from being extinguished.

During these troubles, many families of both parties lost their possessions. In Prussia a subscription was opened for the suffering nobility, and 112 thalers obtained, which was, a long time afterwards, increased by a rich lady to 7,525! Among the Swiss, more than a hundred thousand francs were received immediately for the families of soldiers who had lost husbands or brothers, and in one factory the labourers, eighty-seven in number, taxed themselves for this object, and contributed nine hundred francs, and the proprietors 1,440.

A large debt was left by the princely government, which has been entirely liquidated by their successors.

All Switzerland had for the first time acted in perfect unison. This increased their confidence, showed them the benefit of one united government, and proved to all Europe that neither the Government nor its military were to be despised.

In Switzerland, as in Prussia, every man is required to be a soldier when he arrives at the age of twenty years; but in all things else the systems of the two countries have no resemblance. For military exercises and instruction no Swiss is required to spend so much time as to interfere with his trade or profession, or to prevent his having a home, which will attach him all the more to his country, and make him all the more brave in its defence. Every town and commune has its *muster-ground*, where certain companies are required to practice two afternoons a week, others one, or at specially appointed times. Each furnishes his own uniform, which is very simple; but the Government or State supplies the guns and ammunition, drums, trumpets, and other musical instruments. These companies meet at stated periods for evolutions, and every two years there is a grand review, at which every canton, and perhaps every company, is represented. At *Thoune* there is a military school for the education of officers and those who instruct the companies of the different cantons, which is of course supported by the Federal Government, and in every canton an arsenal.

Besides these, schoolboys from ten to fifteen are formed into companies, in regular uniform, with arms, music, and colours, to be drilled by regular officers with not less care than are those who are required by law to learn the same tactics. We have seen them marching into town in columns half a mile long, with all the regularity of veteran troops.

The willingness with which every man marches, not only to the parade-ground, but to the battle-field, is in striking contrast to the hatred manifested in Germany to a system which requires the sacrifice of the best years of their lives without any hope of reward. In 1854, Austria found, in making her usual enrolments, 1,414 who had voluntarily mutilated themselves for life, to get rid of the detested service ; and in the Bavarian Pfalz of 600,000 inhabitants, during the two years of 1853 and 1854, it is found that 9,341 have secretly fled their country to evade the same requirement.* It is not the battle-field or the defence of their country which they flee, but the waste of time in life's best period, which unfits them for the duties on which life and position depend.

For the defence of important posts, peculiarly exposed to an invading army, strong fortresses have been built; and a fund has been created for the assistance of those who are disabled in war, and the families of those who have fallen in battle. This fund was increased by a legacy of about five hundred thousand dollars, from a rich Genevese, which was certainly a valuable and honourable testimony of his confidence in the Federal Government and its military system. The facility with which they rallied and formed a bulwark on their borders, when the last cry of war resounded throughout Europe, proved their capabilities equal to that of any army in Europe; and that years of discipline do not make legions invulnerable was proved when Austrians fell by thousands on Italian plains before French and Italian enthusiasm.

The eagle of Hohenzollern was not only banished from the land, but also removed from the escutcheon of the Neuchâtelois, where it had been engrafted upon the crown, which was originally upon their national ensign, with three broken rafters of silver upon a shield of red. Now appears a small cross upon a red stripe, which, with two others of white and green, divides the whole into three equal parts, cut vertically. Whether these have any reference to the peculiarity of this canton in possessing three distinct climates, we do not know; but, though only forty square leagues in extent, she is by her lake and her mountains as distinctly divided into three zones of frigid, temperate, and

---

* Dr. Kolb, of Speier.

torrid. Her pastures occupy one, her cultivated fields another, and her vineyards a third.

Her industry is also divided into three distinct branches—the making of lace, printing of calico, and manufacture of watches. Trade and commerce experienced from the earliest times scarcely any restrictions, and in the last few years villages have grown to towns with a rapidity not equalled anywhere on the Continent.

So early as 1700, laces were made, which were carried by *colporteurs* to the south of France and Italy, and in 1742 nearly three thousand persons were employed in this industry. Not only women and children, but aged men are seen with the *kloppers*, which are confined mostly to *Val de Travers*, where now some five or six thousand devote a portion of their time to them, but where agriculture also claims their first attention, and the lace, like the ribbons of Basle and the muslin of Appenzell, is the *knitting-work* for the leisure hours. It lies about till it is black as smoke and dust can make it, and is then rendered beautiful by bleaching and pressing, the whole process being more marvellous than in articles wrought with a needle.

There are still a few of the old houses, where the only chimney is a few planks, to give a little direction to the smoke, which, however, submits itself to no such guidance, till it has converted the walls into soot; but they are fast disappearing, and those which take their place are great square buildings, ample in all their provisions, with stone-floors and brick chimneys, walls and roofs of wood.

Moitiers, where Rousseau lived and wrote his "Letters from the Mountains," is the most ancient village of *Val de Travers;* but here, as well as in some of the others, there are very patrician-looking residences, which may for all we know be inhabited by genuine Swiss patricians.

We are more interested in those who dwell in the cottages which are scattered among the mountains, or stand in long rows along the streets, forming connecting links to the villages. Here are the watchmakers. Though they had long been made elsewhere, the people of Neuchâtel had not seen a watch so late as 1679, when an Englishman, who was travelling through the valley of the Sagne, found his own out of order, and asked, if there was any one who could repair it. A boy fourteen years old, who had become known in the valley for his skill in various handicrafts, was recommended, and not only succeeded in setting it right, but attempted to make one like it. Six months he studied and toiled, and at length completed one, of which every part, not only of the interior, necessary to motion, but the case, gilding, and engraving, were all made by himself. With the aid of his brothers he finished several, all being very simple, and having but one hand. Others learned of them, and in the course of half a century they made two or three hundred with very little improvement in the outward appearance or machinery.

Towards 1750 three brothers, by the name of Perrelet, invented many machines to facilitate the manufacture of watches, and afterwards made important discoveries in science, which are mentioned elsewhere.

Berthoud, who wrote a celebrated treatise on watchmaking, was born in a village of Neuchâtel, and his nephew perfected marine clocks. Breguet was of a refugee family, and afterwards became the most celebrated watchmaker of Paris, where his grandson is now the heir of his genius and his wealth.

Between two and three hundred thousand are finished annually among these villages, a great portion of which go to Geneva, and gain an extra value in the eyes of purchasers by assuming a city name.

It is always a curious problem, but alas! never solved, why people choose such dreary solitudes for their habitations, when there are thousands of sunny slopes and smiling valleys with room enough and to spare.

Among these mountains of the Jura the sky is black, the air is grey, and the snow is blue. In the course of the year they have 230 days of rain, or snow, or clouds, and only 135 of clear weather. The severe storms are not very many, but the summer is one long drizzling rain; the houses are saturated with water, and thus quickly decay, besides having a peculiarly dismal appearance; and the people are not only saddened, but embittered by their climate. They are shut out from all the rest of the world, absorbed in the labour of very little things, and thus become narrow and gloomy in their minds and temperaments.

But the rains keep the summer verdure of a most brilliant green, and the winter nights have a peculiar splendour. The blue of the sky seems darker than elsewhere, so that the stars in their countless myriads seem imbedded in jet, and the little shops, brilliantly illuminated for the long evening toil, seem to answer to the lights of heaven.

The snow sometimes falls to the depth of thirty feet, and when it has attained the height of two feet, it assumes a beautiful azure tint, which cannot be reflected from the firmament, because it is brightest when the sky is overcast with clouds, a fact which no philosopher has yet been able to explain.

Not only the watches, but all the materials necessary to the mechanism are perfected; and men, women, and children are all employed on some article of gold, silver, wood, ivory, glass shell or enamel, and in the larger shops are exhibited all the different kinds of timekeepers for land and sea in every part of the world.

Professor Agassiz is still a citizen of Neuchâtel, where he was formerly professor, and the Museum in return professes to be greatly indebted to him for all sorts of monstrosities in the form of geological, conchological, and zoological specimens.

Purysburg, in South Carolina, was settled by a colony from this canton in 1734 ; and the leader, who gave his name to the settlement, left to his native city, forty years later, the sum of a million of dollars, which he acquired as jeweller, owner of mines, banker, etc.; and a hospital, orphan house, and various other institutions and improvements are the results of his beneficence. From the villages of the Jura two hundred went to North Carolina in 1804, and purchased lands belonging to Kosciusko.

There is scarcely anything remaining of old customs or old life, less, perhaps, than in any other canton. The religion is Protestant, but in all temporal things subject to the State, which takes care of the revenues and pays the pastors. The law makes public instruction obligatory in every commune, and the poor are taught gratis. Teachers are obliged to take the oath of fidelity to the constitution. In the departments of natural history, mechanics, and the fine arts, Neuchâtel has produced many distinguished men. Guyot, Lesquereus, and Matile have also gone to America. Brandt, a distinguished engraver of medals, recently died at Berlin ; and Forster, of Locle, obtained the medal of honour at the Paris Exposition, in 1855.

The Swiss often become famous as individuals without bringing any honour to their country ; because, having either a German or French name, they are supposed by other nations to originate in one of these countries ; and only those who are acquainted with them personally, or happen to read their tombstones, ever learn that they are natives of Switzerland. We have more than once heard English people inform Germans of the works of certain English authors, quite in ignorance that they were American; and the Tauchnitz edition, published at Leipsic, makes no distinction between those of one country and the other, calling all English who speak this notable language.

We cannot help thinking always in Switzerland, it is a pity they have not one national language, though in time, perhaps, German may become so. It is infinitely amusing to be obliged to ask, on all occasions, before addressing a Swiss, what language he speaks; for though we know that upon the eastern borders their language is French, and on the northern German, there are many indefinite limits, where it is far from certain whether they speak one or the other. If in a hotel, we begin with asking for the *pfeffer*, and, not obtaining it, we say *poivre*, to find at last that an English waiter has been procured for the benefit of travellers, and understands nothing but *pepper*. The higher classes generally speak French and German equally well; and coachmen and postilions know as much of one as the other, and sometimes English and Italian in addition. But it is often the case that in the same town one family or individual prefers to speak French and another German; so that one is never sure whether he should say *Monsieur* or *Mein Herr*, *Frau* or *Madame*.

The constitution makes German, French, and Italian national; and all laws and public documents must be printed in these languages; and it is also required that the German be taught in all the public schools. Besides these there are nearly fifty thousand people who speak *Romanish*, or Romane, which has always been retained by those who were longest the subjects of, or mingled with, the Romans. It has eight dialects, and is spoken principally in Graubünden, some parts of the Oberland,

and districts of other cantons. Not many years ago, the Bible was translated into this language, and other books and journals have been printed in the same.

German is the base of forty dialects, and is the language of a majority of the people. It has some peculiarities entirely distinct from any language spoken in Germany; but Schlegel says, the poem of *Niebelungen*, and similar ones of the Middle Ages, when placed before a Swiss peasant, are immediately comprehended. Though the German grammar says the auxiliary verb *thun* corresponds exactly with the English *to do*, the Germans very seldom use it; but in Switzerland they make it answer all purposes in the same way; and other analogies, both in words and phrases, to the English, are many and striking. In some districts they clip all the words, as *I will nit* for *Ich will nicht*, the first sounding very much like *I will not*, and say *Madeli* for *Mädchen*.

We heard a German one day address a woman in the market about her cheese, and not at all understanding him, she said, " I do not speak French !" But we found no difficulty anywhere in understanding those who had been educated in school.

French is spoken in Geneva, Neuchâtel, Vaud, and by two-thirds of the Vallasians. Yet among the peasantry there are at least twenty patois, in which are Latin, Italian, Spanish, and Greek words.

Among the representatives to the Federal Council, fifteen deputies speak German, and seven French. But if you mention these varieties as a reason why they cannot harmonize as one nation, or do not seem fitted to belong together, they ask in answer, " Is not France formed of Celts, Franks, Burgundians, Flemings, Germans, Bretons, Spaniards, and Languedocs? Has not England her Bretons, Anglo-Saxons, Scotch and Irish?

Prussia Brandenburgians, Saxons, Poles, and French? Is not Austria made up of Bohemians, Hungarians, Germans, and Italians? and Germany herself of Suabians, Saxons, Austrians, Prussians, Poles, Swedes, and Westphalians?" Which is true, yet one does not seem to notice it so particulary as in Switzerland. But that there is some common cement, must be true, else they could not have been so long either partially or wholly united. This bond is now becoming more firm every day, and the feeling of brotherhood stronger. A national pride is awakening that leads them to forget cantonal and sectional interests; and though their enemies say there are traitors in Geneva, and restless spirits in Neuchâtel, that would at any time betray their country to France and much prefer to become subjects to the emperor, we doubt whether there are any great number; and there must be very few who would incur the hatred and odium of treason for any reward which France could offer.

CHAPTER XII.

SOLEURE.

PATRICIANS—MATERIAL INTEREST—JOURNALISM—OLD LAWS—HOUSES—
FIRST AGRICULTURAL SOCIETIES—COSTUMES.

THERE are only three or four cantons where families may be found who still live upon rents, and consider it degrading to practise a profession or trade, or know anything of the details of business. Soleure is one of these, and "we the patricians" have always played a conspicuous part in the history of the canton in the old times and in the new.

Among those who are called the lower orders there exists a peculiar hatred towards this class, who are said to have been always the enemies of progress, and to have united in everything that could oppress the mechanics and peasantry. The man behind the plough was considered of no more consequence than the horse before it. The tithes and taxes of every sort robbed him of the fruits of his labour, and there was no motive for attempting to improve his condition.

The patrician class were always believed to be in correspondence with and corrupted by the French nobility, and also by the emissaries of the monarchs who wish to obtain Swiss soldiers,

Swiss money, Swiss neutrality, or in any way Swiss influence and aid. The governments, when in the hands of these oligarchists, were accused of making a regular trade with foreign powers, selling men to war, and receiving money with which to revel in luxury.

Foreign ambassadors and agents were always residing among them, using every art to weaken their principles and render abortive their power, whilst professing for them the greatest admiration and paying them the greatest homage. No canton suffered more from these influences perhaps than Soleure.* No other sent so many of her youth into foreign service, where many of them became estranged from the fatherland, and no longer content with the simple life and manners in which they had been educated.

We see it more and more as a cause of lamentation, that so much of the best talent of the country should have gone to render the annals of other nations illustrious. If the energy of those who had been distinguished as officers alone, had been devoted to any department of usefulness at home, what an age of progress they might have made, which would have given them a so much higher rank in the scale of nations. As it is, all the bravery they have manifested, and the glory they have won, has only covered their own land with shame.

We have met people so democratic in Europe, that they condemned the Americans as severely for building ships and railroads for the autocrat of Russia, as the Swiss for fighting the battles of France and Italy! Whatever analogy there may be in the two cases, as far as the honour of republicanism is concerned, we cannot help thinking it will be a happy day, not only for

* The history of the "foreign service" will be found in the compendium of Swiss history given in the Appendix, and it will there be seen that it no longer exists.

Switzerland, but for Europe, when science, art, and the active employments of material life shall be considered worthy the energies of men, rather than the corrupting idleness to which a soldier is condemned whilst waiting the debasing and brutalizing scenes of a field of battle. What can be the observation, reflection, or religion of a man and philosopher who utters it as a taunt against England and America, that every man and woman is employed in some department of industry, mechanics, agriculture, or in a sphere of mental labour that renders impossible the dreary stupidity and corroding inactivity to which half the people in this old world are doomed, whether willingly or not? Yet we have heard an American utter it.

Russia is fast waking up to the truth ; and whatever the Emperor may be, or whatever his motives, there are no people on the Continent so shrewd, so well informed, so liberal and disposed to adopt modern ideas, as the educated classes of Russia. They were never trammeled by feudalism, they care very little for etiquette, and when they are in the world conform to it, from affability or for the sake of improvement, as a German baron or a Swiss patrician would not do to save his land or his life.

In Switzerland the press is free, but there is no popular journalism, no attractive interesting modern literature, no mental activity on popular questions, no lectures, as these things exist in England and America. It was in Berne that one of their own citizens told me they were in a state bordering on lethargy. In Neuchâtel, Geneva and Zurich, there is more mental activity, and regular contributors to their journals. The "dailies" have a page of items clipped here and there from all foreign and home journals, and the remaining portion of the sheet is devoted to advertisements. They criticise more freely what is done and said, or not done and said, by the Government, and have the liberty to say whatever they please, that is not treason or libel, and yet they say nothing. An editor is a man of no more influence in the community than a shoemaker, and what he does requires no more talent.

In book-publishing it is the same ; nearly all publishers are Germans, and they say reading is not so universal in Switzerland as in Germany. The popular writers are by no means so many, and literature has none of the importance and appreciation it deserves.

We saw in a village paper in canton Zurich a lamentable picture of the morals of the lower classes, a picture too gross for the pages of a book, revealing the secrets of the courts of justice, instances of child-murder and other revolting crimes, in numbers which seemed incredible within the precincts of so small a state. They ascribe the fault to neglect of parents and heads of families ; but it did not seem to occur to them that parents and heads of families cannot impress upon others a moral sentiment they do not feel and have never been educated themselves to regard.

Those lower classes must have a different education, higher subjects of interest and thought, and conversation—exactly what a popular literature and press could furnish.

Jeremias Gotthelf commenced a good work a few years since in a series of popular tales, illustrative of daily life and manners, charming in style and spirit, but his life ended when his work began, and his mantle does not seem to have fallen upon any other.

In Soleure, they say, "my gracious lords" of the Government and Council were always opposed to anything that could create intelligence and awaken thought ; and the same was true in general of the priesthood. As long as the people were ignorant and stupid, they were obedient.

At the beginning of the seventeenth century something was done for education, but the revolt of the peasants in 1633 was an indication to the men in power that it was their duty to revenge this attempt of the people to cast off the yoke of their oppressors; and instead of granting them the hope and relief that would make them content and secure them for friends, they drew tighter their bonds, increased their taxes, and not only discouraged, but forbade all efforts to improve them. It is very curious and sometimes amusing to notice the bitterness with which those who were in office at that period are spoken of by the people. So early as 1612 there is allusion to a schoolmaster, and in the sixteenth century some attempt at collecting the children for the purpose of learning to read and write. But some one wrote of the schools at that time: "A hundred children are together in one small room and taught A B C so diligently, that they learn it in five or six years!" "My gracious lords" did not choose that any one should be forced to go to school; it was easy to see what it would come to, if the people learned reading and writing, and had schoolmasters. If they choose to employ them, "my gracious lords" will not contribute thereto.

At the same time it was ordained, that houses with walls and tiles were to be built only "for my gracious lord the bailiff and the highly worthy pastor." Those for the peasantry were of boards, and covered with straw, dark and dismal as the times in which they lived. There are a few of them still, with the great overhanging roof, shutting out all light, a few beams of which might otherwise enter through the little round panes, and the door a few feet high. The furniture is such as we have described in similar houses elsewhere. The Black-Forest clock ticks in the corner; over a round table hangs a mirror, surmounted by a paper dove, emblem of the Holy Spirit, object of adoration for the family, and favourite resting-place for the flies. A crucifix and Einsiedeln Mother of God hang against the wall, painted and smoke-bedimmed, for the chimney is only an opening in the straw and willow-braided roof, covered with mortar, and the sooty particles are sure to perambulate the apartment before determining to ascend to the upper regions; and here and there, in niches and receptacles, are pictures and *souvenirs* from nuns and capuchins, all black and uncomfortable as it is possible to conceive.

But no new ones are built after this fashion. In every village are pretty cottages, with all modern improvements, tasteful gardens, and all the comforts they know anything about. We hope it will not be long before they will add a few to their catalogue in all Switzerland, which as yet they have never heard of, and life have a higher object than any with which they have ever thought of investing it.

We should not fail to record, that in Soleure, as in Friburg, it was to a Catholic priest that the people were first indebted for anything deserving the name of school. Scarcely a peasant could read or write when Ignatius Glutz determined to put an end to this ignorance, and another, Gabriel Leupi, followed up his efforts. In 1811, the Government created a normal school, and ordained that every commune should support a teacher; but the troubles of 1814 disturbed their operations, and not till 1830 was a regular system of public instruction established. The trouble is, everywhere in Switzerland, that the compensation is so low few can make teaching their profession, and those who do are not properly educated for their calling.

It is only within a short time that all privileges have been abolished, and only since the last French revolution, and the formation of a federal government on the true principles of equality, that gave all an equal interest in the affairs of the whole, that a noble public spirit has begun to awake, and a national feeling to pervade all classes. So long as they were absorbed in their little cantonal affairs, they were narrow-minded. They say of themselves: "So long as the foreign service continued, especially with France, and French aristocracy exerted so much influence in their government and society, a Soleure gentleman was neither French, German, nor Swiss, but a German-French-Swiss monster." But since the war-service and the guilds are at an end, agriculture and manufactures have received a new impulse.

So early as 1537 they built a canal, to connect the waters of the *Dünnen*, several miles long and ten feet wide, by which eighty-five thousand square rods of waste land were rendered fruitful. It was the first attempt of the kind in Switzerland, and the peasants laughed it to scorn; but when it had succeeded, it was the best incitement to new efforts in this and other branches of agriculture.

The Swiss annals allude to the bishops and priests of the earliest period of the Christian Church, as having families and well-ordered households, as working in the field, holding the plough, and harnessing the ox thereto; of their teaching the people to plant and sow, to burn lime, and build with stones, to spin and make cloth, to take the place of the skins of beasts, which they wore. "Work and prayer," was the motto of the Benedictine monks. It was only in later years that they became degenerate, when bad men entered the Church for the sake of the honour and wealth it could bestow, and not for the good they could do. When they ceased to be the true friends of the people, and exercise over them a paternal care, they ceased to improve; and it was this degeneracy of the Church which led to the formation of all manner of benevolent associations and efforts by those who had no connection with it. Among these none are more efficient in promoting the true interests of Christianity and civilization than "economic" and "agricultutal societie."

The first of these founded in Switzerland, was by *Zschiffeli*, in Berne, in 1759, and was composed of members of the government, ecclesiastics, and agriculturists, for the purpose of improving husbandry. The special object of its founder was to popularize useful ideas, and to accomplish this he appealed to the patriótism of all classes, and brought the experience of the lowest, as well as the theories of the highest, to his aid. He said, there could be no permanent improvement without light and knowledge, and therefore scattered publications upon all matters concerning agriculture. It was through the influence of these, that extensive irrigation was introduced, the system of leaving fallow ground done away, and clover substituted, the cultivation of the potato made general, and science applied to the culture of the vine. In a little time industry, commerce, political economy and legislation concerning social interests, fixed the attention of the society, and opened a wider theatre of honourable activity. This was the beginning of all similar efforts on the Continent, and half a century before serfdom was fairly abolished in Germany, and sixty years before a similar society was formed at Leipsic.

In no country are the profits of agriculture so great as in Switzerland, where there are few great proprietors, and most farmers own the soil they till. Nearly four hundred thousand families are engaged in the different departments of husbandry, and only one hundred thousand in the different trades and professions.

Union dairies, and other associations described elsewhere, are now general in Soleure ; nurseries for plants established in many places, and orchards everywhere like forests. Before this new awaking there were only fifteen kinds of fruits and thirty kinds of flowers known in the canton, where now are flourishing those of every climate and soil.

In the good old times, those halcyon days when a few oligarchists ruled and the people obeyed, a peasant could not hunt in the forest on penalty of dungeons and death, but the bailiff was allowed two hunters and twelve dogs, "whenever it pleased his honour to enjoy this pastime." Now each person pays a small sum for the privilege, and it is free to all who care to avail themselves of it at this price.

Fishing is granted in some places by the State, and in some by the communes, and also the privilege of ensnaring frogs and crabs to their destruction, which is done by kindling fires of brushwood on dark nights, and setting nets to entangle them, as the foolish creatures hop out to see what is going on in the world, and soon learn to their sorrow that they are no longer to know anything, even in their own little domain.

They make a curious little cheese in Soleure, which they call "*Geisskäse*," which would indicate that it was made of goats milk, which is not at all the case, but from their diminutiveness they may think it best to give them a humble name. They are only four or five inches in circumference, and cost three or four sous. The process of making them is to place the new milk with the rennet over the fire till it is lukewarm, and removing it, they allow it to stand till the curds are formed, when it is again warmed and put in moulds, where it is cut fine and stirred till it is pulp. It is then poured off, salted, and dried a day or two, and placed in the cellar, where it must remain ten or fifteen days, when it is washed in warm water, moulded, and wrapped in leaves for *keeping*, but, though palatable, they will not serve for heirlooms.

A great portion of the people are shepherds and agriculturists, but in the larger towns and villages there are many factories, and their mechanics are renowned.

Olten is the concentrating point for all the railroads from north, south, east, and west ; and on a summer's day, when all the world is in motion, it seems as if all the world passed through here indeed. Such a running and rushing—such a trundling of baggage—such a confusion of tongues—such a jostling and screaming, as we never elsewhere saw or heard. It seems for a little while impossible that such a crowd can ever get *ticketed* and *numbered* for the right place ; and the two or three hundred names in great letters hung through the length of the long depot must be meant to bewilder rather than to guide. But many times a day the same number come, make the same hurry and rush, and depart, each time leaving the little village as quiet as if only the wheel and the hammer had ever been heard in its midst.

It is especially famous for its coopers, and those who wish to purchase wine in Elsaz often come to Olten for the barrels in which it is to be exported. So expeditiously can a merchant be *fitted out*, that he arrives in the evening not knowing where a single article is to be found, and departs at break of day with tubs, hogsheads, chains, and all the apparatus for shipping tuns of wine.

A thousand hundredweight of iron wire is drawn and rolled, and sent forth yearly. There are ribbon looms in the surrounding country, and stockings woven by the ten thousand dozen.

The cantonal colours are red and white, the robe of the *Landweibel* being white in front from the shoulder down.

The statute-books of the *olden time* are not less curious in this than in the other cantons. Witches were burnt, and not they alone; and those who were guilty of slander had the tongue slit. In 1581, some guild-brothers had quarrelled, and called each other names; in solemn council the Government decided that they should meet and drink wine together, each party furnishing a certain quantity, and *my gracious* lords would condescend to come and drink with them!

In 1661, a watchman who was found drunk and asleep was condemned to stand by the fish-bench, on the market-place, holding a wooden halberd. In 1639, two women, who quarrelled and came to blows, were confined together in a small room, and obliged to eat out of the same dish with the same spoon. In 1798, a man who threatened to cut down the tree of liberty was obliged to stand beside it with a wooden hatchet.

The people are Catholics, but the festivals are not so many as in the other Catholic cantons, baptisms and funerals being the only occasions when the country people make a great display. The national dress, too, is fast disappearing. Formerly the married women wore a black petticoat, and the maidens red, a silver cross upon the bodice, white full sleeves, the hair in long braids hanging behind, and on the head a broad-brimmed hat.

In another district the skirt was fastened to the waist with a great roll like a sausage, filled with straw—a convenient resting-place for the hands in the dance. On festal days they wear a silver wreath with red ribbons braided in the hair; but the skirt is now usually black, the bodice cut low, with a full white chemisette plaited within, and the silver chains passing under the arm.

The cities of Soleure and Trêves are said to have been the first founded by the Romans on this side the Alps, and they have still a *Heidenweg* or road of the Pagans, as well as a statue of Venus in Carrara marble, which prove, with many other relics, that this was occupied by a Roman colony. Their cathedral is a modern edifice, and not so attractive as those which have stood a thousand years, but is not less beautiful than some which claim this additional honour ; but the clock-tower on the market-place is ascribed to a period five hundred years before Christ.

One of the most distinguished of modern sculptors, *Egger-schwyl*, was a native of Soleure, and obtained the prize of honour at the Paris Exhibition in 1802, besides being the recipient of many flattering distinctions from Napoleon. They have also produced many historians and painters. Their heroes rest in foreign graves, but there are monuments to record their valour, and there came one to die among them who was not of them. In this quiet and secluded place, Kosciusko bid farewell to earth, and ceased to dream of his country's glory. We see the house where he lived, and the coffin in which for a little while reposed his remains ; but his dust now mingles with that of his fathers on Cracow's plains, and the foot of the despot marches unheeded over the sod already green above their heads.

CHAPTER XIII.

ZURICH.

MODERN CITY—OLD LAWS—SILK MANUFACTURE—HAPPY HOMES—FROGS AND SNAILS—GREAT SHOOTING FESTIVAL.

So long ago as the thirteenth century, when all the rest of the world was in barbarism, Zurich was known as the *City of Savans*, and one who lives among them, but is not of them, says it deserves still this appellation. By the Romans it was called Turicum; and it embraced Christianity in the seventh century. Yet it is the most modern-looking city we have seen in Europe. It has old narrow streets, and quaint old houses, where knights revelled and troubadours sang;* but they are compressed within a little space, and are not recognized in the general

---

* At the end of the thirteenth century the house of L. Maness was the rendezvous of the *Troubadours*, and the family had very long in their possession a collection of the sentimental poesies of these *knight* and *night-errants*, valuable for their intrinsic worth and rich imagery. It is now in the Bibliothèque of Paris. The poems were not admitted till after rigid examination on the part of the *noblesse* of both sexes in this and other countries. One of the most famous of the Troubadours was *Hartmann von der Aae*, of the family of *Chevaliers de Vesperspiël*. Another was J. Hadlaub, a burger of Zurich, who loved a noble lady, who would not listen to his suit. The verses in which he sang his sorrow are still extant, and very delicate in sentiment and beautiful in construction. The old house is still standing where they met.

physiognomy as we look down upon it from some height, or examine it closely face to face.

We might easily imagine ourselves in the "wooden city" * of New England. It has a similar position on both sides of a river or bay ; and the houses, though not of wood, are white, with green blinds, and after the same model, standing apart, surrounded by gardens and greenswards. But one is infinitely amused in passing them to find they are called by name, or to be directed to the house of some saint or philosopher, and read over the door, "Monk's Cap," or "Sheep's Head." To think of baptizing anything in modern days by the name of *Sodom!* However appropriate it may have been before the days of science, there can be no good reason now for living in a "Rat's Nest," or a "Louse Brush ;" yet, if we were to judge by appearances, some of the most useful of modern improvements are unknown in the city, which has flourished two thousand years. But, though the houses have lost all right to the cognomens, they are probably allowed to remain as relics of that time-honoured past for which the respect is so universal that even the exposition of its foibles only increases our veneration. So when we read the above-mentioned names, or "Garter," "Fool," and "Longface," over the doors, we have no idea of concluding these signs to be true indications of what is within !

Zurich is not only the city of *savans*,† but "my lady bounti-

---

* Providence, R. I.

† To enumerate Zurich's wise men would be as useless as impossible. Their name is legion, both in the past and present. *Conrad Gessner* was among the first as physician, botanist, geologist, and in all learning the Pliny of modern times. *Solomon Gessner* is denominated the modern Theocritus, and no German poet of the last century has so many readers. The translation of his works was the introduction of German literature into France. His essays were equally renowned, and he was also painter and engraver. *Felix Faber* wrote travels in Palestine, which Robinson, the great American Eastern traveller, alludes to as remarkable for correctness. *Scheuchzer* wrote travels among

ful" for all Switzerland. If there is an avalanche or land-slide in any canton or any village, a flood, or famine, or fire, the appeal is always made to Zurich, "Come over and help us," and never in vain. It is almost a proverb, and heard everywhere, "Had it not been for Zurich, we should have starved." In 1834 they taxed themselves nearly five thousand dollars for the Greeks. In the days of persecution she was the "city of refuge" for every country; and it is owing to the Huguenots, to whom they opened their dwellings, and to the Locarners, who fled to them from Italy, that they were so early a manufacturing people, and verified the words of the Preacher, "Cast your bread upon the waters, and it shall return to you after many days." They received at one time a whole troop from the French galleys, who had been condemned for political offences, and distributed them about in families, till they could support themselves. English theologians and Catholic priests, all, of every faith and nation, have experienced their hospitality. In all the cities it was the custom to have corn-houses, or granaries, where corn was deposited during years of plenty, and sold at a low price in years of

the Alps, and was called to the court of Peter the Great by recommendation of Leibnitz. Sulzer, author of "Theory of the Fine Arts," was called to the chair of philosophy at Berlin by Frederick the Great. Bodmer was denominated the Plato of the modern Athens.

It was when meditating, "By the margin of Zurich's fair waters," that Zimmerman was inspired to write the delights of solitude, and Goethe penned the productions which acquired him most renown in the midst of the same scenes. The "good works" of the great Lavater live still in the memory of every inhabitant of Zurich, for it was not less by his deeds of love than by his words of wisdom that he deserved to be known. It was also the noble heart of Pestalozzi which inspired the marvellous labours he accomplished. The fame of these two is the most enviable which can be acquired by man, for it is owing to the *good they did*.

There are fifty more whose names are not less familiar in the circles of science and literature, and those who are now the lights of her University will be recorded with equal honour; and here as in all other things we have to remember, that Zurich is only one small canton of a small republic.

scarcity. The revelutions of science, improvements in agriculture, and introduction of many new kinds of food, have diminished the dangers of famine, so that the granaries are no longer so important. But in 1636, there occurred a famine, from the failure of the crops, and more than 20,000 dollars' worth of grain was *given* to the people in the country, besides what was sold at a price within their means.

The universities, schools, and benevolent institutions of Zurich, correspond with the age, though now she does not give citizenship to all who come, but sells it to all who can pay the price, which, to be sure, is not a large sum.

Her savings-bank is the oldest in Switzerland, and the second in Europe. So early as 1558, we read of soup-houses, where her own poor, and those from many other lands, were fed gratis, and with far better food than the cloisters had been in the habit of furnishing. Immediately after the Reformation, the State undertook the care of the poor and sick, and Church-property was confiscated to create a fund.

In the last half century more than fifty thousand patients have been received into her hospital, nearly five thousand being from other cantons, and eight thousand from other lands.

One must be continually reminded, in reading of Switzerland, of its size, in order to appreciate its importance. When we think that the twenty-two cantons together are not larger than a third of the State of New York, we can conceive what one canton must be. Yet the population is one-seventh of the whole United States of America. There are ninety-two cities of a thousand inhabitants, sixty-three communes or hamlets, and seven thousand four hundred villages. There are more inhabitants, in proportion to the land, than in any other country, which must not be forgotten when we read of their industry or their poverty.

Zurich is seventeen square leagues in extent, and has between two and three hundred thousand inhabitants. They are an agricultural and manufacturing people, and in both those departments aim at the highest possible perfection. Their silks rival those of Lyons, and their fields those of England in beauty.

It is not less interesting in Zurich than in Lucerne, to trace step by step the social development and progress of the people.

In 1358, there were only two hundred and sixty-three servants in all the families of the city, because it was the custom for the wives and daughters to perform the domestic labour; and there are several instances recorded of women being punished for scolding. In 1329, a burgomaster was fined two thousand, seven hundred and fifty dollars for insulting a woman.

In 1280, there was a great fire, and the clergy said it was a judgment upon the city for its extravagance, especially for the *folly of the women in dress and finery;* and they began to make laws to restrain this propensity! The unmarried were allowed to dress more than the married. Neither men nor women were permitted to wear pointed shoes. Sometimes gold and precious stones were to be seen on the head, and even on the dress. This consisted of a long underdress without sleeves, sometimes only a mantle thrown over, and sometimes a short dress reaching to the knee, having sleeves, and the hair fell in curls on the neck. Men wore something like a monk's gown, making it always shorter and shorter, and red or blue stockings, or one side blue and the other red. These were the Zurich stockings, so famous at the battle of Morgarten.

The inventory of articles in an inn for travellers in 1380, enumerates four table-cloths for a long table, and four for a round one, sixteen pillows, eight baskets, one for bread and one for keys, a chest for trumpery; forty dishes and plates, one cauldron, one great wash-tub, one reel, one foot-stool to stand before a bed, and six flat irons, etc.

When burghers resorted to an inn, to talk and drink in the evening, the bells of the city rang at the proper hour for them to return home, and no one was allowed to walk in the streets afterwards without a light.

It was forbidden to invite more than twenty persons to a wedding, and the god-parents must not make presents worth more than seventy-five cents. Only two singers and two fiddlers could be present. A bride at her first marriage could receive a morning gift; widows, of course, received none.

In the sixteenth century, the people were commanded to make a pilgrimage to Einsiedeln, the first Sunday after Pfingsten, consisting of twenty-four priests, and one grown person from each house, and at the next State-Council a report was made of disobedience and misdemeanors. Priests were reproved for talking and laughing so loud during confession that the voices of those confessing could not be heard!

In 1480, a feast was given at the choice of a new burgomaster, at which two thousand persons were present. The inventory of articles in a rich burgher's house enumerates eighty linen sheets, sixty table-cloths, and seventy-nine pieces of silver.

In this century men and women wore grey mantles, but no woman was allowed to wear a girdle that cost more than five dollars, and not then unless her husband was worth four hundred dollars!

In the course of the fifteenth century three hundred and eighty-eight persons were condemned to death, twenty-one being women; one hundred and eighty-two were led with blinded eyes to the gallows and hung; one hundred and ten died by the sword; twenty-one were broken on the wheel; and thirty-seven drowned. Mention is often made of cutting off ears and noses; and two were buried alive. This is after the Gospel had been preached five hundred years in their midst, and its words are said to be "sharper than any two-edged sword."

Those punishments were the remnants of heathenism, and some of them, or laws as disgraceful, exist still in every Christian land. How slow is the progress of truth and righteousness, notwithstanding their power.

Zwinglius said of Zurich he hoped his field of labour would never be in such a wicked place; yet he afterwards came and accomplished much good. He was the reformer in whom the people had most confidence, as he not only preached against the oppression of the Church, but of the Government. In the war of the peasants, Luther was with the princes, merely because his life had not made him acquainted with the wrongs and oppressions of the poor. But Zwinglius had never lived in a monastery, and knew nothing of dreams and theories. He was opposed to all wrong, and advocated freedom in its broadest sense. Yet he was superstitious, and believed the appearance of a comet foreboded evil, and saw no sin in trying and burning witches.

In this century the ladies are said to have become more domestic; those of the highest rank worked in the kitchen, spun, and sewed, and wove their household linen. It was the custom to make great preparation for the new-born child; all the silver of the house was present. The cradle furniture was of the finest embroidery, and the oldest daughter, though not more than ten years of age, stood by as its *femme de chambre*. Very costly presents were made, and sixteen god-parents were present at its baptism.

In 1688, Bishop Burnet travelled in Switzerland, and wrote of Zurich : " Here we find the simplicity of the old times, and ladies devoted to their households instead of intrigues and dress." Having studied diligently, we have not been able to learn when the *old times* ended and the *new times* commenced.

In 1550, a young lady received for her marriage dower a double bed with curtains, and two foot-stools to climb up to it; six table-cloths, six hand-towels, and twelve dish-towels, twenty-four chemises, and twelve caps, thirty-four doyleys, five ornamented dresses, fourteen other articles of dress, bracelets of thirteen rows of agate, garnet, and cornelian; silver girdles for keys, and a psalm-book with silver clasps. This trousseau cost about three hundred dollars and she received four hundred dollars in money.

In 1663, ladies are forbidden to wear girdles worth more than three guineas English; and gentlemen must not sport wigs weighing several pounds, costing perhaps $75 or a $100. In the beginning of this century, Sunday began to be observed in the modern way. No one was allowed to labour except shoemakers and tailors, who were permitted to finish a piece of work already commenced, if they could get it done before the sermon.

It was at this period that powder began to be worn upon the hair, and that gentlemen first tried the influence of presents in wooing. Women of bad reputation were obliged to wear red caps in the street and in church.

In 1614, the law prescribed the limits of a wedding dinner.

FIRST COURSE.

A pastry.	Smoked sausage.
Two dishes of warm soup.	Smoked beef.
Two dishes of cold soup.	Two dishes of rice.
One boiled fowl.	Two dishes of beets and other
One piece of smoked meat.	vegetables.
Half a calf's head and pluck.	

SECOND COURSE.

Two joints of roast veal.	Half of a roast hare.
One pair of fowls.	Two dishes of pears.
One pair of doves.	Two dishes of plums.
Roast sausage.	

EVENING.

One dish of wafers and wine.

If any one wished to give a larger entertainment than this, he must ask permission of government.

During the last half of this century, tea and chocolate became common, and people smoked mastic and little tapers of juniper-wood and berries.

During the seventeenth century, three hundred and thirty-six persons were condemned to death ; ninety-eight of whom were women, and no amelioration occurred in the modes of punishment.

In the beginning of the eighteenth century, coffee became as common as wine, and snuff was used, but was forbidden in church "as a hindrance to heart culture !"

People began, at this time, to invite company on certain days, and the ladies used to sit on benches before the doors to gossip. The burghers met according to their guilds in front of the churches, each guild having its exact line, so that no one trespassed upon the stone that belonged to another.

Clergymen commenced kneeling on entering the pulpit, and praying softly to themselves. Families lived together in one great room, where the father studied, the wife spun, and the maids shelled peas.

In 1739, a Frenchman wrote of the Zurich people : "The men talk as loud at table as when they are scolding their wives, and take such long steps that one would think a postilion were striding through the room. The women are the best creatures in the world, but cannot hold a conversation."

In the beginning of this century parasols began to be used.

It is the custom in Zurich, when a child is born, for a young girl to take an enormous bouquet, ornamented with long ribbons, and go from house to house to announce to the relatives and friends the happy event. It originated in the eighteenth century. Baptism took place immediately after birth. If there were several to be baptized, the boys received the rite first, lest they should have no beard when men. Those who carried the children ran through the street, in order to make them active.*

Country people began to come to the city to be married, and often in procession, with violins and trumpets. The bride and bridegroom kneeled during the ceremony. If the bride could not in honour wear the wreath, she could not receive the blessing on the wedding-day, but waited till Saturday evening. Golden weddings were celebrated in church by *re*marriage, and with gifts and great rejoicings at home.

At funerals, the house was entirely draped in black, within and without. The friends were informed by a special messenger, and assembled at two o'clock in the afternoon; the men receiving expressions of condolence at the door, and the women forming a circle in one large room. The service and procession were in the ordinary manner.

In 1753, ladies first began to attend public concerts; but in the middle ages the Zurichers were famous for their music. Phrenologists say, their heads exhibit a remarkable development, indicating their taste and talent for this branch of the fine arts; but the discovery would not indicate any special discern-

---

* This custom precisely as in the northern part of Germany.

ment in a phrenologist, by which we do not intend to implicate their discernment in general.

The taste and skill in the mechanic arts is not less decided, and the hum of industry is heard literally in all her borders. The manufactures are not crowded into one corner of a great city, but occupy the leisure hours of those who live in the country. Especially is this the case in the weaving of silk. All those beautiful fabrics, which now equal those of any part of the world, are produced in the cottages scattered over hill and dale, and by those who perhaps work in the field in summer and weave silk in the winter, or devote only the leisure hours of every season to this light and tasteful labour.

Lord Canning once said, "he believed everything but figures;" and surely it is difficult to believe the figures which state the amount of wealth this little canton produces in this desultory way. Five millions of dollars' worth of silk alone go to North America; and at least five millions more to other countries; and nearly twenty thousand individuals are employed on them. The looms belong to the families who use them, and they exercise their own judgment and pleasure concerning the time to devote to one labour or another.

We need not apologize for introducing our readers to one of these cottages, that they may see the companions of the loom, in which is a web that may one day flourish in an English palace or American saloon, or whirl in the dizzy dance at Newport or Saratoga. It is of the beautiful kind called *gros de Naples*, which you need not imagine to have been made in Italy because it has an Italian name, or that it is less beautiful because it is woven on Swiss soil.

First, you must see the weavers, who wear a white linen cap, ornamented with glass beads on both sides, and tied under the chin with a velvet ribbon. A short blue jacket, with light blue bodice, on which appears the letter V, wrought, or formed with coloured velvet ribbon. What the letter signifies we do not know, and they do not know themselves.

The house is of two stories, built first of timbers, and then a wall of coarse bricks or stones, covered with plaster. On the first floor are a sitting-room, two small rooms, and a kitchen These are finished with panels, painted light green, looking beautifully neat. The most conspicuous object is the great stove of potters' work, veneered and painted, and wrought into three walls, so as to spread its genial influence in every apartment below and above. These stoves are everywhere at the north, and very comfortable when thoroughly heated night and day, but require much wood, and in the mild weather of spring or autumn not very economical, unless permitted to remain cold, which is often the case !

Under the windows are long wooden benches, and before these the table, set around with wooden chairs. The unfailing chest, with its various compartments, is near, and on it a tin pail and copper wash-basin ; a book-shelf is suspended over, and on a nail at its side a towel and a brush. On a little table in the corner is the folio family Bible, and upon two nails over the door rests the family gun, polished to brightness. The next article is a curious relic of the olden times, and here we are able to state exactly what marked the times as *old*. When they use this term, they mean the age of oatmeal pudding made so thick that the spoon would stand upright in the centre. These are the days their grandmothers still remember, and the great wooden spoon hangs by a string to the wall, as does also the bread-knife, with the initials of the heads of the household thereon, and the date of their marriage. It is a curious article on which to preserve the record of so important an event; but being the one they would oftenest have to use, it is not on the whole so inappropriate. A slate, an almanac, a looking-glass, and a pair of scales, occupy their wonted posts, and in accordance with their humble offices, the cat's dish, the cricket, the cradle, and standing-stool. Under the stove are the unoccupied shoes and playthings, and in the most honourable positions pictures from the Bible, Swiss history, and the never-to-be-forgotten Black Forest clock.

Near the window is the loom! Does it seem marvellous how one of those beautiful and delicate tissues of green, or gold, or purple, can come forth from the midst of such a medley without spot or blemish? We can only answer, that we wonder all the same, though everything is remarkably neat. The loom is like any other, except that it is more light and delicate in its construction. The reed, through which the *warp* is drawn, is fine as gossamer, and the *shuttle* for the *filling* might answer for a fairy. The web goes underneath, and winds on a beam like any other web, of tow or of more plebeian pretensions. The threads break, and fingers which are not at all fairylike tie them together with marvellous celerity, and we watch the checks and stripes or figures form with never-ceasing interest and amazement.

In the second story are the large double-canopied beds for children and servants, and in the same room and adjoining apartments are linen and clothing chests, boxes for dried fruit and old trumpery, barrels, full of meal, clover seed, and salt, swallows' nests, and dried sausage, ham, bacon and bundles of yarn in all their luxuriance, and, one would think, detrimental proximity!

In the deep cellar are stored the beer, and apples, and cider, sauerkraut, potatoes, and other vegetables.

These are the homes, and the happy homes, of free and industrious people, who may be said to lack nothing that is absolutely necessary to comfort and happiness. There is none of the abject poverty which is seen in exclusively manufacturing districts, and none of the luxury attendant upon suddenly acquired and immense fortunes.

The manufacture of cotton in Switzerland is more extensive than that of silk, and occupies at least fifty thousand people. The whole number of spindles is six hundred and sixty-six thousand, and the half of these are turned in Zurich. There are also six thousand employed in bleaching, dyeing, and printing cloths; and of those, Zurich has also the greatest number. There are five hundred tanneries in Switzerland, with three thousand labourers, confined mostly to three cantons, of which Zurich is one. The manufacture of woollen is confined principally to four cantons, of which Zurich is one. These are the most important branches of industry, and yet agriculture has attained here the highest perfection. Of the fifty thousand people who weave silk or spin cotton, make paper or braid straw, a great proportion devote part of their time to some department of labour in field or garden.

There are in the canton no Alps, yet they possess fifty thousand head of cattle; besides horses, sheep, goats; pigs also number by thousands. Their vines, like those in Germany, were first planted by Charlemagne; and of the four hundred and eighty thousand acres of land belonging to the canton, one hundred and twenty thousand are devoted to pasturage and cereals, fifteen thousand to vines, and one hundred and sixty thousand to various culture.

The farms are very small, but the soil is made to produce to the utmost of its capacity. We are very sorry to be obliged to offend our fastidious readers with the revolting details of agriculture, and especially to introduce them again to a *manure-heap*, but as this is the agriculturist's wealth, and as in Switzerland they seem to have learned the art of converting it particle by particle into gold, we cannot pass it by. We write for those whose duty it is to learn and practise in the same way, and those whom we have usually found as refined as some who profess to be shocked at being told that fruits and flowers do not grow spontaneously, or that science aids in anything so vulgar as enriching the soil.

This same "manure-heap" was the first thing that attracted our attention on passing a farmhouse, because it was made with so much care and so peculiarly, and because it occupied the most pleasant position near the house in the shade of some elms. We afterwards learned that the shade it must necessarily have, from the principle on which it is constructed ; and if it were near the stable, it must, of course, be near the house, as they are in close contiguity. It is appointed to receive all the waste juices of the house as well as barn.

If there are no trees in the right place, and of the right size, they plant them ; not to beautify, but to shield this most important portion of their treasures.

A pit is made some two or three feet deep, walled tight with stones or boards. Beams are placed across, covered with branches of trees, so that when the manure is placed thereon, the fluids drain through and leave the solids dry above.

The stable where the cattle stand has a floor of plates of stone or boards, with gravel earth in front, that they may lie down and get up without slipping. Between them and the wall is a drain from ten to fifteen inches wide, which connects with the reservoir, without. There are also two or three ditches of hewn stone, or boards, into which the manure is first thrown from the stables in order to be moistened with water, and then placed upon the heap; or if thrown directly upon it, it is often wetted, in order to cause fermentation and decay, and to enrich the fluid beneath, which is made accessible through an opening at one corner, and dipped out with a long-handled pail. One sees everywhere women and children watering gardens and fields of vegetables with this liquid.

The stables are carpeted with clean straw before each milking, and sometimes four or five times daily ; and with this, and often new straw taken for the purpose, they make each layer separate, and twist the straw so neatly around the edges that it looks as if it were braided, and is thus preserved from falling down and wasting.

The sink-drains from the house connect with this reservoir, and farmers often build them near cities, to gather the treasures which are to them invaluable, and would otherwise do no man any good.

Compost heaps are also made of weeds and all refuse which is not food for cattle. Leaves of trees are collected in another place and used for a peculiar soil. Gypsum and marl are also used, as well as ashes, turf ashes being considered better than wood.

This is the secret of their agriculture, and explains how so many people can live upon so small a space. Red clover often furnishes four and six mowings a year, and other grasses are fruitful in proportion.

We have sometimes seen an aqueduct and reservoir in front of a stable, with an engine for spouting pure water over the cows and their stalls, to keep them clean.

Hunting is free to all, with a few slight restrictions for the protection of fields and gardens ; and the forests are open to joiners, carpenters, and basket-makers for all the wood they need in their several callings, and the wild berries and *broom stuff* may be gathered by all who eat and sweep.

There are one or two other articles of commerce in Switzerland which we are sure no Englishman or American ever thought of "*trading in ;*" and yet which might be made profitable perhaps, for the marshes bring forth as abundantly there as here. Catholics not being allowed to eat meat on Fridays, and various other days in the year, and Catholics being many in the land, all manner of fish are in great demand. Frogs and snails belong to the genus fish, and are collected in great numbers for cloisters, monks being among those who preach, but do not practise, fasting. It is not necessary to enjoin the peasants to deny themselves meat, as they seldom eat it except on Sundays. Snails are fattened in gardens on certain kinds of leaves, and one may hear the chattering of their teeth as they eat, in passing by. From Zurich they are exported to Italy in the autumn. It is only frogs' legs that are eaten, and formerly they used to catch them and cut off their legs, leaving the animal to die a painful and cruel death.* In a period of four years, the cloister Rheinau disposed of forty thousand snails, and thirty-six thousand pairs of frogs' legs.

Zurich was among the first to subject the Church and her priesthood to the law, allowing them no preference above other citizens. In 1379, it is recorded that they permitted a priest to go for half a week to Baden for his health, but if he remained any longer, his salary would cease ; and they were often deposed for immorality and punished for crime.

The sacrament was administered for the first time after the method of the reformed churches, April 13, 1525. Formerly,

* This is now prohibited.

all the bells in the city rang for church service, but now only those of the church where the people assemble. The ceremonies are nearly the same as in America, except that there is only one session. The Sunday-school is in the afternoon.

Fairs and festivals are not so many in Zurich as in Lucerne, and not so many in the Protestant cantons generally as in the Catholic. Fires are kindled on all the surrounding heights in the spring, but now they call it burning the last vestige of winter, and it is a sport only for boys. They gather stealthily the materials, and allow no sign of their preparations to be visible, till at a given signal all blaze forth at once, and their songs through "all the welkin ring." In the evening there are a few holding sports around the fireside, merely to make glad the hearts of the little ones.

There is a meeting every year of the old men who are of the same age, to enjoy a dinner and a talk of the olden time. They first met in 1824, on the 8th of October. When there are not enough born in the same year for a respectable tableful, they include those of two years. They do not confine themselves to the simple cookery of the Bremen burghers, but allow the wine to flow merrily, and " their hearts do beat cheerily," yet it is no day of revel, only of gladness.

On the day of ascension, the young people from the country ascend Mount Uetliberg, near Zurich, where those from the city join them, and sing psalms and hymns of praise to the Giver of all blessings. It is one of the prettiest of the festal days. The processions, like all peasant processions, are gay with flowers and bright ribbons, but their mirth is on this occasion chastened, without destroying their gaiety.

Shooting companies are universal in Switzerland, and every two years they hold a great festival in one of the principal cities. It is now a federal *fête*, and one which enlists the sympathies and co-operation of the whole people. The first was held at Aarau in 1824, where a society was formed ; and though they were at first very simple they have now attained to an almost fabulous splendour. This year it took place in Zurich, the first ten days in July. A volume would be necessary to describe it in detail, and then one would have little idea of the effect of the whole, enlivened by the enthusiasm of these liberty loving people, thronging from their mountains and their valleys in the true spirit of brotherhood, to celebrate their oldest and best beloved national *fête*.

To Zurich belonged the preparations for the reception of the guests, and she lavished her money and her taste with her usual spirit, of allowing nothing to fail of beauty or comfort in all the arrangements.

The expediency of holding the festival when all Europe was trembling with "wars and rumours of war," was for a long time doubted, and when at length it was decided that there could be no serious reason for deferring it, the lateness of the hour obliged them to hasten the work.

Three sides of a parallelogram were devoted to the necessary buildings, and displayed the light graceful architecture of the Swiss cottage, familiar to all by pictures and miniatures in sugar or wood. It included a dining-room which could accommodate several thousand persons, a spacious saloon, telegraph and post-office bureaux, kitchen, storeroom, and various lesser apartments. The background was devoted to the targets, which were a hundred in number, raised six or eight feet from the ground, and behind each an immense block of hewn granite to receive the bullets, and prevent all possibility of accidents.

In the dining-room was a fountain with four jets, sparkling in the midst of shrubbery and flowers, and the whole was lighted by hundreds of *burners*, making a very fairyland in beauty and brilliancy.

Finding that they were in danger of not being ready at the appointed time, the Austrian soldiers who had trespassed on the neutral soil of the Republic were invited to become helpers in erecting the temple of freedom, to which they did not seem at all averse, and performed diligently whatever their hands could find to do !

In the centre of the parallelogram arose a Gothic temple, with twenty-three towers, the centre surmounted by the flag of the Confederacy, and those of the twenty-two cantons waving around. There was no interior to the building, but on its outer walls were suspended the *prizes* for those who should win in this rivalry of sharp-shooters. The prizes were numbered, and each competitor had the privilege of selecting the one which he would try to win, in the division to which he belonged. The targets were of different kinds, some requiring more skill than others.

The united value of the prizes was more than fifty thousand dollars, and presented a curious spectacle in their individual character, disposed, according to their worth and nature, on little nails, so thickly as to form a covering like tapestry for the walls. The most of them were purses of different size and workmanship, containing gold of every possible amount. But as the Swiss in all countries contribute to this feature of the festival, there are some things characteristic of the lands in which they now dwell. Such is a Mexican saddle, of beautiful finish; purses of fifty, eighty, and a hundred dollars, from New York and Philadelphia; one of four hundred dollars from Memphis, Tennessee; a similar one from Valparaiso and Constantinople. There are also silver cups and pitchers, china tea and coffee sets, watches, and rifles, all tastefully displayed and decorated. Each one pays a certain sum for the privilege of shooting, graduated according to the prize he strives to win. During the time of the festival there were between six and seven hundred thousand shots, and sometimes ninety in a moment.* It was like being within the sound of a battle, but the sight was one to be remembered with joy, and not with sorrow.

The concourse of people was a multitude which no man could number. Every day came a new deputation, which was received at the railroad station by a committee from Zurich, who escorted them to the city with music and colours, showing them the town, and introducing them to the festal palace, to reach which all must pass through the triumphal arch, which was erected at one of the portals of the city, not far from the festal scene, which was without the gates. This beautiful specimen of art was designed and finished entirely by the inhabitants of the neighbouring commune of Riesbach, and consisted of three arches, the centre being sufficiently large for carriages, and surmounted by a colossal statue of Tell, with his bow in one hand, and in the other the arrow which remained after he had cleft the apple from the head of his son. He is in the act of showing it to the tyrant, as he exclaims, "Now, if you would indeed know the truth, had I killed my child, your heart this second arrow had not failed," and beneath appeared the three men of Grutli, in the attitude of taking the oath. The whole was wreathed with evergreens and flowers, and was of singular beauty and effect. After the *fête* it was purchased and transferred to the garden of a wealthy citizen of Zurich.

Especially attractive was the deputation from the four forest

* For the numbers in the two highest of the three divisions each person could shoot only once.

cantons, accompanied by the martial music of Lucerne, the four cantonal banners, William Tell and his boy, and three men bearing the *notable horns*, in the costume of the twelfth century. They were many hundreds in number, and were greeted by cannon, by cheers, by music, and every possible demonstration of joy from the countless throng through which they passed; and very affecting was their surprise and pleasure as they halted before the triumphal arch, and with more slow and measured step proceeded to the *Schützenplatz*. Here deafening cheers awaited them, and a speech from the temporary throne, which produced a solemn stillness; and many a strong man might have been seen wiping the eye from which it had caused "the silent tear to flow."

The *star-spangled banner* waved proudly from a conspicuous height, and thé 4th of July happening on one day of the *fête*, was duly celebrated by the American Consul and some fifty Americans, who were granted the privilege of the festal hall for the occasion. Some grey-haired clergymen thought it no sin to drink wine on such a day; and their toasts were none the worse for the exhilaration of the sparkling beverage. The Swiss, not less than the Americans, seemed to enjoy the moment that enabled the two Republics to celebrate their national *fête* under the united banners of each.

The field for the exhibition of the skill of the *wrestlers* was opposite the *Schützenplatz*, in the grounds of a private citizen, who offered them freely for the occasion. They entered the city in one phalanx, though coming from every valley in Switzerland, and bore aloft nearly fifty banners with original devices. They occupied the two last days of the *fête*, and attracted a multitude which increased by hundreds and thousands as they marched; the long trains of railway-cars were crowded; every diligence was laden with a gala-dressed group; and from every pathway, over mountain and through valley, came the rustic vehicles like moving parterres, with happy villagers, their banners and streamers fluttering in the breeze, till the city was one dense mass of human beings in grand jubilee, yet nowhere exhibiting coarse revelry or unseemly mirth.

The feats of the wrestlers we have elsewhere described; and here they lasted from six in the morning till four in the afternoon. This was the first time they had shared the prizes with the *shooting parties*, and the value of these was doubly enhanced by the manner of offering them. Young girls, in white robes and red scarfs, stood upon a platform beneath a tent of blue and white, and each victor was called by name, and crowned with oak and laurel wreaths by those fair hands, besides receiving appropriate prizes. One of these prizes appeared in the form of four white sheep, also wearing wreaths and ornamented with ribbons.

On Sunday there was no shooting or wrestling, but all gathered together in the open air, a united Church as well as united people, to listen to the solemn services of the Sabbath, and a sermon which evinced the spirit and power of the divines of the Reformation.

On one day the Duchess of Parma and her four children were conspicuous guests in the amphitheatre among the spectators, and at the table in the hall. For the third time an exile she fled for refuge to a free people; and soon after came the plenipotentiaries to the same city, to settle by the wiles of diplomacy what war could not effect. Strange that princes will not learn to make their own people free, that they may rule over them in peace. The Italian diplomatists evinced great interest in the institutions of the Republic; visited the schools, and inquired diligently concerning all that could furnish them knowledge of the practical workings of freedom ; but. the Austrian walked about in dogged silence and contempt, determined to believe in nothing but grinding oppression, and to attach importance to nothing but the etiquette, barbarity, and ignorance of the middle ages.

We have no room for the speeches which were the daily events of the *fête*. They all had for their motto, " Union is strength !" and were very much like those which are heard every 4th of July in America, full of national pride, some vain boasting, and glowing with the enthusiasm which can only be exhibited by a free people.

The last day was the anniversary of the entrance of Basle into the Confederacy three hundred and fifty-eight years before ; and they remained the last to lower their colours and say farewell. Eight peals from the booming cannons announced the fall of the curtain upon the festal scene ; and all returned to tell the wonders they had seen to those who had remained in the huts of the mountains and in the cots of the valleys.

CHAPTER XIV.

SCHAFFHAUSEN.

OLD CITY—PRIDE AND EXCLUSIVENESS—JEWS—COSTUME—RHINEFALL—DISTINGUISHED MEN.

SCHAFFHAUSEN is the only canton where the people secured their freedom of church and state without dissensions and divisions between the city and country, the aristocracy and peasantry. They pride themselves on being a quiet and orderly people, and there is more of the sober and antique in their physiognomy than in any other city. They have not experienced so often or so lately the calamity of fire, and the old roofs look as if they might have passed through the flood. The coats-of-arms of many centuries are still to be seen on their fronts, and carvings and paintings, of which no man knows the signification, still adorn half the buildings.

We think there must be funny old customs in such an old place, but the people are more modern than the walls within which they dwell. They profess to be more hospitable than any of their confederates; but they have the same pride of birth, and the same boast of "old families," though now their aristocracy is more of wealth than of pedigree. There are those among them who count ten centuries of illustrious ancestors, and some who can prove their blood to be coloured by a few drops of some distant cousin of the House of Hapsburg, which surely ought to make it very red, and yet are more proud of the coin in their coffers, and strive day and night for the gold that perisheth.

One is as lawful as the other when made a reason for exclusiveness and oppression, and the sole reason that Switzerland did not earlier settle into harmony and steadily increasing prosperity with her free spirit and enterprising people, was, that the Government was *based on privileges*, and a class of people in almost every city assumed to themselves the right of enjoying something which the others could not obtain. Not till 1848 did they succeed in getting rid of these haughty aristocrats, and the people of true republican spirit became so much in the majority, that they could say to all, of every class, "You are indeed free." Those who composed these supercilious oligarchies, being deprived of their political power, endeavour to show their resentment and superiority by shutting themselves within a narrow circle, and boasting of what they were, determined not to believe, or at least not to acknowledge, that *new* men can equal them, or a Government which they did not form can exist and prosper. They would not acknowledge a king or a foreign bailiff, but they arrogated to themselves a power not less tyrannical, and used it in a manner not less opposed to every principle of equality and justice.

It was the restlessness of the people in those bonds that kept them forever in turbulence and rebellion; and though the devastation of Napoleon's armies was a curse, and their invasion unjustifiable, his *mediation* was a blessing. He saw that he could not rule them, and he undertook to teach them to rule themselves.

They had demolished feudalism in form, but the spirit still lived. Whatever may have been his motive, his mission was the same in Switzerland as in Germany—to crush this hydra-headed monster.

During the period of his ten years' mediation, there was peace and prosperity; he was dethroned, and all was again in confusion. But had he remained on the throne, it is not probable the people of Switzerland would have been long content to acknowledge his sceptre. A foreign ruler by any name was always their special aversion. "We are a free people, and a free people we will be," is the inborn spirit of the Swiss. But they learned of him a lesson, and what is more wonderful, they profited by it. There was no more rest till the native, as well as the foreign, oppressors were dethroned. The power has been entirely taken from their hands, but not till time has laid some of them still lower will Switzerland be entirely delivered from their corrupt and demoralizing influence in her institutions. Their hatred of the genuine freedom of the present Government is gall, wormwood, and bitterness. In one city we heard a family belonging to this aristocracy say they would not attend a party where a member of the Government was to be present; and the caste of the Hindoo is not more prescribed than the line they have drawn between themselves and those whom they denominate *plebeians*. Whether they attend the same church I do not know; but they are here, as elsewhere, the people who make the greatest pretensions to piety, and profess to be the disciples of Christ whilst ignoring every principle which He preached and practised.

There is less of this spirit in Schaffhausen than in some other cities, and it thrives most in Berne, Soleure, and Geneva.

Yet the laws concerning the Jews are of the most oppressive

and unchristian nature in Schaffhausen, while in Berne and Geneva they are free in every respect as other citizens Here they are forbidden by the law to trade, to own real estate or cattle, and are not allowed equal privileges with other citizens in the courts of justice. They can reside in the canton only eight days, which is a permission evidently for their own interest, as Jews are permitted to trade in cattle at the public market, and in the stables of those who sell; any infringement of this provision is punished by fine.

They do not even recognise a bargain between a Jew and Christian as binding, unless it is made in the presence of the President of the Commune or the blood relatives of the Christian. If a Jew lend money to a Christian, the law does not oblige it to be repaid; he must do it at his own risk. A Jew cannot take a greater interest than five per cent.; and in no instance is allowed compound interest for whatever sum he may lend.

Letters of exchange, promissory notes, and other business transactions, are subject to the same restrictions; and if a Jew should inherit real estate, he is obliged to sell it within a year.

These are strange laws to remain on the statute-book of a free and Christian land, yet in six other cantons they are the same.* There is no anomaly so incomprehensible as that of a free people imposing slavery—of those who would die for a right or a privi-

---

* We are indebted for these facts to an able document presented to the Swiss Federal Council by the Honourable Theodore S. Fay, resident minister of the United States at Berne, and now published in several languages. A remonstrance was made by Jews, who had become citizens of America, on account of the expense and trouble to which they were subjected when business obliged them to visit Switzerland, and it became the duty of the minister to secure to them the protection every American had a right to demand.

lege, denying it to others who are equally entitled to the utmost liberty.

We are sorry to be obliged to expose the existence of so dark a stain upon this fair land, and hope that it will soon be blotted out. In all else it is a "goodly land and a pleasant," and the people who dwell therein right friendly to the stranger and the pilgrim who may happen to be within their borders.

Agriculture is the occupation of the great proportion, and has adopted all modern improvements. In 1771, there was a great famine in Switzerland, which was followed by a new impulse to agriculture. Men of science and influence devoted themselves to the study of soils, and the adaptation of different kinds of grains and fruits to their climate and tillage. There had existed a great prejudice against potatoes, which was overcome; and since their multiplication and general use, want has disappeared. Nurseries were established to raise seed, and soil improved by artificial meadows and irrigation.

The Napoleonic period is mentioned as a prosperous one for agriculture. Very old and unjust laws were abrogated, one of which was, that every third year the land should lie fallow; tithes were abolished, as well as the right to free pasture, by which the cattle occupied an extent of ground, that could be made to produce three times as much by cultivation, and their food became richer and more abundant.

In Schaffhausen one half the land is in productive fields, and vineyards occupy thirty-five thousand acres. It is a rule in the northern cantons, where it is colder, to plant vines where wheat would ripen in ordinary years by St. Jacob's day.* Until 1798 the law forbade every one to plant vines without permission of

---

* There are several St. Jacob's days in the calendar, but the one to which this refers is probably the 25th of July.

Government; the reason being given that it was necessary to be sure vines should not be planted in an ungenial soil and clime. In some places where they are exposed to slides from heavy rains, they are planted in the form of the letter V; often have no particular form, but are set here and there so far apart that one can easily pass between the stocks. Often the principal branch is bent in the form of a circle, and bound to a stake, on the principle that the lower the stock the better is the wine; but the nearer they are to the earth, the more they are in danger of frost. In winter the stakes are removed, and the vines laid upon the earth, and covered with manure, or merely loosened and left to the protection of the snow. Different methods are practised everywhere according to the climate and soil. In Zurich they have vines a hundred years old.

In Schaffhausen they are very utilitarian, and do not encourage vine culture, saying it requires six times more outlay in the beginning, and four times more labour, and is the most precarious of all products.

The peasant costume is a dark blue skirt with a red border, red stockings, and shoes bound with blue; a yellow apron, which forms part of the bodice, and blue kerchief round the neck, with the ends hanging below the waist. The hair is brought to the top of the head, and arranged in two large braids. The men wear small clothes and blue stockings, a jacket, with the lappets of yellow, a red vest and blue neckerchief.

There are no Alps and no shepherds, and very few flocks.

There is a school in every commune, and all the children can attend as early as five years of age, and *must* as early as seven, continuing in summer till they are eleven, and in winter till they are fourteen. In the city there are high schools, and a superior one for young ladies.

The Church affairs are regulated upon the most republican plan, by an equal number of delegates from the Church and State, and the laity possessing an equal voice in all things with the clergy. To all the thirty-five pastors in the canton the State allows about one thousand seven hundred and fifty dollars, which cannot afford to each a very luxurious life. Everywhere in the country in Switzerland the church service commences on Sunday as early as seven or eight o'clock in the morning. When we asked why they assembled so early, they said, "Oh, the people would become sleepy before it was over, if it began later." The clergyman enters the church first, and when the people are assembled, all sing together. The pastor then ascends the pulpit and reads a prayer, during which all the people stand. The law forbids the sermon to be more than an hour in length. After this is again prayer, and then publication of marriages, if there are any, and other notices, when they again sing, and the blessing is pronounced.

Between twelve o'clock and one they have the Sunday-school.

In all the churches we have seen, the baptismal font is of hewn stone, in front of the pulpit, large enough to hold several gallons. Here it is the same, but the baptisms take place on Wednesday and Friday afternoon, at four o'clock. The sacrament is administered five times during the year, on Sunday, the table being spread by placing a board upon the font, and the bread, which is unleavened, is broken and laid upon plates. The cups are of silver in the city, but sometimes of tin in the country. All pass in a row to the table, the men having the precedence, taste the bread and wine, saying at the same time, "This bread which we break, and this cup which we drink." There is a service on the Saturday afternoon previous, and also on the ordinary festival days.

There are no Catholics in the canton except in one little commune, which was not united to Schaffhausen till 1799.

They have a custom, similar to that which exists in Zurich, of announcing a birth by sending a young girl to each house, ornamented with flowers; but she does not carry a bouquet in her hand except for a boy. At every house she receives a present for her message.

At weddings the bridal pair receive presents from guests, but do not also exchange them with each other, but they exhibit a curious peculiarity in employing the tailor of the bridegroom to invite the guests.

Funerals are announced first by a woman, who wears a black veil or mask; and the next day a man clothed in black goes to every house, rings or knocks, pronouncing the name of each person whom he invites. Expressions of sympathy and shaking of hands are received at the door, between twelve and one o'clock. The moment the clock strikes one, the coffin is covered with black, and taken up by the bearers, who are in number according to the rank of the deceased. The procession is formed, first by the male relations, the guild brothers, and then the poor, who afterwards receive gifts. Whilst the coffin is being lowered into the grave, all assemble in church, where a simple prayer is offered

Every Sunday, men in long brown striped mantles knock at each door to obtain money, which forms a fund for those who are afflicted with some incurable disease. As they pass from house to house they sing, in no very musical chorus.

The cantonal colours are black and green, the long robe of the *Landweibel* being quite black, with a narrow green stripe in the skirt. Upon their shield appears, in full length, a *sheep;* but the origin of such a promotion of these unpretending animals we do not know.

In the eighth century there were only a few boatmen's huts where the city stands, and little *skiffs* the only vessels on the water. Thus it derived its name, *scapha* being the Latin for skiff, and the whole name *Scafhusum*. From the Swiss we have often heard this pronunciation, which is in accordance with their custom of leaving out the first letter of a diphthong, and placing the accent on the last.

It is mentioned as a curious fact, that the Rhinefalls are not alluded to by any ancient or classic author. Yet they are not the less famous in these days, and the one attraction of modern Schaffhausen. We went to see them, of course ; and when we came in sight of a cascade, said to some one standing near, " What is this ?" " The Rhinefall, to be sure ; is it not wonderful ?" " Are you sure it is the Rhinefall ?" " Yes ; why do you doubt it ?" " It is not so large as I expected, and does not seem so very grand." There had been a smile on our face, which spoke even plainer than our words, that it appeared very insignificant. " But where can you find anything to equal it ?" pursued the gentleman, who was a German, from Russia. We answered very quietly, " We are from America." " Oh," answered he, and burst out laughing, " it is not so strange : but for me, I have seen nothing finer, though I have read of Niagara.

We were not so foolish as to expect a second Niagara, but we expected the Rhinefall to surpass all lesser ones, yet in this we were also disappointed. We have seen some that struck us as much finer, on the whole, even in Switzerland ; yet it is the grandest they have in Europe, and is beautiful, as are all waterfalls. The greatest height is one hundred feet. The river alone is three hundred feet broad, and when the banks are full, the volume of water very large. It is certainly strange that it should not have been mentioned by those who wrote of the city in its early days.

There is a salmon fishing in the bay below, which belongs to the cloister Allenherlingen, and catching trout, a privilege which must be bought of the old monks who dwell there. They are said to be worth the price, and never to sell for less than twenty sous a pound.

Hunting is a privilege of the State, which they grant to all who will pay two or three dollars, for it ; thus deriving an income from the forests of some hundreds of dollars every year.

This canton, as will be seen by the map, is a little circle, almost surrounded by the Duchy of Baden. It is infinitely curious to observe the difference of the people, divided only by an imaginary line, and the problem which presents itself everywhere, and which we are never able entirely to solve, is here more intricate than in many other places, how these few people were able to throw off the yoke of foreign oppression, while those around them still groan under its burden. A French author, who wrote some thirty years since, said, in travelling along the borders, between Baden and Schaffhausen, that on one side the people looked thriving and happy ; and on the other they were " covered with dirt, and half begged while the other half collected taxes !" They are a little improved from this picture since, but yet not very much. The taxes in Baden are nearly five times as great as in Schaffhausen, yet the people live by the same toil, and have the same resources. The rates of taxation, which we give on the next page, will show plainer than anything else the reason of the absence of that extreme poverty in Switzerland which is to be found everywhere else in Europe. Their Goverment machinery costs scarcely anything ; for with them, as in America, no one expects to live by a Government office,

10*

and there is no class of people supported in idleness by the toil of others.*

Schaffhausen was a great acquisition to the Confederacy, because of its position of defence, and as a post for the commerce of transit, and she has proved not less valuable in her fidelity to the spirit of the republic, and the support of its institutions. The greatest historian of Europe was a native of this little canton, and she has given many to the ranks of usefulness and honour. Wagner is known as among the reformers scarcely less influential than Luther and Zwinglius, and the celebrated "Elegy of Folly," written by Erasmus, owed much of its spirit to the "Library of Fools," by Geiler, of Schaffhausen, who lived in the fifteenth century. There originated the first effort to in-

* Rate of taxation in different countries, in francs and centimes, a franc being a little less than twenty cents, and five centimes equal to a cent.

	F. C.		F. C.		F. C.
Great Britain	33 20	Sachs Weimer	5 77		
France	12 85	Kurhessen	5 47	Valais	1 60
Holland	12 67	Hanover	5 38	St. Gall	2 8
Baden	9 95	Wurtemberg	4 76		
Prussia	9 87			Neuchatel	2 7
Darmstadt	8 75	Zurich	2 85	Berne	2 54
Denmark	8 70	Schaffhausen	1 23	Basil Land	2 63
Portugal	7 73	Lucerne	1 68	Soleure	2 98
Bavaria	6 85	Argovia	1 74	Vaud	0 9

We give the expense of supporting the three governments of Zurich, Weimer, and Brunswick, states nearly of the same size and population. A thaler is about twenty cents less than a dollar.

	Zurich.	Weimer.	Brunswick.
Court		250,000	260,000 Thalers.
State Debt	3,600	306,103	428,407 "
Military	122,000	153,825	315,287 "
Pensions	4,000	106,493	127,990 "
	129,600	815 921	1,131,684 Thalers.

struct the deaf and dumb, in a treatise written by Annan, a physician and botanist, whose works are still read with interest.

The celebrated astronomical clocks of the cathedrals of Cologne and 'Strasburg were constructed by artists of Schaffhausen, and Mosier, sculptor and painter, was President of the Academy of Painting of Great Britain. Trippel, who studied at Copenhagen, Paris, and Rome, had Canova among his pupils, and was one of the first sculptors of his age. He died, 1775.

But the name of which they, and perhaps Switzerland, is most proud, is Müller, who was for a long time almost their only historian, and who was honoured by every court of Europe. Having been professor of Greek many years in his own country, he was invited to Cassel and Berlin, and afterwards was sent as *diplomat* from Mayence to Rome. At Vienna he was created Chevalier of the Empire, and director of the Imperial Library Napoleon constituted him Minister of State at Westphalia, and Director of Public Instruction, and he was long the life and soul of several German universities. He died at Cassel, in 1809, where Louis of Bavaria has erected a monument to his memory. His birthplace was the humble home of a poor citizen of Schaffhausen. His maternal grandfather was *Pastor* Schoop, who collected a considerable library of history for those times; and one day, calling his little grandson into the room where they were, he said, " I have collected these books and written these chronicles for you. Take good care of them and read them attentively." The face of the boy lighted up with a new expression, and he exclaimed, " Grandpa, I wish also to write a book." The old man little dreamed how faithfully his treasures would be preserved and pondered on. At five years old he assisted at the nuptials of one of his parents, and mounting a chair, recited dramatically a portion of history in such a manner that all were enchanted. At nine years of age, he commenced the history of his native city.

When at Göttingen, a professor tried to detach him from his country, and the love of its free institutions, but he wrote to his father, "No, I will come back to live with you in the bosom of my country, and beloved by friends of virtue. It is better to eat black bread, dipped in water, than commit one act unworthy of the nobility of our souls." When at Geneva, speaking of his household, he said, "My servants love me, accustomed as I am to despise no man, however humble. We are the children of one God, and pride is one of the greatest curses of humanity."

When he was writing his history, his brother wrote to ask why he was so slow in producing it? He said, "I must be sure that it is correct; there is not a chapter that I have not re-written many times, not a phrase which has not cost me many perusals in my chamber." Long years after it was finished, he was travelling among the people of the little cantons, and coming to the ruins of an old castle, he saw a peasant, and asked him what it was. The man immediately gave him the story, and when questioned as to its authority and authenticity, he exclaimed, "Have I not read it all in the history of Müller, of Schaffhausen?" All who would learn anything of Swiss history must read the same, as it is the standard and true record of the glory and the shame of his country.*

* Having decided to describe Switzerland by cantons, we found the most difficult part of the task to be a correct representation of each, without indulging in repetition. Many of the most interesting things are common to all, much in the general life, customs, agriculture, and history are the same everywhere, but we confine ourselves entirely to that which differs in each, as the only way of presenting a complete idea of the whole. They cannot, therefore, be judged separately, though thus written. Together they form Switzerland, and like the parts of the body, each is necessary to the beauty and perfection of the whole, but a very indifferent and uninteresting object when standing alone. The country life and manners of Schaffhausen would in detail too much resemble those of Zurich and Argovie to allow of particular description.

CHAPTER XV.

BASLE.

SOCIAL LIFE—OPINIONS OF OLD AUTHORS—REVOLUTIONS—JEWS—ROBBERS
—LOOMS—CELEBRATED—MEN.

BASLE is at the same time the most ancient and the most modern of cities. In some things its inhabitants have made the greatest progress, and in others they still remain at the very beginning of the middle ages. Ever since anything has been said of them at all, they have been called "cold, haughty, and exclusive." Strangers who dwell among them at this day say the same, and in one of their own journals, published not many years since, we find what they say of themselves in the following editorial remarks : " Basle people are not favourites at home, or abroad, and for this they are somewhat at fault. They are thought to be excessively economical, but this is true only of the rich. They have equipages, to be sure—a country house, and a house in town ; they travel and visit watering-places, but they keep few servants, and spread a frugal table. They seldom make parties, and never go to theatres or plays. The furniture is very plain in their houses, and their dress very simple. One ieason of these habits of economy may be that they usually make their own fortunes, and have for them a peculiar affection. When they part with a little gold, they feel as if parting with their identity.

"Most fathers retain their fortunes till death, and sons are not educated to live on independent incomes. They are not more avaricious than elsewhere, but on the contrary remarkably benevolent. Taxes and subscriptions for objects of charity are very frequent, and also legacies to found benevolent institutions. But it is very seldom that a man parts with any portion of his fortune during his lifetime for the public good. Even when childless, he never thinks of promoting the happiness of his fellow-citizens or the beauty of the State.

"They are social in a certain way, but a public, noble, social life is not known among them. They are not idlers. Very few are ever to be seen at inns, clubs, or reading-rooms, but their life is business.

"Among women there are sewing circles and family parties ; but such a thing as a *soirée* or mixed company, never. There are a few concerts for the rich, and two or three balls in the course of the winter. There are no coffee-gardens, and no people in the public walks. How the marriageable youth ever become acquainted with each other is a mystery.

"If this is the way they comport themselves to each other, what can strangers expect? and it is true, that they are not only not cordial to strangers, but glad to get rid of them. Whether it is the result of pride, self-complacency, or easy indifference, we cannot tell. One reason is, that no marriages take place out of their own circles, and thus no ties are formed to lead them to take an interest in any who dwell not among them.

"Another reason is the influence of the guilds. Every mechanic is jealous of strangers, and sees in each one a competitor who will by some production rival and depreciate his own. This leads to a secret war of all towards all, or a reserve, which prevents all cordiality and friendliness. They are often heard to deplore this among themselves, and say they ought to change ; but nothing is done towards effecting so important a social revolution."

This is a true picture, but it is not true of Basle alone. In many towns of Switzerland and Germany there is the same cold, stiff unsociality, often merely because they do not know any other way. If a family or an individual comes into the place, to whom they really wish to be polite, they give a ball for them, and of course think it a great trouble and great expense, dread it and groan over it, and end with the conclusion, "that strangers are a great nuisance," and the resolution to let them alone. They have friends and society enough for their own pleasure ; and neither as a matter of Christian duty or benevolence or common kindness will they make an effort to promote the happiness of another. They never go where they see anything different, and how can they practise what they never heard of? Their balls are insufferably stupid, a constant whirl of dances, without the relief of conversation, after the manner of the middle ages, when "brave knights and fair ladies," stiff with brocade and powder, whirled each other round, because they were not capable of any higher amusement. There was some excuse for them, because knowledge was not within their reach, and intelligence had then not even a name. But it is a still more ridiculous sight to see gentlemen and ladies in these days, who call themselves educated, spend a whole evening in these puppet performances. Yet they are not a great way from France, where conversation is the highest accomplishment, where at a ball the dancing is only secondary, and where little unceremonious gatherings foi the sole purpose of conversation are the occurrences of every evening.

There can be no such thing as hospitality where great dinners or great suppers are the *ne plus ultra;* and until this idea is banished from Switzerland and Germany, they will never be either hospitable or intelligent, elegant in manners or liberal in opinion ; because these accomplishments can only be acquired by an easy and cordial intercourse with others of different nations and different customs, and those who affect to be religious without hospitality, must study something besides the New Testament for example and precept.

At the time of the great Council in Basle in 1438, when five hundred ecclesiastics assembled and remained months within its walls, *Æneas Sylvius*, afterwards Pope Pius the Second, acted as secretary. He wrote also some familiar letters to Cardinal Julian concerning the manners and customs of the people. In one of them he says, " There are no old houses, because the city has experienced so many earthquakes, and no remnants of the middle ages ! They have gardens and brunnens, and eat and sleep in heated rooms, which are finished very beautifully with panels and glass windows, and furnished like Florentine houses. The rich people have apartments in front like palaces for richness, and beautiful fountains before almost every door. They are very pious, but have no fancy for heathen literature, and never heard of Cicero. The nobility have a winter and summer residence and large buildings for balls. The rich dress in black, and eat a great part of the day. The boys go barefoot, and the women wear white or black shoes. They are very upright, and rather *be* honest than appear so."

We are always particularly interested in the transactions of the year 1492, and find at this period in Basle the Government principally concerned in enacting laws against extravagance in dress, but they are too similar to those in Zurich and Lucerne to need repetition; and during two or three centuries the magistrates were employed a good portion of the time in the same way. They constituted a police to regulate customs, and ascribe the simplicity of the people to this measure.

Castles were almost as numerous in the region of Basle as in Graubünden, and the city beset with nobility; but so early as 1260 the privileges of the burgesses were formally written, and they insisted that emperors and bishops and *noblesse* should respect their rights. Before the seventeenth century nearly all the noble families had died out, moved away, or incorporated themselves with the citizens.

In 1571, an author wrote, " Basle is a very beautiful city and the people very honest. A chest of gold or silver might stand in the street, and no one would touch it. Men have no need of arms, and the women no need of protectors."

Yet only ten years later, Montaigne wrote, "The people are Calvinists, Zwinglians, and heathen; the women without modesty, and thé men drunken."

In 1610, some one says, "The houses are very beautiful, and the women beautiful beyond example, and dress richer than in any other land. There is scarcely any difference between masters and servants in dress or manners; they sit at the same table, only the servants take their places later, and rise earlier."

In 1658, we find in the book of a Bernese, "The people of Basle dress more than in any other city of Switzerland. They wear velvet shoes embroidered with pearls; but they are coarse in their manners. Some merchants went the other day to the fair at Strasburg, and entered the inn, where were already set many tables for dinner. The innkeeper sent the servant with a roast goose, and told him to set it before the Basle people 'Where are they?' asked the servant. 'Oh, look around when you go in, and where they are the noisiest and most ill-bred, set down the goose, and you will make no mistake.'

"The servant had no sooner opened the door, than some one cried out, 'Here, you dog, hand us the goose.' He thought to himself, 'Surely these are the Basilians,' and obeyed their command, finding afterwards that he was right."

Yet twenty years later a Parisian says of them, "They are upright and courteous beyond most people. They have been called coarse and awkward, but it is not true."

Dr. Moore wrote of them in 1779, "They are very exclusive and earnest, and the few I saw very stiff. Whether this is real or affected, I could not tell, but how it ever became an opinion that solemn gravity in the every-day business and intercourse of life is evidence of uncommon understanding, I never could conceive."

A Saxon who visited them in 1785 writes, "They never have any but family parties, and know nothing of mixed assemblies. Every one, when he leaves, must express his thanks to the hostess in a formal manner, and not to say 'Good evening' to the host is a breach of politeness ! The ladies are handsome, and the burghers' daughters usually learn French and dancing."

In 1786, a Swiss author says, "They live too much in families, and become narrow-minded and obstinate in opinion."

In 1809, one of their own citizens says of them, "Their social life is too earnest and serious ; they do not know enough of modern literature or the times. Coffee is seldom allowed even in rich families, and the style of dress which a lady has when she is married must be worn through life ; a man would think he was traitor to his country if he allowed her to do otherwise.

When the men are not engaged in business, they assist their wives and train their daughters. The family festivals are new year's, name days, harvest and vintage."

These various testimonies in the early periods leave the impression, that exclusiveness was originally the characteristic of the people of Basle ; and still, in 1837, a German says of them, " As proud and earnest as their Münster are the Basilians. Even aristocratic Berne does not compete with patrician Basle, where piety and quiet contrast with gilt and glitter."

And in the same year a Frenchman writes, " One would think the whole city was to let, judging from the closed windows and doors, where neither ladies nor children are to be seen on the balconies, nor pretty maidens chatting at the fountains, nothing but servants with their everlasting mops, scrubbing, scrubbing. The fronts of the houses are all closed, but one need not conclude from this that the ladies never look out of the window and have no curiosity. They have little glasses, which are arranged at the side of the window, and reflect all that passes in the street without any greater effort than turning their eyes.* This is the unsociality of all the Swiss. Whether it is republican exclusiveness, or aversion to social pleasure, or burgher pride, or the egotism of small states, which is the greatest hindrance to small governments, we cannot decide."

These are the opinions of many people of various positions, who saw all classes ; and if we add the testimony of 1859, it would not differ materially. They are determined not to change.

Yet there is a strange inconsistency between this selfish social evil and the interest and benevolence they manifest towards all

---

* These glasses we saw also in Germany and other cities in Switzerland, and they are very convenient for those who are willing to be seen, and those who are not.

classes of poor, and towards the heathen of other lands. They support one hundred and fifty colporteurs in France, and distribute seven thousand Bibles annually.

The whole canton is twenty square leagues in extent, of which the city occupies scarcly two. The whole population is seventy-eight thousand, and the city numbers about thirty thousand. Their separation and the cause we have elsewhere explained, as being entirely in consequence of the unwillingness of the city to grant to the country an equality in representation and in the enjoyment of rights and privileges. They remonstrated and remonstrated in vain, and then rebelled, fomenting and retaining a bitter spirit, which is alike detrimental to the interests of all.

But the influence of the Federal Government is everywhere to harmonize and create a national feeling. If they can now only remain in peace long enough to carry out the measures of the Federal Council, and prove the wisdom of unity, they will in the next ten years progress more than they have in the last hundred.

The insurrections and disputes of which we read so much in Switzerland are misunderstood and misrepresented. Monarchists quote them to prove the instability of republics, and the unfitness of the people to govern themselves ; when the truth is, they prove exactly the contrary. So long as oppression existed in any form, and rights and privileges were secured to one class, which were entirely beyond the reach of others, however worthy they might become, or however they might struggle and toil to obtain them, so long there was restlessness and discontent. The country people of Canton Basle asked only what it was right they should have, and though the Federal Diet and the Federal troops came to force them to yield, they resisted unto blood.

And when they found the city would not yield and admit them on an equality, they withdrew and formed a distinct Government by themselves. As soon as they were free, they were content; and it is only eleven years since this equality was spread over all the republic.

In Basle the guilds are still in full operation, with the same laws and restrictions as existed in the thirteenth century. In 1798 they were abolished, and all protection removed; but during the period of mediation, in 1803, they were restored, as far as mechanical trades are concerned. Under this head they number sixteen in the city, and to one of these every citizen must belong, enrolling his name at the age of twenty, at which period he begins to exercise the right of suffrage; those who have a trade inscribing their names in the *guild-book* of the trade or calling to which they belong; and those who follow a business or profession not included among the number of guild corporations, are recorded members where their fathers are.

These corporations superintend the different benevolent societies for the support of widows, and the guardianship of orphans.

The guild-regulations are the same of those we described at length in Germany. Each one must learn his trade by a regular apprenticeship; travel a certain period, finish a masterpiece, and be regularly received into the guild, conforming to all its laws and requirements. No one who has not been thus approved can work at any trade; no one can make articles belonging to the trade of another; and nothing made elsewhere of the same kind as that produced in the city can be sold. Compensation is fixed, and the time of payment. Formerly, legitimate birth was one of the requisitions to brotherhood, but this statute is repealed. Each guild is taxed for the aid of the apprentices, and for those who are sick.

The liberal-minded among themselves say that the object of protection, which is professed, is not secured; and the whole system is evil, and not good.

The number of inns is prescribed by law; but the small coffee-houses and restaurants are not limited, except to ordain that only citizens can establish them. It is not strange to find people who are thus exclusive to Christians, exercising the most unjust and illiberal policy towards the Jews.

In the city no Jew is allowed to have a residence unless born there, and the children of these must obtain special permission in order to remain.

In the country all trade and commerce are denied to Jews without exception. Whoever employs a Jew in business or in the family is liable to a fine of sixty dollars. In case of repetition of the offence, the punishment is seventy-five days' imprisonment. Thus a father may have a son in America who cannot visit his home or participate in the employment of his family without incurring the penalty of the law.

On the days of fairs and markets, Jews may expose their wares, but a peddler is not allowed in the land.

If any one rents a shop to a Jew, he is fined ten dollars.

They may travel through the canton if furnished with a good passport, but any one who will inform against a Jew is allowed a third of the fine which is demanded for transgression.

There are no restrictions in city or country concerning trades carried on after the manner of manufactures. These include silk, cotton, woollen, straw, paper, tobacco, burning tiles, and calico printing.

The first paper-mill established in Switzerland was at Basle, in 1470; the first printing-press in 1460; and we may see specimens of their books in the Library printed in 1474.

One thousand persons are employed in the different processes of cotton manufacturing, but it is the ribbons which have gained for Basle its modern "wonder and renown."

As in Zurich, the looms for this species of industry are scattered all over the country; and should we enter any house, the scene would be nearly the same as that we described where the web was *gros de Naples*. In weaving ribbons the loom is filled with many webs instead of one. Besides those who weave, are those who *quill*. This is done by the aged and children; and there are some also who twist and reel. Often all these may be seen in the same house in full operation, and sometimes three or four looms working together. They have, too, the art of dyeing to perfection, with the knowledge of chemical proportions and combinations which enables them to produce all the colours of the rainbow, and many more, with an exactness that defies competition. But more curious it is to see those delicate offices performed by hands that cook, and sweep, and dig, and scrub, with equal ease and indifference. Behold a loom filled with the richest scarlet ribbon in brocade and flowers. The notable housewife weaves a yard or two, and attends to her potatoes for dinner,—weaves another yard, and fries her sausage and boils her *sauerkraut*. The table is laid, and while the "gude man" is washing the dust of the field from his hands, she steps into the loom, and adds a mite to the silken treasure; and thus are finished, in all their elaborate details, these beautiful fabrics.

Scattered over the country are between four and five thousand looms, which employ in weaving, quilling, reeling, dyeing, etc. nearly twenty thousand people, who yet spend a goodly portion of their time in other ways. These looms have increased two or three thousand in the course of the last century.

But in the city there are large manufactories, which employ

each three thousand persons. It is a still prettier and more wonderful sight to see hundreds of looms each filled with a different colour, or with webs each of many colours, developing by a process, which is to us so incomprehensible, flowers and figures and checks, without the variation of a thread; all the machinery regulated upon the same principle, and moved by the same power. We have wondered where the webs were all white and of the same length and width, but here we stood wondering almost like

"Katterfelto with his hair on end."

To describe the machinery would be as impossible to us as to measure the stars. The noise is a buzz, more torturing than the loud thumping of coarser and heavier looms; and in the details there are many variations from the ordinary construction of reeds and shuttles and beams.

In one factory are produced fifty thousand yards a day, and three millions of dollars' worth go every year to America. We said to the obliging proprietor, who accompanied us over every part of the establishment, "They are very dear when they get to us;" and he said he was very happy to hear it! But what is stranger, they are no cheaper right here within the sound of the buzz, than when they have crossed the Atlantic.

In another room they are assorting the skeins, and finding "*a thread that will run;*" and in different apartments are twistings and twirlings of all descriptions, with every nail and reel and beam and spindle wreathed with the brilliant threads. The floors are also covered with the same, and it seemed to us almost like scattering gold-dust in such profusion.

There must be a great waste of the *raw material* in the different processes, but they understand very well how to *calculate* loss and profit, so as to make the prices atone for each particle that falls.

The spinners and weavers, all women, have a neat, tidy look, which is not usual in factories, and in no instance seem haggard and life-weary. The average wages paid each is three dollars and seventy-five cents per week, and sometimes whole families are employed ; and if there are four persons, this amounts to fifteen dollars. But some individuals are paid five dollars or five dollars and fifty cents a week : and if any one is sick so that she cannot work, her wages are continued just the same, and those who have spent their lives in the factory, receive their accustomed wages in old age till they die. Among the operatives there is an association, to which all belong, taxing themselves to provide a fund for the sick and aged, and to this the proprietors contribute a sum equal in amount to that furnished by the members.

The buildings stand in an open, healthy place, and are furnished with air and water in abundance, and we could not see that there was anything lacking, that justice or humanity required, which it would be possible to have in the performance of such labour.

So late as the last century a law was made prohibiting ladies to dress entirely in silk ; and on the Sabbath all were required to wear black in church. No citizen was allowed to have a footman mounted behind his carriage within the city, or to clothe him in livery.

In 1771, it was prohibited to perambulate the city after ten o'clock in the evening ; and no person could drive a carriage with four horses, unless he could prove that he had at least three leagues to travel.

At the time the University of Basle was founded, in 1460,

there were only seven in Europe ;* and it had the first year two hundred and twenty students.

In 1521, Erasmus was enrolled among its professors, and many of the theologians of the Reformation added to its celebrity.

The city derives its name from a fortified castle named Basilia' built in 360 by Valentinian I., and from that day to this it has been renowned, first in one way and then in another, but always renowned

There is an old house here, as well as in Zurich, where a troubadour is said to have poured forth his sighs in song beneath the lattice ; and many a legend of the dark ages clings to its towers.

For centuries their clocks had the peculiarity of striking an hour in advance, and when from the great tower one pealed forth, the watchman cried twelve. The members of the great council were accused of regulating them in a way to do this in order to prolong their sessions. But from whatever cause they went wrong, they utterly refused to be set right till a few years since.

The glory of Basle in the field of science is Euler, who was born in 1707. He founded the Academy of Sciences in Berlin, and was called by Catherine to be President of the Imperial Academy of Sciences at St. Petersburg. His works on mathematics are the study of all who wish to be renowned in the same department of learning.

The first botanical garden of which we have any knowledge flourished on Basilian soil, and was planted by Felix Plates, who died in 1614 ; and the first local *flora* originated also with a professor in the same University. It was the school of all the

---

* Bologne, Paris, Cologne, Heidelberg, Friburg in Baden, Erfurt, and Vienna.

Swiss and many German reformers. Basilian diplomatists and generals have added lustre to every European court and army ; and her poets and artists have received the homage of a world. The elder Holbein was born in Augsburg, and was invited to Basle to paint the Hotel de Ville. It was the native city of his sons, the younger of whom went to England recommended by Erasmus ; none of them painted the famous "Dance of Death," as is often stated, which is due to an artist of Berne. Ornamenting houses with frescoes was first commenced in this city, and the interior of their Münster seems to us more beautiful than any other we have seen in Europe.

We hope we have done justice to their good works, and that they will so model their manners after Christian and humanitarian principles, as to do justice to themselves !

CHAPTER XVI.

ST. GALL.

MONEY-MAKING—VICES OF MATERIAL LIFE—EMBROIDERIES—SWISS MUSLINS—CHERRY WATER—CITY LIFE.

By way of reproach, St. Gall is called the *Yankee Canton* of Switzerland,* because they are a money-making people, and care too much for the things of this world. They have the vices of ambition, industry, perseverance, and love of the luxuries and comforts of life, rather than idleness, poverty, and destitution. A distinguished German philosopher says, "The vices engendered by material life are not so many or so gross as those of dreamy idleness, and not so many die of melancholy and madness in manufacturing towns and great cities, as in the country ; those who spend their time in solitude and dreams, are

---

* We are here reminded of a curious incident, related to us by Mr. Mason, the American Minister at Paris. In an official interview with the Persian Ambassador, he noticed that in speaking of Americans he called them always *Yanghe* and the new world *Yanghe-donia*. *Yangee* was the term applied to the first English by the North American Indians, as our readers well know, and afterwards changed by the British soldiers in the time of the Revolution to *Yankee*, and made a term of reproach to America. We leave to philologists to philosophise upon the resemblances between Indian and Persian tongues.

more likely to be corrupt than those who enjoy merry company and the activity of thickly populated places." *

Our observation has led us to the conclusion, that *calculating to make* money, has not so bad an influence on the character, as calculating to *save* it; and those who study and contrive so assiduously to save a few kreutzers might be better employed in *making* a few francs.

The north of Switzerland is infested with beggars, but a German author † says, they are from Bavaria, and other provinces of Southern Germany. They come in troops to join the pilgrims to Einsiedeln, and afterwards wander through the land. Many children are born and left by the mothers at the doors of the people in the night, whilst they return to their poverty-stricken homes. Almost all the servants are from among the same people, and in the cantons where their labour is most needed, the immorality is frightful.

Statistics will prove that the poor of Switzerland are few in comparison with those of all the nations which surround them. For every species of labour the wages are a third, and sometimes one half more, than in Germany.‡ In Bavaria, and some other provinces of Germany, the illegitimate children are more than the legitimate. In Wurtemburg, the proportion is one in eight, while in no canton of Switzerland is it greater than one in sixteen, and, in some one in a hundred, and in others none at all!

Who would believe, if figures did not prove it, that the average number of deaths in the crowded city of London is not so great as in the Duchy of Nassau, where there is no great city, and most of the people live in the country? ‡

---

* Man and his Physical Relations, by Dr. Oesterlen.   † Ebel.   ‡ Dr. Oesterlen.

One great reason of this is the want of proper food and cleanliness, and those are lacking, because the women are employed in unsuitable labour, and are also utterly ignorant of the art of cooking. The same *German* physician and philosopher whom we have quoted, says, " The construction of the houses everywhere in Germany, with reference to ventilation and cleanliness, is *barbarous*, and it is impossible for people to live in them, to be wholly Christian, civilized, or healthy."

The universal want of aqueducts, and the consequent deficiency of water for all household purposes, is another great cause. This is the same in Switzerland, only that the fountains are more plentiful, and the water, though carried on the heads of women, needs not to be transported quite so far.

In England, the average quantity of water used by each family daily is three hundred quarts, making from thirty to forty to each individual, while in Germany, the average proportion in every family is only ten quarts! * Yet for those ten quarts each family pays three times as much as is paid in England for three hundred, if the time of the women is taken into account, and also the destruction of clothing and health, which must necessarily be immense.

These are statistics which have been carefully gathered by a *German* and *published concerning his native land*, not in malice, but with the hope of awakening attention to the matter, instead of sitting down in pride and self-complacency to deny what everybody can see who has eyes.

If there is no way for individuals to improve except by being told their faults, the same is not the less true of nations ; and would that some mighty whirlwind would sweep over this great conti-

---

* Dr. Oesterlen : " Man and his Physical Relations."

nent, and scatter for ever the dust and cobwebs of centuries from their habitations, and some purifying flood wash out the dank and mould that cover with the gloom of ages their minds and hearts.

St. Gall is one of the manufacturing cantons, but adds to her spinning and her weaving the embroidering of the fabrics after they leave the loom. The Swiss muslins we need not describe; there is not a city or a village in America where they are not, and perhaps not a family which has not in some form a specimen of the beautiful tissues here produced. The value of the embroideries alone amounts to one million dollars, and the ladies of England and America buy it for Parisian work, as it is bought by the merchants of Paris, and sold by them under this name. No Parisian, however skillful, could produce anything more beautiful.

Our attention was first attracted to them in the carriages on our way, when an old woman and a young girl opened their boxes for the display of their wares. They had been on a tour to sell the products of their labour, and had not parted with all. Some gentlemen thought it a nice opportunity to secure a pretty gift to the ladies at home, when they should return; but alas, they did not know enough of "style and fashion" to select. They turned them over and over, and finally appealed to us to tell them, if "this was the fashion," and that a "reasonable price;" and another inquired if the one he held up would be sure to please his wife? We would answer the one about as well as the other, the *modes* not being our province of inquiry; but we did the best we could, and hesitated not to say that a neat little collar would become the good Frau, and that no doubt it would be considered entirely *comme il faut* in the little village where they lived on the Caspian Sea.

When the gentlemen were satisfied, we talked with the owners of the pretty things, and learned they had a *stickstube*—an embroidery room—in Appenzell, where they employed twenty-five maidens, and paid them each twenty sous a day besides their board. The muslin was purchased in St. Gall, and furnished to each person, who embroidered it, and, when finished, it was bleached, and the greater proportion carried to St. Gall again to sell. We thanked them for their information, and promised, when in Appenzell, to call and see them in the midst of their maidens, which we afterwards did.

From our window in the old city we looked out upon the market-place and a fountain. If the aqueducts should be constructed, they would certainly spoil very much of our travelling pleasure, for not less in Switzerland than in Germany are the fountains never-ending sources of amusement, as they are the universal rendezvous for gossip and the discussion of village affairs.

Here the horses came to be watered and washed, the children to drink, the servants to fill their tubs ; and though there are four large *spouts* to the great pump stock, they are not able to supply the demand. The receiving vessel is a great octagon-formed basin, and little tubes conduct from the spout to the edge of the basin, which are only used when clean water is wanted. At other times they are pushed on one side, and the stream falls into the trough. But often they forget to remove them, and soon there is a river pouring over street and pavement, and the next comer scolds merrily that she cannot get near without wetting herself from top to toe. The vessels in which they transport the water on their heads, are copper kettles, with a rim round the bottom, and from six to ten in the evening of one day, we watched the process of making these and others bright as mirrors, all being done at the "Brunnen," and then *splashed* in the water.

On the evening before market, the bushels of potatoes and bags of meal begin to assemble, and arrange themselves in rows on the square ; and in the morning, long before we are there, the beets, cabbages, and "other vegetables," have paraded themselves with due formality near. Then come horses and cows, and pigs and goats, *bleating* and *baaing* their aversion to being made the objects of barter and gain ; while old women with cheese, and young women with knick-knacks, erect little tents and booths for exhibiting their stores ; and baskets of berries, and balls of butter, peep temptingly out from the green leaves, which keep them cool and clean. The markets are all alike, not furnishing variety enough to give material for description.

But the days when the damsels come with their embroideries, and the merchants meet them to pay their wages, and measure to them new pieces, offer a novel scene. Not only from Switzerland, but from Bavaria and Baden, from Alsatia, Wurtemberg, and Tyrol, they arrive with their little boxes, containing the beautiful fabric over which their fingers have ached and their eyes wearied—which please to remember, fair reader, when you *beat down* the price of some fine handkerchief or "set of collar and sleeves." They get a much better reward for their labours than the lace-makers of Saxony ; but we asked one young girl how long it would take her to embroider the handkerchief she had begun, and she said, a quarter of a year—three months day and evening, all the time she could see to work !

In Appenzell, the little canton lying entirely within the limits of St. Gall, still more are employed in this species of labour, and in the two cantons together, seven thousand persons, who

11*

finish from one hundred and fifty to two hundred thousand pieces every year, and earn nearly four hundred thousand dollars.

In all the different processes of spinning, weaving, bleaching, etc., fifty thousand persons are employed the whole or a part of the year, whose united wages amount to one million five hundred thousand dollars, and the average wages of each are fifty dollars. They include many aged and children, who perform light labour, and work but a small portion of the time.

We had never thought of inquiring how webs of muslin were bleached, till we saw them stretched by means of wooden pins and stakes in long rows in the sun. They are too delicate to lie on the grass, and stand *slanting wise*, two or three feet from the ground. They are, of course, yellow, like any other cotton, when they leave the mill or loom, and when perfectly white, must be starched, ironed, and pressed.

When factories were first established in St. Gall, nine bleaching houses, several for pressing, ironing and packing were built by Government, and laws made to prevent all fraud.

1st.—That all webs before being laid to bleach be examined by a committee, and when unfit for use, should be cut to pieces and burnt.

2d.—To see that every piece has one hundred and thirty-four ells.

3d.—That whilst bleaching, it should be watched by men sworn to fidelity.

4th.—That all webs after being bleached, should be examined with the same exactness.

5th.—All webs which are to be coloured should be subject to the same examination.

6th.—A fraud in any department should be severely punished.

Pieces of muslin, richly embroidered with gold and silver, sell for between two and three hundred dollars.

Through all the cantons St. Gall and Appenzell, one sees the wheels turning, and hears the looms thumping from almost every house in some villages, especially in the northern part. The weaving room is usually on the ground-floor, to which they descend from above by a trap-door. They say, the muslin is not so good unless woven in the cellar, and to increase its beauty, or the facility for weaving, they wet the threads with meal and water.

For the finest muslins a half-ounce of cotton spins a thread from sixteen to twenty thousand feet long, but the ordinary length from the same quantity is only from nine to ten thousand.

Those who weave at home, own their looms and buy their cotton. When the webs are finished, they are given to a *collector*, who goes from house to house to receive them, and carry them to St. Gall. If necessity does not compel them to sell immediately, they keep the pieces till there are several, and dispose of them to better advantage.

The muslin which is embroidered in other states is returned unbleached and almost black ; but that which is embroidered with gold and silver cannot be washed, and is therefore all done in Switzerland under their own eyes.

In Zurich and St. Gall both silks and crapes are made, which merchants sell for India goods.

The first attempt at weaving muslin was in 1753 ; but St. Gall was famous for its cloths in the thirteenth century, which were known as *Constance Cloths*, many having emigrated thither from Constance in 1414 at the time of the session of the council, and given great activity to industry. In 1790, forty thousand persons were already employed in embroidering ; and agents were sent into other countries to establish factories. In 1734 appeared the first loom set in motion by water, and in 1740 the first calicoes and handkerchiefs were printed. The revolution of 1798 destroyed all monopolies ; and English markets being closed, a great impetus was given to industry in Switzerland, and they held their first exposition, a Crystal Palace on a small scale, in 1813, which was successful as an experiment.

In the southern part of the canton agriculture flourishes, and in the Rhine valley we see here and there large patches of Indian corn which the Indians might be willing to own ; and in the alpine pastures are some sixty thousand cattle, goats, and sheep.

Everywhere in the northern cantons fruit-trees are standing like forests ; and there is not only a brandy distillery in almost every commune, but also a cider mill. Pears are pressed for their juice, and cherries crushed to make what they call *cherry water*.

We one day saw a decanter upon a table filled with what we supposed to be water, as it was colourless, and we had never seen any stronger liquid without some slight tinge of yellow, red, or purple. Being thirsty, we thought to help ourselves, and took a generous draught, which in an instant had pervaded every drop of blood in our veins. It was *cherry water*, but it surely deserves a more significant appellation.

It is made by crushing fresh cherries and pounding them, as the juice is expressed from grapes. They are then kept slightly warm till fermentation takes place, which sometimes happens the second, and often not till the fourth week. The tub remains covered, and the pulp is stirred every two days. It can then remain a long time without injury, or be immediately distilled like brandy. So long as it runs clear, it is of the right taste and consistency, but when the liquid is thick, it is put back with the pulp in the still. To prevent its taking fire before it begins to boil, it is stirred violently. Like good wine, it improves with age. An imitation is sometimes made of plums, but can easily be detected by mixing it with a few drops of water, when it looks murky, and, if rubbed upon the hands, has a different flavour.

In all Switzerland are from fifteen to twenty millions of *quarters* of fruit, making eight quarters to each person, and more than in any other country. It is the staple article of food among the peasantry, cooked in various ways, dried and preserved as well as distilled.

St. Gall has a majority of Catholics, but Protestants are also numerous, and they live very harmoniously together,—the two sects in a village often occupying the same church, the one in the morning and the other in the afternoon. The old abbey, founded in the seventh century, was long the ruling power, and the cause of continual wars and dissensions till it was finally suppressed by the Government in 1805.* It was the seat of learning in the olden time ; and the sons of kings and emperors from all parts of Europe came to be educated by its wise monks. They not only preserved the writings of others, but wrote themselves what have proved the most valuable chronicles concerning the middle ages, and also the ancient ballad-poetry of Germany, which a Swiss peasant can read now, while to the most learned German philosopher they are an unknown tongue. The Ger-

---

* We may conclude, however, that superstition is not quite extinct in this commercial community, when we read that on last *Three Kings day*, some boys made quite a speculation by wheeling about on a hand-cart a hogshead of *holy water*, which they sold from house to house to those who believed in its efficacy.

man of Germany became so Latinized that very little of the original language remained, while in Switzerland it retained more of its original simplicity, and for this reason is still more like the Saxon.

The city looks very city-like, the houses standing thickly, and every place open to the sun and air is filled with the bleaching webs. There are many quaint features, yet over all a modern air, and also an appearance of equality among the people, very pleasant to observe in a manufacturing town. Toil does not depress the lower classes, and anxiety does not mark the countenances of those who *calculate* and grow rich.

It is strange to see the little cantons of Switzerland defying all the powers of the Vatican, and subjecting her priesthood to the law, and obliging monks and cloisters to give up their possessions, unless they will make a proper use of them; while in Austria, even the Emperor himself fears the mere shadow to which the See of Rome is reduced, and the most senseless mummeries of the dark ages are still practised as the means of salvation by the Imperial court and people.

In Rome there is a church to every hundred people, and a new one erected almost every year, and the want, misery, ignorance, and degradation are beyond what any human pen can describe. In ancient Rome there were fifty public baths where now there is not one; and in all Italy there is the same destitution of everything which modern civilization demands for the physical, moral, and mental health of the people. The King of Naples died last year of a disease which had no other cause than the filth by which he was surrounded, and thousands are dying in Italy of the same. Whilst it is confined to the poor, they heed it not; but palaces become at length infected, or rather infested, and then they begin to ask what can be done to avert it? If half the money which has been spent on palaces and churches had been devoted to aqueducts and other means of cleanliness, thrones and steeples would not now be tottering as they are to their foundations, and dukes and princes fleeing everywhere for life. To people who are never troubled with human sympathy, these will be very revolting statements, and those who travel only to admire architecture and fine paintings, will think it unpardonable to expose what is beneath. But it is becoming impossible for the most sentimental travellers to spend even a day in any city in Italy for any purpose whatever, for these reasons and others which it is impossible to expose.

We read with horror of those who fall by the sword, and all the terrors of the battle-field, but the horrors of hospitals are far greater.

Among soldiers in time of peace, full six per cent. are on the sick list, and among from three to four hundred thousand men, one hundred thousand are disabled by illness. While among other classes of men only one in ninety or a hundred die on an average, among military men in barracks forty or fifty die out of the same period of life! In the Crimean war the French lost eighty thousand men, but one-fifth died in consequence of bad food and unhealthy arrangements.

We have heard Americans in Europe deplore that they had not a more stable government! and people who travel in Switzerland, and happen to see a cantonal election, go away to say there is nothing but anarchy and confusion, and those who rule are ignorant boors and noisy democrats.

The governments of continental Europe have not shown themselves very stable during the last year. While every empire, dukedom, and principality has felt as being shattered by an earthquake, not a nerve of Switzerland has trembled. There has not been a single fear of insurrection or revolt from her populace.

The quiet of despotic governments is numbness and stupidity, instead of obedience and content ; but they are not only stupid, indolent, and depressed, but immoral, wicked, poor, and sickly. The clamour and flourish of trumpets at a Swiss or American election are only safety valves, and the surest preservations of permanent order. When they have spoken and clamoured, the effervescence is departed, and any sort of a whirlpool is better than a stagnant marsh.

CHAPTER XVII.

APPENZELL.

SPIRIT OF LIBERTY—MURDER BY A YOUNG GIRL—STICKSTUBE—COSTUME—
ALPS—AMUSEMENTS.

WE have elsewhere sufficiently illustrated the heroic deeds of "the men of Appenzell." "We are a free people," has been their boast for four hundred years. They laid down their shepherd's staff to take up arms, and when their warrior work was finished they took again the simple crook and sang their songs as gaily as if no wilder strain had broken in upon their melody.

All that they knew or understood of freedom, they demanded and secured. When they were enjoined not to eat milk in Lent, it being animal food, they said they saw no sense or reason in such an injunction, and ate milk all the same. The Pope, as usual, knowing that it was better they should do it with his permission than without, granted it to them in 1459, *proprio motu*. A few years later, in 1489, the Landamman obtained the consent of "His Holiness" to marry his god-daughter, by passing a stipulated sum for dispensation. The people then decided in council, that what was no longer a sin for the Landamman to *purchase*, should be granted to a simple citizen free ; and so in future they married without consulting the Pope or Church, and nobody undertook to compel them to change their decrees.

In 1525, Capuchins were sent among them to counteract the influence of the reformers, but they brought so much discord with them, that Catholics and Protestants both wished they had stayed away.

Those who first came were Peter Ludwig and his friend Jacob. A boy met them in the forest, and their dress was so strange that he thought they were not men, and cried for help. They said to him, "We are holy fathers, and do no man any harm." He fell on his knees and cried, "Oh, holy devils, I pray you, touch me not."

But the two religions were the means of dividing them into two parts, though in the whole canton there were not twenty square leagues. Appenzell is entirely enclosed in the canton St. Gall, looking as if it were fastened by a button to the banks of the river. It must be distinguished, not only by the name Appenzell, but the two divisions as "outer" and "inner Rhoden," the word Rhode meaning district. They were threatened with civil war on account of the dissensions concerning religious tenents, when some, more wise and prudent than the rest, suggested that it was better to divide the land. So, like the patriarchs of old, they said, "You go to the east, and I will go to the west; and there will be no more strife between your herdsmen and my herdsmen." So it was agreed. They met in council on the 1st of August, 1597, and arranged the separation so quickly and peaceably, that on the 28th they held the election in Outer Rhoden, which was the one set apart. They were to remain divided so long as it was agreeable to both parties. Each Rhode chooses its own Landamman and other officers; yet, there is also a common council, in which delegates from both meet for the administration of common affairs.

The council-house is an old building with time-stained walls, and the statute-books and instruments of punishment are not less ancient. By the side of the door is a bench, on which criminals are still stretched, and over it an *iron collar*, which is the yoke still worn by stiffnecked offenders.

On the walls of the council chamber are painted the heroic battles of the early period of their history. Underneath is the bastinado, which is also still retained among their means of punishing the guilty. The person to whom it is applied must lie upon his face, with the arms stretched as for swimming, and when bound hand and foot, the "raw hide" begins its work. The little cages, like those of a menagerie, are also here, placed immediately under the roof, with a narrow opening, through which air and food in very small quantities are admitted. It is not possible to stand upright in them, or to lie at full length. When it was remarked to the cicerone, "They must soon be brought to confession here," she said, "Yes, in winter ;" for no warmth can come to them the coldest winter day. Yet no one is kept there after confessing his guilt; but one might be tempted to confess to a crime he never committed in order to get out.

We have heard of an instance of endurance, in one of those cages, which finally revealed a sad story of crime, and shows the power of fashion among the simplest people, and that diamonds and rubies are not the only tempters of the frail and fair.

It is only ten years ago, that two young girls were returning from a festival in the city to their homes, to reach which they must pass a lonely meadow. They had been friends from childhood, and nothing had disturbed the pleasant relationship which bound them together. The one was beautiful, but she was poor, and it is a proverb in Appenzell, "that every maiden to win a lover early must have a silver chain." Her beauty, and perhaps her worth, had already won a lover, but still she was not content. Her companion was every way better dressed than herself, and had also a silver chain, which she coveted. Suddenly pretending to discover that she had lost her paternoster, and would return to find it, they both hastened back to a pool which they had passed, and while both were stooping to search eagerly, Anna Maria quickly seized her unsuspicious friend, tore the chain from her neck, and pushed her into the water, where she was drowned.

The corpse was found the same day, and when it was prepared for burial, Anna Maria stood with others around the bier a mourner, and joined in the prayers! But soon the chain attracted suspicion, and as one sin prepares the way for another, she said, "her lover had given it to her." That a man might have committed the murder did not seem improbable, and for such a reason; but that a girl nineteen years of age should have been guilty of so horrible a deed did not seem possible to any human mind.

The lover was arrested, and experienced the tortures of the bastinado without confessing the deed, and was then confined in the most dismal of the cages, where he submitted patiently to the ordeal, but remained silent.

Anna Maria was free, and came often to Appenzell, always going to the prison to inquire for her lover. One evening some of her young companions returned with her home, but she spoke not all the way till they reached the place of the murder, when she stopped, and turning pale exclaimed, "See there!" They looked, but saw nothing. This again excited suspicion; but others thought it natural that she should be troubled and see ghosts, though not herself guilty.

The woman who had charge of the prison felt more than suspicion from her manner when she called to inquire, and one day said to her bluntly, "You committed the murder yourself." She was white as marble, and trembled like the aspen. On being closely questioned afterwards, she confessed, and gave herself up for trial.

No long process was necessary to establish her guilt, and according to the law of the land she was condemned to death. When this was communicated to her by the clergyman she refused to listen, and said, "I will not die." How little she had thought of death when depriving another of life! Her father and sister prayed for mercy, but ninety voices had confirmed the sentence, and only six were heard in favour of pardon. There was no more hope; she must die.

When they came to lead her before the judge, she threw herself upon the ground, and screeching and screaming repeated, "I will not die, I will not die!" Four men dragged her to the council chamber, and when the sentence was read, her cries drowned the voice of the speaker. The pastor came to her, but she cast him off, and they were obliged to bind her on a sled to take her to the place of execution. When there, she kicked and strove, and bent her head to her breast, to avoid the fatal stroke, so that they despaired of bringing her head to the block, and sent to the council, yet in session, to know what they should do. The answer was, "that they must finish the work." The short respite had encouraged her to hope, and when she heard the words of the messenger, her screams became more frightful than before, declaring she would not die.

At length a grey-headed man suggested that they tie her long hair to a stake, which they succeeded in doing, and the death-blow fell. "It was finished," indeed.

A few years ago, a young girl was condemned for child murder, and the nuns of the Franciscan convent begged permission to receive her, and lead her in the way of repentance and truth, instead of putting her to death, and it was finally decided to grant their prayer, which we cannot help thinking was "the better way."

If a young girl accuses a young man of being the father of her child, he is put in one cage, to produce confession, and she in another, to compel her to tell the truth. If he insists that her statement is false, the oath is administered to her, and if it is proved that she has slandered him, he takes the oath of purification, and is restored to citizenship and respectability. If her words are proved, he can sign a paper promising to marry her, and is free.

Appenzell is the only canton where the *Kiltgang* is not the custom, and the guilty man is here more thoroughly abused than in Glarus. He cannot even vote at election, or rather, would not dare appear there, as the hissing and scorn would be unendurable. The maiden must wear a cap, and cannot put the silver pin in her hair.

In the olden time, "the men of Appenzell" were a rude and quarrelsome people. A game at *fisticuffs*, authorized by law, was an every day amusement, and death often the consequence. Men wore *schlagrings* on their little fingers, and no one dared go alone from village to village. Till within half a century the law existed, that he who killed another in this way, "could not drink wine nor cider nor take part in public festival."

He who committed intentional murder could be pardoned with consent of the relatives; but must never meet them in any public place, or pass any road where they were in the habit of going. He must take the murderous weapon in one hand, and a candle in the other, and go to church in funeral procession, kneel there and at the grave, and pray three times to God for pardon. He must furnish two hundred candles for mass-service, and set a cross where the relations wished, and pay them a sum of money prescribed by law, and sit always apart in church.

The election ceremonies are nearly the same as in Glarus, and the cantonal colours black and white. The salary of the Landamman in Outer Rhoden is forty dollars, and of the Mayor six.

When we passed the house of the Landamman, a young girl in the *diligence* pointed to it with great reverence and pride. It was a large wooden domicile, looking just then very nice and new, with bright shingles and clapboards. Opposite was a large orchard and a pretty summer-house of pink stucco outside, and white painted window frames, all looking as if some new fortune had come to the possessor, and he was enlarging his borders accordingly, yet without ostentation or display.

The houses stand dotted about on the hill-sides and greenswards, having often, upon the old ones, the date of their erection, figures made with the shingles on the roof, and various ornaments, verses from the Bible, paintings, sentimental phrases, and gilded points and crosses. But the new ones are plain and comfortable. Nowhere, perhaps, is neatness more truly the characteristic of the people than in Appenzell.

We did not forget to visit the *stickstube* of the woman we met on the railway, and found her in the midst of her maidens, some twenty-five, seated round the room, with their frames fastened to a light three-legged stand of convenient height, which they carry about with them as easily as a parasol or roll of embroidery. The muslin is pulled tight over one frame, and fastened by a loop shutting on to the other, which we have often seen used, but without the stand. Oh ! the beautiful flowers, figures, animals, landscapes, everything that artist can invent, which appear at the command of their fingers ! Why, are they not as truly evidences of genius as those which are made by a brush on canvas ? Never did we see anything more wonderful than the designs which were furnished them, and the skill is not less marvellous which perfects them—so graceful, delicate and true.* All the day, all the evening, all the year, they bend over the little frame ; but we should think it would not take years to make them blind.

The woman, as we stated, gives each twenty sous a day and board, and finds the muslin. She, of course, has all the risk and trouble of selling. But there was no air of poverty about them, and they looked very cheerful and in good health. Besides these, many daughters work at home, and at almost every window we see them, and also in the gardens, under the trees, or in the street, always with the frames in their hands.

In Outer Rhoden there are twelve thousand persons engaged in the different departments of the manufacture of muslins and embroideries. The bright coloured papers which are laid under the corners of the handkerchiefs, and beneath the collars and sleeves, to exhibit the pattern, are also manufactured here ; and in the *Hotel Hecht*, the ancient costume, in all its details, is exhibited by a woman, who evidently wears it for this purpose. The skirt is purple woollen stuff, looking as if it had been quilted, the little plaits commencing at the waist and reaching to the hem, without losing their form. The bodice, bright scarlet silk, pointed before and behind, shows a white muslin chemisette

---

* It is true that many artists are employed in furnishing the designs for this work, who would otherwise, perhaps, be employed with the easel.

under the arms and over the bosom. The sleeves are short and full, and above the elbow are broad hair bracelets with silver clasps. Around the bodice is also a border of silver ; and the silver chain, coveted by all maidens, is upon her neck, and consists of many fine strings, making more than an inch in breadth; one of the same kind passes under the arm, linking the points of the embroidered collar. Her cap is also of bright scarlet like the bodice, trimmed with various ornaments in lace and silver. One would think from the description, that it must look *finical*, but it is remarkably neat and pretty, and on a young pretty maiden must be charming. She who wears it has evidently been "handsome in her day," but is now stricken in years, and very pale. But she understands well the duties of her vocation. She has a word to say to everybody, and presents herself upon all occasions, with a sort of theatrical manner, which seems to say, " Do you observe ?" and it is certainly worth while to take one dinner at her table, to be served by so gracious a hostess, and observe both her air and costume.

In the embroidery rooms, also, they retain some peculiarities, a sort of uniform ; but the people one meets in the streets daily are in the fashion now universal. A traveller, who wrote more than half a century ago, says at that time the men wore *hosen*, which left a wide space between the top and the vest ; and when he entered the hotel, where many people were assembled on election day, dressed in the modern style, he saw all the people looking at him and laughing. Fearing something was wrong in his attire, which he could not see, he asked what excited them to such mirth, and they said : " Oh, it was too funny ; such a costume !" Small clothes are sometimes still seen in the country—a red vest and leathern girdle, long stockings, and shoes with silver buckles.

In different years, from the middle of the sixteenth to the nineteenth century, we find various laws concerning dress, endeavouring to restrain extravagance. But custom is stronger than law, and all enactments which infringe upon personal liberty were constantly evaded.

Servants were scarcely known in families till 1830, but when embroidery became so common, servants were necessary, as the daughters could not perform the labours of the household and those of the needle too.

As everywhere else in Switzerland, the menials are from Suabia; but they are generally treated like those of the family, and have the same life. Their wages are very small, being only as much for a week as the embroiderers receive for a day.

Appenzell is a miniature Switzerland in itself. The prairies are very few, and the mountains among the grandest of the snowy Alps. The whole of Inner Rhoden is covered with shepherds and their herds; and the hum of industry in the canton has in no wise drowned the wild melody of the mountaineer. Here one may listen to the *Ranz des Vaches* in its primitive pathos; and the wild *ragusa* is hummed with no diminution of its power by the maidens of the valley.

The dance has been long forbidden in Outer Rhoden, except at the four principal festivals of the year; and it is on these occasions that the young people meet, and wooers have an opportunity to sing their loves. When they are betrothed, the young man and maiden can walk together any time in the day before evening, not arm in arm, but with the little fingers locked together; and each young maiden has some notes of a *ragusa*, which she sings when she is abroad, that her lover instantly recognizes as a signal to join her, if he is at leisure.

All gambling is also forbidden, and money won at play is not allowed to be retained. No person is allowed to invest money in lotteries at home or abroad, and no journal is allowed to advertise a lottery.

No innkeeper can permit a dance in his house of young persons unless their parents are present. For all those offences a fine is the penalty; but to avoid them, people go over the borders, a distance which is not very far, and dance and play, perhaps with more injurious consequences. Suicide, madness, and melancholy, are more common than among the Inner Rhodens, who are much poorer, and live not half so well. The ceremonies of the Protestant Church are not interesting except to those whose hearts are concerned; and when so many restraints are imposed, without a culture that elevates the mind and soul above self-indulgences, the effects are evil, and not good.

Among the Catholics, a little money purchases the pardon of all their sins, and evidently satisfies their consciences, whether it should or not, and they dance all care away. It is a subject worthy of theologian and philosopher, and should have a good deal more consideration from Christians than they have ever given it.

We often hear such reproaches against the peasantry both in Switzerland and Germany from those who will live side by side with them year after year without one effort to understand them or improve their condition. This never struck us more forcibly than one evening when we went to a peasant's dance, and, after leaving them, entered the saloon of a patrician, who made the greatest professions to being a Christian and a friend of liberty. He sat in his elegant room, leaned back among the velvet cushions of his *fautenil*, and exclaimed: "How disgusting— how dreadfully disgusting—those peasant dances, their noise, .heir beer-drinking, and their unseemly deportment!" His cellar was filled with the choicest of wines, and his wife dressed in silks, and velvets, and jewellery, to the amount of many thousand dollars. They could afford it, and there was no reason why they should not indulge in all the luxuries civilization has invented. Not long before, they had given a ball, for which they rented a hotel, invited several hundred people, and gave an entertainment that in all must have cost considerably more than five hundred dollars. A lady informed us how the peasant girls "tried to get married." In the society in which she moves did she never see any similar efforts? I think it was the same lady who told us that among the higher classes, when daughters became of a marriageable age, their mothers had already engaged a husband for them; and we have heard of intrigues among young ladies themselves such as would not have disgraced the court of Francis I. and Louis XIV., for this same purpose of "getting married," which is so shocking among peasant girls. If, instead of spending five hundred dollars for a ball—which does not occur on Sunday, to be sure, but furnishes work and conversation for many holy Sabbaths—one hundred had been devoted to a pleasant and proper festival for the poor, where their manners would be improved and their character softened, would it not have been a more Christian way of treating them than to call them heathen, and let them alone? In how many ways could five hundred dollars benefit a peasant village, if a man really wished to perform a Christian duty, and to work as well as pray in the vineyard of the Lord! We do not wish to condemn giving balls to lords and nobles, though we think there is a better way even for them; but we doubt whether those who meet in cottages to dance and sing are more reprehensible characters than those who meet in castles.

It is the most imcomprehensible of all things, if the Bible was given for a guide to man, that people can read it a lifetime and never get one idea of Christian love and duty as exemplified on its pages. They read the life of Jesus of Nazareth, and scorn the person who follows the most nearly his example. They profess to have no other enjoyment than "religious exercises," and exhibit not the fruits of patience, long-suffering, and kindness, but envy, hatred, malice and evil-speaking.

The peasantry are forbidden to dance, and called low and vulgar, and beyond the reach of elevation, because they still delight in so many amusements. But can anybody say what they shall do in the hours they have been accustomed to devote to play? They are now all taught to read, but of what use is it so long as there is nothing within their means upon which to practise the art? Five hundred dollars, or so, would furnish one village with a library within their comprehension, which spent in feasting lords and ladies is worse than wasted.

The law in the United States of America that provides for every school a library, is doing infinitely more good than the one which provides a school. Interesting books excite the ambition to learn to read them, and do away with all necessity for making laws against dancing. What a new world would it create for the lonely shepherd in his cot on the mountain, to fill it with pleasant stories that give him food for thought, and awake in him nobler aspirations. There are those who think it is better to let him alone to his songs, and his dreams, and his rovings. Alas, how little they know of the shepherd or of humanity who come to this conclusion ; and why is it that Mission and Bible Societies so readily spend their money for the heathen of other lands, while thousands are in the darkest ignorance and superstition around them, to whom they will not speak even a word of Christian kindness?

The schools in Appenzell have been increased and improved within the last thirty years, so that they exist in every commune in Outer Rhoden, and the number of scholars has doubled. A high school has been endowed by private citizens at Trogen, and another at Heiden ; and there are, besides, secondary schools for the upper classes supported by the State. In the Catholic portion of the canton there are not so many, and the law does not require the parents to send the children unless they choose. There are two convents where girls are instructed by the nuns, who have the reputation of being good and benevolent, as they have also in many other places in Switzerland.

The amusements are very many among those of both religions. So early as 1646, a law was made, that all should sing in church ; and that those who sang in inns, and at plays, and not in church, should pay a fine of twenty-five dollars. They were also required to sing in schools, and the clergyman named from the pulpit on Sunday what psalms should be practised during the week.

A society of mutual improvement was founded in 1832, a slight admission fee providing lectures on agriculture, art, etc.

But the *shooting fêtes* are better attended, and date from a period unknown. From the year 1780 to 1808, they spent in prizes and various *fêtes* five thousand dollars. But fewer men have gone into foreign service from Appenzell than from any other canton.

The first reading-room was opened in 1725, and they are now very general ; but the variety of journals and books is not very extensive. In some villages, museums are connected with them, and natural history illustrated.

The weddings of the olden time were very sumptuous affairs. We read of one which took place in 1651, when the bridal train consisted of thirty horses, and ninety-six guests were present; the whole costing about thirty dollars! and one in 1654, at which were fifty pairs and two hundred and sixty-two guests; and one in 1685, where were four hundred and thirty-three guests. Then the law interfered, and ordained that no bride should invite more than eighty persons, or have more than eight bridesmaids.

Now the law says nothing about it, and the custom is prevailing more and more to have the ceremony performed in a quiet manner, and take a journey or make a visit. Wreaths and flowers are still worn, and the bridesmaid sews a bouquet to the left side of the skirt of the bride, which costs her nearly a dollar.

Those who wish to marry must obtain the consent of the Landamman.

Baptism is performed in church, and the baby is arrayed in all the fine swaddling-clothes it can carry. The ceremony is seldom put off more than three days, as they fear it will die unbaptized; and many do not allow the infant to lie upon the mother's bosom till it has been thus purified. The godfather stands on one side of the font and the godmother upon the other. They exchange bows, when the godfather hands the child to the pastor, on a cushion, who holds it over the water, which is always warm, and wets its brow three times, "in the name of the Father, Son, and Holy Ghost."

Among the superstitious, they rejoice when an infant dies, and say, "Now we have an angel in heaven." Often they send for a priest to say mass, instead of the doctor to cure the sick one.

The election is the great national *fête*, to which all come, men, women, and children; and the military review and *kirchweih* are almost as widely celebrated.

A peculiar custom in Outer Rhoden, on the 17th of February, is to mount the trunk of a tree upon a wagon ornamented with flowers and garlands. An old man and woman, clothed in the ancient Swiss costume, and carrying little bells, precede the *cortége*, walking in the gravest manner. The king of the day is seated upon the tree, and makes gracious salutations to the multitude, while the whole pass through the length of the street and back again, when they end the festival at an inn.

At carnival, the fires are kindled on all the hills, and Christmas is celebrated with great parade.

There are several bathing establishments for strangers, and at *Heinrichsbad*, one of the largest in Switzerland, are elegant *salons*, reading-rooms, and dancing-halls, surrounded by a beautiful country, affording delightful promenades.

When we left the pleasant land of Appenzell, it was to go southward, by the railroad to Chur ; but in order to reach the station we were obliged to take a post-chaise to Alstacten. Seeing the horse nearly harnessed that was to take us, we went out and stood by the carriage. Just then a neighbour appeared, to ask the owner of the vehicle if his daughter could not ride to Alstacten in the same carriage with the lady, as she wished to visit her aunt. There was much talk and hesitation before we understood the cause, but finally the father appealed to us, and said, "Sure it will not annoy you, she is a young girl, and there is plenty of room ?" We answered most heartily, "Indeed we had much rather she would go than not ; to have some one to talk with is far pleasanter than to sit silent." He ran immediately to call her, and she soon appeared, and looked so exactly like a cousin we left among the Green Mountains at home, that we could almost have called her by name. She was a coy maiden of sixteen, blond and pretty, dressed neatly in black, for she had lately lost her mother. We found her a pleasant travelling companion indeed, blushing like a summer rose at every remark or question, but very intelligent concerning anything by the way.

Our road was through the neat villages, fruitful orchards, and waving harvests of this prim little canton, till we came to the top of a hill that overlooked the valley of the Rhine. What a contrast is suddenly presented. The sky has become, as it seems, instantaneously black with clouds, the thunder rolls, and the lightning flashes among the dark gorges which open in the opposite banks, while the dense forests upon the hillsides look as if a fire had just imparted to them its scathing hues, without depriving a branch or twig of its rich clothing. We realize the fulness of the expression "blackness of darkness." It is strange and fearful beyond description. Whilst gazing upon it, we are slowly descending from peak to peak, surrounded by woods which would present the same appearance to a distant observer, while the rain pours in torrents, making a road, never safe, perilous at every step. But our young companion has seen it a hundred times, and heeds it no more than a gentle shower. These are to them every-day scenes, the pastime of their Alpine skies and snowy heights. To us it has been ever like a vision of another world, a glimpse of something terrific beyond the limits of mortal vision.

Soon the clouds were dispelled, and the sun shone out in splendour. On the railroad our way was beneath the bold, frowning cliffs, whether on the banks of the Rhine or the stormy *Wallen See:* though not so frightful in sunshine as in tempest, they present some of the most peculiar and grandest features of Swiss scenery. If we could enjoy but one, we would rather trace the Rhine from Constance to its source than trace any other portion of its way to the sea. The castle-crowned peaks have an interest which these wild, untenanted cliffs have not, but they are few in comparison, and have not that solemn impressing sublimity which becomes every moment more awful till we approach the *Via Mala* and the eternal snows which gave birth to the "father of waters."

CHAPTER XVIII.

GLARUS.

SCENE IN STREET—OLD FAMILIES—ZWINGLIUS—BROTHERHOOD—SCHABZIEGER CHEESE—ALPIN ETEA—CALICO—INCIDENT ON RAILWAY—ELECTION—SUPERSTITIONS—OLD LAWS AND CUSTOMS.

Not since we left New England have we heard such a hooting and tooting, such a horn-blowing and trumpeting, such a snapping of whips and singing of songs, as in this old town of Glarus. It is by no means a noise which indicates rudeness and uproar, but merely the exuberance of youthful spirits, where people do not consider the State in danger from allowing "boys to be boys," instead of keeping them under the surveillance of a police, lest a little excess of mirth should increase, and become rebellion, and end in revolution! We are reminded of the words of one of their own poets—

> Oh Lustgesang, Oh Hirtensang!
> Wie schallest Du so schön,
> Durch wonnevollen Sennenklang!
> Herab von grünen Höh'n!
> Ich frag' Euch alle, stolze Länder,
> Habt Ihr so süssen Jubelsang?
> Nein, nein, nein, nein, das habt Ihr nicht,
> Euch fehlt der Freiheit süsses Licht!

To translate this would be to spoil it, but the sentiment is, "Why are the pleasure ' songs,' and ' shepherd songs' here so thrilling and so beautiful, from the green heights of the Sennhut to the valley beneath. All ye proud lands I ask, have you festal songs like these? No, no, no, no ; because you breathe not the air of the free !"

The wordless notes of the *Ranz des Vaches* are said to be nowhere so thrilling and musical as upon the hills of Glarus and Appenzell, and nowhere was freedom more bravely won, and by none more sacredly preserved.

The day in their heroic history of which they are most proud, is that which saw the battle of *Näfles*, April 9, 1588, which left one hundred and eighty three Austrian chevaliers on the field, and two thousand five hundred soldiers, their own loss being only fifty-five. The enemy had come upon them unawares, obtaining an entrance at the gates which protected the valley on the north, by treachery, and pouring down upon the astonished people came near, crushing them before they had time to seize their clubs. But three hundred and fifty defended the narrow passage for five hours against the whole Austrian army, and by that time messengers had reached the town, when the Landamman collected a few shepherds, and met the retreating party at Näfles, where some ascended the heights, and pelted them with stones, which so threw them into confusion they were easily put to rout on the plain. Austrians then, as now, knew no other way, but to "march" and "wheel" and "face about" according to rule, and, therefore, then as now, could be very easily wheeled to destruction by a little ingenuity.

Appenzell had the aid of the Glarners in throwing off the yoke of the bailiffs, and on all occasions, when soldiers were necessary, they were ready with their fortunes and their lives.

During four hundred and ten years no foreign army had set foot upon their soil, when it fell into the hands of the French in 1798, and they lost all their possessions, and in the course of five months five battles were fought between the French and Austrians within their limits. This ended their experience of wars, and, more fortunate than many of their neighbours, they have never been torn by internal dissensions. They have had no trouble with the Federal Diet, and none with their own Government, as it has always been upon the broad basis of the utmost freedom to all.

Their constitution is curious for the liberality shown to Catholics when Protestants were a large majority; and the two confessions live together in perfect harmony, having an equal share, in proportion to numbers, in all public administration, and in the capital of the canton using the same church, the one in the morning and the other in the afternoon. This liberality is perhaps owing to the influence of one of their pastors, Valentin Tschudi, who died in 1555, and was the author of the History of the Reformation, and the burden of whose sermons was, " Live like brethren, the disciples of one Lord and Master !" For many years he was a Catholic, and afterwards, inclining towards the reformation, he still retained his pastoral office, performing mass in the morning, and preaching to a Protestant congregation in the evening, but at all times carefully avoiding every subject of controversy. To some people who remonstrated against such tolerance, he said, " Do you think it impossible to be a Catholic in the morning and a reformer in the evening, and yet a Christian all day ?" Eventually, however, he embraced the new religion in full.

He belonged to one of those *noble families* of whom we find so many in Switzerland, who are reverenced by the people for their antiquity and for the noble deeds of their fathers. For this reason they invest them for a series of years, perhaps for centuries, with the highest offices of the State. Fastidious critics and travellers think this too aristocratic, but we see in it only a proper regard to worth and a just reverence to heroes. The officers are re-elected every year, or at certain periods differing in different cantons, and they choose to select them from the same family, which is not at all likely they would do if they were not also worthy.

Christianity was first preached in Glarus by an Irish monk, who came among them in 490, and founded a convent, which was dependent upon one which he had previously established at Seckingen, on the Baden side of the Rhine. Subsequently, all the country became subject to the abbots of this convent, except forty families, among which that of Tschudi was one. The present pastor of Glarus belongs to the same family. It is not necessary to be so democratic as to discard worthy men *because* they belong to "old families," when they themselves do not make this a reason for demanding honors and emoluments. In the cantons where this has been done, they are almost certainly deprived of those they might otherwise have enjoyed.

A Tschudi, who died in 1572, wrote one of the best histories of Switzerland, and others have distinguished themselves in various ways, proving that worth is sometimes an inheritance. The children in the hotel, where we were, brought us their reading book, which we saw was also prepared by their pastor, Tschudi. It contained a good selection of prose and poetry ; and we were a little gratified to find two or three stories of Washington and American history side by side with those of William Tell and the men of Grütli, and the children taught to repeat them with almost as much enthusiasm.

Zwinglius was pastor in Glarus nine years, and the liberality and practical piety of the people may be in some measure owing to these elements in his teachings. In his sermons there is not so much of denunciation either of pope or prince as characterised many of those of his day, and no flattery of their subjects. In his counsels are no exhortation to the selfish enjoyment of solitude, or the indulgence of the spirit in dreamy idleness, which many people flatter themselves is " communion with heaven," and therefore meritorious, when it is only an excuse for inaction, and an escape from responsibility. What better is it to shut one's self in a closet or a church than in a monk's cell or a hermit's cave ; and what example or precept of Christ are those following who spend their lives in the " holy delights and joys of meditation," instead of going forth into the world to meet its trials, temptations, and sacrifices, in the spirit of Him who made his examples the great sermon of his life, and carried it to the tables of wine-bibbers and into the halls of money-changers ? We were never able to understand how it came to be considered any part of the religion of Christ among Catholics or Protestants to live as hermits either by one name or another.

These are thoughts, though not the words, which Zwinglius a thousand times uttered, and the *Glarner Volk* evidently profited by his instructions.

It is a proverb in Switzerland, that " No *Glarner* was ever known to remain behind when the honour and good name of the land were at stake." When they are abroad, they keep constantly in remembrance that they are the representatives of their country, and must be sure to conduct themselves in such a manner as to bring no reproach upon the name they bear.

They seem to think it would be a disgrace to have among

them many sects, and say, "We have no Pietists, no Separatists, and few Baptists." Yet the religious feeling and sense of honour are very strong; and self-denial and sacrifice have no bounds when their land's-people are in need. If a calamity befall a family or district, all contribute to remove it; and houses are everywhere being built by those who agree, one to draw the wood, another the stone, a third to hew, a fourth to hammer, and all to do something till it is within the means of the owner to finish. It is the same in their factories. Employer and employed are scarcely distinctions;—they are all citizens, brothers, and friends.

Like those of Tessino and Graubünden, they, too, are a wandering people. All the way from Madrid to St. Petersburg they may be seen either settled as merchants or travelling as agents, with their calicoes, handkerchiefs, slates and tea. These are their especial articles of commerce.

How curiously great events spring out of trifles! It is related that in the sixteenth century some poor people in the Sernfthal thought the stones they found in the neighbourhood were very smooth and pretty; and without any idea that they could be made useful, offered some for sale. Another person, with scarcely more thought, framed a piece, and used it for keeping his accounts, and any little writing he had to do; and still another thought, it would make a nice table. This was the origin of the use of slates. Some fifty or sixty persons were employed in breaking the stone from the quarry, and as many joiners to fit them to frames, till the commerce spread into all Europe. For them the business is now confined mostly to Switzerland, as slate stone was discovered in other countries, but their wandering commenced with these, and taught them new wants for themselves and new wants for the world.

Their next article of commerce was a kind of tea, which grows upon their hills, and which is very palatable ; and being cheaper than that which comes from China, is in great demand by the lovers of tea who cannot afford young Hyson or Bohea.

They were once famous for all manner of little boxes, game-boards, and fanciful articles made of different kinds of wood, which they climbed every mountain and searched every forest to find ; but they say, since America sent her beautiful woods to Europe, " this trade is spoiled."

They are still renowned for peculiar cheese, which is made nowhere else, and for which no other country seems to furnish the material. It bears the distinctive name of *Schabzieger Cheese*. We used to see them in Germany in the form of little pyramids, the size of a quart measure, and the colour of sage. They are very hard, and must be grated to use, the powder being sprinkled upon the *butterbrod* for " a relish."

The herb from which it receives its name was called originally *ziegenklee*, or *kraut*, and also *siebenzeit*, because the flavour changed seven times daily ! It was known to the Greeks as a medicinal plant, and was transplanted to the gardens of cloisters for this reason. It is alluded to among the botanical plants of the cloister garden of St. Gall in the ninth century. The first definite knowledge of the cheese dates to the fifteenth century, when the nuns of St. Gall taught the nuns of Glarus how to make it. It is mentioned as one of the articles of food furnished by Abbot Ulrich the Eighth to the army he stationed to watch the enemy on the borders of Germany.

In 1464 it was ordained by the Government, " that each one should make his cheese good and clean, turn it, salt it, and stamp his name on the rind ;" and declared at this time to be a well-known article of commerce and exported into all other lands.

Conrad Gessner, of Zurich, wrote in his book published in 1541, and dedicated to the " Glarner Volk," " Your people are principally engaged in the care of cattle and in making all kinds of food from milk, among which is the *schabzieger*, that is known everywhere and deserves to be."

They bring the curds from the Sennhut in hempen bags to the village dairy, and when drained till very dry, the powdered herb is mixed with it by means of a sort of mill of large stones, which grind it very fine, till the two have become one substance, when it is put in moulds to be pressed, and set in the air to dry. Much care and experience are necessary to be sure that every process is rightly performed—when it is in the right state to press, to rub, to dry, and to grate ; and none but the Glarner people have ever succeeded in making it exactly right. When the little cheeses are ready, they are packed in boxes containing forty each, and sent to all the world ; and wherever we go we shall be happy to meet them, for they are the only Swiss cheese we cordially like.

In 1714 a man taught the servant in his family and some poor people to spin, which was the origin of the cloth-making, though for many years they sent their yarn to Zurich to be woven. But now they spin it, and weave it, and print it for themselves. Their grass plats are not covered with webs of gossamer or fine linen, but long rows of *turkey-red*, which look very warm on a hot summer's day. Their calicoes, like the ribbons of Basle, are no cheaper at the mills than a thousand miles away ; from this reason they say, that "if they were, everybody would come to the mills to buy, and the merchants would have no profit."

Those who go out into the world to make a little fortune, often come home to spend it in the old homestead ; and though adding a little to their comforts and luxuries, make no display that contrasts unpleasantly with those around. They have a thoroughly upright, sensible, respectable look, which would attract the attention of the most ordinary observer. We happened to see half the town one day—indeed, half the canton—first at one station, and then at another, on a *fête* occasion, and thought we had never seen so many fine faces; and the friendly greetings prompted us to exclaim: "Are they all brothers and sisters and cousins here?" and they were not less friendly to a stranger.

We were some miles from the station where we had stopped, when we discovered that our "guide-book" was left behind. A lady, with a face we should notice among a thousand, and never forget, seeing us look for something, kindly asked what we had lost. On hearing, she said: "But you can get it by telegraphing; ask the conducteur to send for it." "But do you think it would be of any use? there were hundreds of people there, and no person would know to whom it belonged, and there was no name in it." The conductor appearing at that moment, we told him our calamity, and he said: "But you should not be so careless; there is no telegraph for miles yet;" and went along. But soon he came back, and asked the address to which it would be sent, still repeating: "You should take care of your things; how do you expect to get a book where there is such a crowd of people?" His words were rather harsh, but his manners were not; yet we had little hope of seeing the book, though two gentlemen kindly assured us, "There was no doubt of it; nobody would touch it."

The incident had introduced us to the friendly lady, and we scarcely regretted the loss with such a 'gain. She was one of those whom nature produces now and then, and to whom all the art and polish of courts would not add a charm. She had never seen the world, and knew nothing of airs and graces, but these would not have made her more refined, and might have detracted from her loveliness, and taught her that it was vulgar to be frank and unsuspicious. Not often in a lifetime have we experienced such genuine kindness or been so won by native grace and beauty.

The next morning the red "guide-book" walked into our room in the hands of one of those black-eyed, red-cheeked Swiss officials, and we asked, "What is to pay?" He said, "Nothing," and doffed his cap. "But nothing for the telegraph or the trouble?" "Nothing." The conductor had given it to him, and told him to bring it to me. This was all he knew. The pleasant man had scolded us for our carelessness, and rewarded us in this way. We shall be in no danger of forgetting either the one deed or the other.

The hum of the factory has not silenced the shepherd's song; and the Alps are still the principal dependence of the people, but are now chiefly private property, yet subject to general laws. Only so many cattle can be kept upon a certain space, and persons are appointed to count them and attend to the clearing of the pastures. Every Senn is bound by oath to give the number correctly. No one is allowed to have a great flock of sheep to the injury of the wild hay, and no one is allowed to begin cutting it before August. This is to prevent accidents to those in the valleys, who must receive notice of the time, because it comes tumbling down from the heights with such force, that persons may be killed or seriously injured if they do not keep out of the way. Those who cut it are obliged to fasten themselves to the cliffs with hooks or cramping irons, by which they hold with one hand and use the sickle with the other, and in this way they gather a hundred pounds a day, where neither goat nor chamois would think of browsing.

The ceremonies of election day are the same as we have seen in Canton Uri, with slight variations; and we could not expect any great bribery or corruption to be used in obtaining an office, the emoluments of which amount to barely one hundred and fifty dollars a year. This is all the Landamman receives, and the treasurer seventy dollars. The whole expenses of the Government of the canton for a year amount to *six hundred dollars*.

The people assemble on the second Sunday in May; and no man who is eighteen thinks of staying at home on an occasion when he is to show that he is one of the sovereigns of the land. The streets are filled as with a procession, and they are as earnest talking of "the candidates" and the new road or tax, or whatever is to be voted upon, as if the whole nation was put up at auction. The benches are placed upon the square in the form of an amphitheatre, exactly as they were at the first election ever held in the canton. The ringing of bells is the signal for the procession to form, when the trumpeter takes the lead, and the Landweibel follow with sceptre of silver and sword. Their mantles are red, with a stripe of black behind, and their sense of importance not less than that of the chamberlains of the King. When the officers arrive, all the people rise and uncover their heads. The oath of office is then repeated by Landamman and Statthalter, when the assembly is called upon to do the same. Every man holds up his fore-finger while the formula is read, and when it is finished, with bare head and finger * still raised, repeats the following words: "That which has been read to me,

---

* The reader will remember, that in the case mentioned in Brunswick in "Peasant Life in Germany," when the fingers fell, the witness felt at liberty to swerve from the truth. In both cases, to hold it uprightly is an oath of fidelity.

and which my office, condition, and country's oath require, I have understood plainly and fully. I swear to live for them in all truth and fidelity. This I swear so truly as I pray, 'God me to help.'" The Catholics add, "And the Holy Virgin." This is said by all in a half tone; but as soon as the last word is uttered, a quick and earnest expression of assent, as with one voice, goes through the assembly.

The voting is by raising the hand, though there are eight or ten thousand persons present. No proposition can be considered which has not been presented to the council a month in advance.

Whoever speaks, begins his address in the following manner: "Highly respected Sir Landammon, highly respected, highly honoured gentlemen, high and worthy pastors, trustworthy, free, and beloved countrymen."

In front of the platform a place is always left for boys, that they may be solemnly impressed with the duties of citizens, and they evidently enjoy the privilege, and attend like those who are by and by to share the honours and responsibilities.

If it rains on election day, messengers are sent to say it will be deferred. If a storm comes suddenly, they finish only the important business, though they often stand hours in a pelting rain, to settle all questions; so jealous are they of sovereign rights!

Usually there is remarkable order; but sometimes storms of words arise, more frightful than the clouds furnish, which the subjects of despotism think an indication of the evil tendencies of liberty, but at which an American would only be amused. When people are permitted "to speak their minds," there is no smothering of wrath, and those who are defeated always have the hope and consolation of being the victors next time.

A pastor in 1765 preached a sermon, censuring severely various customs and practices, which he thought unworthy of such a people. It was received very kindly, but a clergyman in Zurich, to whom it was lent, caused it to be printed, and this excited the indignation of the whole land. The good pastor was called the betrayer of his country, and summoned before the council to answer for his sins. As he appeared, he was met with execrations; but when he arose to make his defence, his voice was so gentle, and his words so earnest and kind, that they were softened, and before he finished, they cried out, that he was right, and just, and good.

A Landamman in 1775 was denounced as false to his country, because he had defended his brother, whom he believed to have been wrongfully accused. But when he appeared before them, and in all honour stated the whole case and showed that he would have been verily guilty, if fear of the people had led him to punish an innocent man, because he was his relative, they exonerated him, and collected a sum of money for the slandered brother.

These incidents show that an excited popular assembly may be controlled by reason and truth, calmly and seriously presented.

One of the old statutes ordained that a man who married two wives should be bound hand and foot, and thrown into the river, to "drown his false heart."

If fruit-trees were planted so that the branches hung over another man's field, he could have all the apples he could reach with his hands and with hooks.

Children under sixteen cannot marry without the consent of parents, but after that age may do as they please. Children who are forced to marry against their will, can be released by law.

Betrothed persons must marry within three months. A woman who runs away from her husband, and returns without being invited, is assailed by all the boys, who assemble before the house, and serenade her with cat noises, calling her out, and obliging her to depart, escorted by their music.

A man who is guilty of adultery is branded by public opinion as a forger or bigamist is elsewhere, and not eligible to any public office during the whole of his life, which under such a Government is the greatest punishment which can be inflicted. The man who breaks his promise of betrothal, or in any way betrays a woman to mortification and shame, is heaped with the same scorn as women receive elsewhere. The woman who is betrayed is also censured, but the man is henceforth an outcast. How curious to find in this one little corner of the earth the law and custom of the whole civilized world reversed! The consequence is, that the falsehood and crime so common elsewhere are here unknown. If a girl allows herself to be ruined by a stranger in the canton over whom their laws and customs have no power, she is placed in the pillory an hour, with a straw wreath on her head, and then banished for three years. The illegitimate children are not so many as one in a hundred of the births; and these occur not among their own people.

In some places the superstitions are still many. The crow and the woodpecker are evil omens; and witches have lost none of their power. *Thor* and *Woden* were evidently the gods of those who once inhabited the land; and remnants of the ancient mythology are still to be traced in the credulity of the ignorant. To sit upon a house where one is sick will bring death. Whoever meets a white chamois will die. The blossoming of the nightshade, the striking of the clock when the bells ring, are tokens of evil; but if one has money in his pocket when he first hears the cuckoo sing in the spring, he will have money all the year.

Hunting and fishing are free, except for the chamois, and with some restrictions for seasons when game is not good.

The dissecting knife of Professor Agassiz has been among the tenants of the Linth, and he has found more than forty different species of fish in its waters. The stories of chamois hunters are marvellous as fairy tales. In German *Jagdgeschichte* has about the same signification as *sailors yarn* in English, and when the hunter relates what they cannot believe, they say he tells *Jagdgeschichten, he spins long yarns.* Many of them remind one of "leather stocking" and the trappers of Kentucky in the olden time in America. Hunting is to them a passion, and its hardships only incitements; but they often faint and die among the glaciers, or fall and break their limbs, and thus perish before help can reach them. They relate the fate of one who used to go every Monday morning, with only bread and cheese in his pocket, and return on Saturday night to attend church and spend Sunday with his family. At length the accustomed hour did not bring him; and the next day those who went to search found him sitting with his head upon his hand, and elbow upon one knee, the other having been broken so that he could not move. He had been frozen to death. He had acquired a little fortune of three thousand dollars from his perilous profession. Another killed one beast every day for four successive days, and brought them home; but the fifth he came not; and they found him alive, but so deep in a snowy ravine, that it was impossible to save him. They could only stretch out their hands in pity; they could not reach him. He had killed three hundred chamois.

The paths among the glaciers of Graubünden were a long

time known only to the chamois hunter; and those of Chamouni were not discovered by tourists till 1794. The unknown regions were called "valleys accursed," and supposed to be inhabited by savages. Messrs. Windham and Pococke, who went from Geneva, determined to explore them, were considered as committing a sin and condemned. They returned in safety to say the inhabitants were good Christians, though unknown to the Pope, and good Savoyards, though unknown to the King of Sardinia. Their taxes soon became heavier than their glaciers, and their poverty is greater than among any of the Swiss Alps.

Around *Bernina*, in Graubünden, there are more glaciers than around *Mont Blanc*, and they are not less grand, but it has not yet become the *fashion* to climb them. The hunter has them still all to himself. In 1837 one died, who numbered two thousand seven hundred chamois as the victims of his rifle. His son used to kill from forty to fifty a day, but in 1854 the number amounted to only eleven, as the gentle creatures have learned that the chase is forbidden in the Valtline, and flee there for refuge. Now and then a tame one may be seen, who has been brought up with the goats, but they do not learn of him grace, and he never quite conforms to goatish habits. The hunter says they are not shy in their youth, neither are they so skilful and expert in bounding over the glens. The young ones are taught as a child is taught to walk, the mother going back and forward, performing a succession of leaps, and then looking anxiously on while they are imitated, by first a little jump, and then a longer one, till they fear no height, and pause at no depth. Whether this is true, or a *Jagdgeschichte*, we do not know, but there is not a prettier sight than a troop of the beautiful creatures put to flight by a hunter's gun, and bounding, with the swiftness of birds, over mountain and valley and stream.

But the brave men of Glarus are not all hunters. Gallati, who was sixty-nine years field-marshal of France, was a native of this canton, a shepherd boy on the Alps ; and they have given to the armies of Italy and France many of their most distinguished generals.

A nobler man still was *Escher von der Linth*, who was instrumental in turning the course of the river Linth, so as to convert two thousand acres of marsh into fruitful fields, and thus give a pure air to hundreds who had before breathed only pestilence.

The Lake of Zurich and the Wallen sea are thus connected by a navigable canal, and a profitable commerce opened to the people.

The proposal of Escher was adopted in 1807, and in ten years the work was finished by means of a subscription throughout the country, obtained by the eloquence of one man. The title of *von der Linth* was conferred upon him by the Federal Council as a reward for his labours. But by the sentimentalists of despotism this would be considered evidence of a practical and mercenary mind, and the projector far inferior to him who has successfully slaughtered a few thousand innocent men on the field of battle.

They have also furnished many eminent historians and jurists, as well as useful men in all the various callings of life. It was a man of Glarus who first introduced potatoes into Switzerland, which is a deed to which attaches no *éclat*, but, perhaps, no other has proved a greater good to the people.

All summer there is a throng of mountain climbers, and every morning parties set out on expeditions to the surrounding heights behind which the sun sinks so early, that the long summer days are short, affording in winter scarcely six hours of daylight. We were more interested in the expeditions of a little boy, who used to go every morning with his little herd of goats, and return in the evening with his charge. He did not look more than six years old, and was often scarcely awake when he set out, with a little whip in his hand, and two or three animals, who followed him slowly, being joined by others here and there as they passed the houses of the owners, till the full number was complete. We always pitied him in the morning, he looked so sleepy, and was so small to go far away alone among the hills, but in the evening he came merrily home, and a very opposite sentiment was inspired as the children ran out to welcome him, putting their arms around the goats, patting and kissing them, while the little herdsman laughed and snapped his whip full of glee.

Thus all our journeyings were strewn with pleasant incidents that will be furnished in the future "sunny memories" in "foreign lands."

CHAPTER XIX.

THURGOVIE.

TALK IN A DILIGENCE—COACHMAN'S LIVERY—THURGOVIAN VILLAGE—POST OFFICE—NAPOLEON IN THURGOVIE—CUSTOM-HOUSE—SCHOOLS—WEDDINGS.

THE first acquaintance we made with *Thurgovie* was, when occupying the traveller's seat in a post-chaise, with a very young and very good-natured looking little coachman, seated within speaking distance in front.

We do not wait long for an occasion of addressing him ; for this is our principle in Switzerland as in Germany, to learn all we can about the people from the people themselves, not understanding how there can be a better authority for any custom, than those who practise it !

But in this case, as in a multitude of others, we learn that it is not a Swiss, but a German, with whom we are thrown in contact.

" What part of Germany are you from ?"

" Würtemberg."

" What did you come to Switzerland for ?"

" Ach, man kann hier besser machen !"* (Oh, one can do better here !)

* A German suggests that this is not good German, but it is an expression often heard in Switzerland.

"Why?"

"We get more wages."

"Oh, you do ; and how much do you get a week or year in your office of coachman?"

"Five francs a week and found."

"What did you do in Germany?"

"I was coachman there too."

"How much did you have a week?"

"Sixty sous."

"O yes, I see, it is a little better ; and is this all the reason why you prefer Switzerland?"

"Oh, nein—die Freiheit."

"You think it is freer here than in Germany?"

Upon which he laughed, as if we must be very stupid to ask such a question ; but immediately said, "Are you from Germany?"

"No ; but we have lived there some time ; and we also like the Freiheit here better than the absence of it there."

In the course of conversation we learned that he was not yet twenty-one, and had only been in Switzerland a year—that he was to receive from the Federal Government a whole new suit of clothes the first day of every May. When we asked him how much the clothes cost, he did not know, because it had never occurred to him to ask. He went to the tailor and was measured, and when they were finished he received them. He went to the hatter and the bootmaker in the same way. The clothes were of Prussian blue ; and before we had journeyed many miles, as we passed a house a similar suit was brought to him to carry to the coachman on the next road. These being on the seat, we examined them more closely, and saw that the buttons had for ornament the great cord and tassels with the trumpet attached, which our driver wore over his shoulder. So we ask, "Are the buttons of all the coachman's coats in Switzerland like these?"

"Yes, they are all alike; it is our uniform; so we always know one another."

The collar and seams were of bright red, with some white stripes for beauty. As we turned it over, he said, "Schön, nicht wahr?" (They are beautiful, are they not?) And a look of conscious pride spread over his face as he glanced at his own federal livery.

We afterwards had occasion to notice many, and saw the never-failing cord and tassels on all the buttons, and also the invariable pattern of roses and butterflies, on all the cushions and coach linings in the twenty-two cantons.

The trumpet was of course to blow, when he came to a post-office or other place where it was his duty to stop; but instead of this he snapped his whip and waited long, sometimes in vain, going on without seeing the people.

"Why do you not blow the horn?" we ask. His face turned a deeper scarlet than his coat collar, while he laughed but spoke not.

"Why do you not blow the horn?" we repeat, seeing that he is determined not to do it, whether anybody hears or not.

"Oh, niemand thut es," nobody does it.

"But in Germany they blow the horn continually; why do you not like to blow the horn? We think it is beautiful."

"Yes, in Germany, but in Switzerland nobody does; and they would all laugh at me."

So, as the Germans say, we learned the secret; still we could not be quite certain why nobody liked to blow horns in Switzerland; and the little man was evidently not a philosopher. He did not ask the price of his coat, being quite content to get it; he carried the horn, because the rest did; and he did not blow it, because the others did not.

It was the same with what he ate and drank; he never asked how much was paid for his board. All his wants were supplied; his duty was to take all the travellers who went that way to a certain village, which required only three or four hours. The next day he returned; and when not on the road, he cared for the horses. Surely no philosopher could be more content.

But either because we are neither coachman nor philosopher, or for some other reason, we are not so content, and begin to wonder what should create this insignificant point of difference between those of the same class in these two countries, lying side by side. But the difference is not in those of this class alone, in matters of equal importance. Whoever is *angestellt* in Germany, must blow his trumpet, whether it is tied with cord and tassels over his shoulder, or appears in a string of long titles to his name; some grand parade must be made to let all the people know that they are Government *employés*. In Switzerland, those who are Government *employés* are usually something else, for all the Government furnishes them would not supply their daily bread. The magistrates, professors, and literary men often have a trade or some business by which they live; literature and the duties of office being only pastime. A Frenchman in writing on Zurich says: "An artisan knows more of literature than the *beaux esprits* of Paris. A man is not merely a geometrician or a naturalist, but a useful man in some sphere of active life. Lavater was *curé* to the orphan-house, and is remembered only for the good he did. Their books are everywhere, and their names have filled the world."

But whilst we are philosophizing, the post-chaise has set us down at a nice-looking inn, where we are to observe a little while, and leave moralizing for another day.

Fortunately for our purpose, we are again by the village brunnen, which, however, has not the usual hero or saint placed to protect it, and probably is not thought worthy this honour, as the reservoir is only a large trough, into which the water is conducted by the simplest of *wooden spouts*. But the *frauen* are there all the same, with great tubs and baskets of clothes, and nod to us so familiarly that we look again to see if it is any one we have known before. This we noticed, too, in passing in the coach; the women looked up and greeted us in so friendly a manner that we could not at first believe they regarded us as quite a stranger. But we afterwards learned it is their custom, and a very pleasant one it seems. How many such pleasant customs there are among unsophisticated people. What a contrast to the cold, inhospitable "Who are you?" manner of the high-bred and world-wise!

Passing by the village post-office, we look in at the windows, and see that the duties are performed by an old lady and a very pretty young one; and as here the post wagons from three different ways meet, there is quite a bustle, as the great and little bags, containing great and little letters, are untied, and their contents poured forth. We walk in, and ask for a letter, though we know that by no possibility can one reach us here, where no person in the world has been informed that we shall ever come. But being once within, on any proper pretext, we sit down and observe the operations. The room is small, and a gate separates the *postmistress* from those who come in, but does not at all conceal the bags or their contents; and soon comes a village maiden, blushing like a tulip or peony, to ask if there is no letter for her. How sad she looks as they tell her "No," in a chilling

13*

business tone, and she turns slowly away. Then comes an old man, whose son is in a strange land ; a little boy, whose sister is on a journey; a mother, who has not heard from her daughter for very, very long. Alas ! how many family and heart-histories are revealed in this one hour : and our thoughts are ever recurring to that one village scene with an interest we have seldom felt in strangers.

How very respectable looks that portly middle-aged man, with his straw hat bound with black, and large white-headed brown and yellow cane, walking with his *frau*, who has the same *first people of the village look*, on their way to make a neighbourly call, or take a social cup of tea.

We like the looks of things in Thurgovie very well. The canton makes almost an equilateral triangle between St. Gall and Zurich, and has Lake Constance for her northern boundary. Her name she derives from the principal river flowing through the land ; but we cannot learn the signification of the lions in full length on her escutcheon, upon fields of green and white, climbing up an inclined plane. The mantles of the Landweibel are also green and white ; and her Government is now entirely democratic. But this was not brought about till a few years since ; and Thurgovie was a subject province of the seven original cantons after the Austrians were expelled in 1499 till after the revolution of 1798. She has experienced only a short period anything like liberty, yet her territory is called the garden and granary of Helvetia.

The original Helvetian League was dissolved by the Romans, who occupied the country till they were driven out by the Germans. They were conquered by Clovis ; and the Francs became masters, and introduced missionaries, one bishop having a seat at Constance and another at Arbun. Then came the

Suabian Counts, who by various rights and with various degrees of power, ruled till 1264, when the whole fell by inheritance to the House of Hapsburg. The castles of Thurgovie were like a network, completely linking and overlooking the land; the ruins of seventy-two are still visible, and there are only forty three square leagues of territory. The monasteries, churches, and chapels, were almost as many; and the tyranny of their lords and bishops was like a millstone on the necks of the people.

It is another curious subject for moralizing, to see the ruins of the castle of a Hapsburg Prince not very far from the new Imperial palace of the French Emperor. In the castle of Gottlieben, on Lake Constance, John Huss and Jerome of Prague were imprisoned, and two miles from this is Arenenberg, where Hortense Beauharnais took refuge, when *ex-Queen* of Holland. Her son, Louis Napoleon, repaired thither on his return from America, when he was made citizen by the Government of Thurgovie and captain of a company of artillery. He practised under General Dufour, the commander-in-chief of the Swiss republican army, when the soldiers met for a grand review at Thun, and took great pride in his Thurgovian regiment.

When he received his patent of citizenship, he wrote in acknowledgment, " With great pleasure I have received the offer which you have made me of citizenship of Thurgovie. I am happy to be linked by new bonds to the land which has so long extended to me its hospitality. I am an exile. Believe me, that under all relations, as Frenchman and Bonaparte, I shall be proud to call myself citizen of Thurgovie, and my mother joins me in the expression of this feeling."

The command of the artillery company was given by the Federal Council. This he acknowledged too, in the following manner :

"Mr. President,

"I have received the patent by which I am made captain of artillery by the little council of Berne. I hasten to express my thanks, that you have thus fulfilled my most ardent wish. My fatherland, or rather the French Government, has banished me, because I am the nephew of a great man. You treat me more justly. *I am proud to be numbered among the defenders of a state in which the people are recognized as sovereign, and where each citizen is ready to sacrifice himself for the good of the fatherland.*

"Accept, Mr. President, the assurance of my highest respect," etc., etc.

Is it possible he can ever forget this hospitality; or that, when they were afterwards asked to give him up, twenty thousand Swiss soldiers were armed almost in a day to defend his rights, not as Louis Napoleon, but as citizen of Thurgovie? *

One would think, he would be ready to say, "If I forget thee, O Jerusalem, let my right hand forget its cunning. If I do not

---

* As a matter of curiosity we add the letter he addressed to the President of the United States when he left America:

"Mr. President,

"I will not leave the United States without expressing to your Excellency how sincerely I regret being obliged to leave your country before fulfilling my intention of going to Washington to become personally acquainted with you. A cruel destiny has thrown me upon your shores; but I hoped to improve the opportunity this banishment would give me of seeing the great men for whom your land is renowned. I wished to learn the customs and understand the Government of a country which has made more lasting conquests by its industry and commerce than we in Europe by our arms.

"I hoped to travel under the protection of your excellent laws, and to study the genius of a people which has excited my whole sympathy. But an imperative duty calls me back to the Old World.

"My mother is dangerously ill; and as no political consideration can detain me under such circumstances, I shall immediately return to England, and attempt to go from there to Switzerland," etc., etc.

remember thee, let my tongue cleave to the roof of my mouth." Where would he have been now, had there been no land of refuge—no England, no America? Woe to him when he forgets the hand that protected him in the day of his affliction. The son of Hortense Beauharnais and grandson of Josephine, should be more than prince or emperor—a noble man!

The schools he founded in Thurgovie are still flourishing, and still receive the aid he promised, and many children are taught to call him blessed. But while performing the duties of humble citizen and seemingly content, he was probably spinning the purple threads of his imperial robe. When it was finished, and he became fairly invested with it, he sold the noble castle, with all the relics and souvenirs which had accumulated during the misfortunes of his family, to a Neufchatelois for the sum of one hundred and eighty-five thousand dollars. Twelve years later the Empress Eugénie repurchased it for a gift to her husband, and has fitted it up anew, in the most *recherché* style of construction and ornament. Almost within sight are the ruins of four other castles, one of them having been built by Eugène Beauharnais, when *Viceroy of Italy*. Kings and emperors surely are the sport of the fickle goddess. How marvellous that they should so devotedly worship at her shrine!

In the early historical battles, Morgarten, Sempach, and Näfles, the nobles of Thurgovie were in the Austrian army, and many of them were among the slain. Afterwards they were entirely subdued, and their castles demolished by the people of Appenzell; and though the Emperor regained a measure of his power and some of his rights in the Landgravate, the nobility never again recovered from the blow.

But the poor people were no more fortunate under the bailiffs which the cantons set over them. These officials often paid four thousand dollars for the office, which was to last only two years, and repaid themselves by exactions from their subjects. This is the dark spot of Swiss history. Having fought so bravely for their own independence, and especially to secure this very right of choosing their own rulers, they governed with scarcely less tyranny and injustice their conquered provinces, instead of receiving them as brothers and allies.

The Reformation again made foes of friends ; and during all the Thirty Years' War the influence of the nobles was with the imperialists, and the people had to guard against traitors within and enemies without ; yet they succeeded in securing a little more of political freedom, and establishing the reformed religion. But still they were the subjects of the Confederacy till 1798, when a popular assembly demanded admission on an equality ; and the fear of the French, and the necessity of unity, made it impossible to refuse. Then followed stormy debates about their own constitution, which was not framed upon the basis which can alone secure peace and contentment till 1831.

During all those changes, Constance remained a city apart ; but this we quite forgot one dark, rainy night, when the diligence rolled us over its rickety pavements, and set us down at the custom-house door. Half a sleep and half frozen, we entered the lighted apartment, not at all understanding why, or what was to be done, when we heard the man of office order our boxes and bundles to be opened, that he might inspect them. We were so fortunate as not to betray our ignorance, and made no remonstrance, but kept wondering to ourselves why we were obliged to submit to this departure from Swiss laws and politeness in this one city. The man who filled the honourable office of examining ladies' toilet boxes exhibited a peculiar exultation as the knots of the cords were being loosened, evidently feeling quite sure of booty because of the care with which they had been secured. We had come to our senses, and began to enjoy his impatience, and to triumph in anticipation over his disappointment. They succeeded at length, and without allowing us to perform the office ourselves of exhibiting our wardrobe, this honourable dignitary thrust his rude hands into the depths of woollens, silks, and cottons, without ceremony, and found of course—nothing—nothing that belonged to him.

He looked sufficiently ashamed when he had finished to excite our compassion rather than our contempt; and we doubt not, the next lady traveller would benefit by our experience.

A few days afterwards we were at Rorschach, quite as ignorant or forgetful that it was a border town, and the same boxes, secured with the same care, were set down by the porter upon the very scales of the custom-house. But the official, with a peculiar scrutiny which such officers only have, looked in our eyes, and said, not only politely, but graciously, "You have nothing in this but your wardrobe?" "Nothing, mein Herr:" upon which he lifted it to test its weight, and ordered it to be passed on, bowing to us to do the same.

When people remain a long time, or take up their residence in any town in Switzerland, they are obliged, we believe, to deliver their passports, and obtain permission to dwell in their midst. But we can say for ourselves, that during a residence of many months in the country, staying days in one place, and weeks in another, we never saw a policeman that we knew to be such; and when we asked a gentleman, one day, who had lived in the capital a year or two, if a certain man in cap and cloak was a member of the police, he said he did not know, he had never seen a policeman that he knew of, and could not tell whether there were any in the city ; which was perhaps quite as creditable to him as to the government and people.

From no government official, high or low, did we experience anything but the utmost kindness and politeness, with one exception, which was on the railroad, leaving this same town of Rorschach. The conductor being a very good-looking man, was so absorbed in talking with pretty maidens, that, when we asked if this was the carriage we should take, he did not pay sufficient attention to answer rightly, and not till we had gone some miles in the wrong direction did we learn the mistake. He was so rude and boisterous, evidently because he was disturbed in his favourite amusement, that we were nearly thrown from the carriage into a little village of which we knew not the name, nor how we were ever to get out of it. But we had a pleasanter experience in the kindness of the station-master, who provided for our return to the starting-point gratis, with some one who should testify to the treatment we had received, and with the injunction that our original ticket was to cover all expenses.

Constance does not belong to Switzerland, and therefore, comes not within our sphere of criticism or description. But only a mile from there is *Kreuzlingen* on Swiss soil, where travellers who know enough, or who are thoughtful enough, often go to avoid the custom-house, and come into the city *sans* baggage, to review it at their leisure.

We were interested in Kreuzlingen for another reason. Here exists one of the best agricultural schools and teachers' seminaries in Switzerland, or on the Continent. The free Government was no sooner established than schools became their first care. Primary schools were immediately instituted, which children are obliged to attend from the age of five till twelve, and higher schools, in which they must continue till fifteen, at least one month of every year. Besides these, the Government has created secondary schools throughout the canton, so situated that no child has more than four miles to go in order to attend one.

The school buildings at Kreuzlingen were formerly an old Augustine convent, dating to the tenth century, and rebuilt, after its destruction in the Thirty Years' War. The site commands a beautiful view of the lake, stretching seventy miles east and west. To the left rise the towers of the time-honoured, and martyr-famed city ; to the right the snow-clad peaks of Appenzell, and in front, the forest-crowned hills of Wurtemberg.

Mr. Vehrle, who is at the head of the institution, was a pupil of Pestalozzi, and his son distinguished himself as scholar and teacher in the school of Fellenberg, at Hofwyl, near Berne. He is now an old man, but with a bright, intelligent face, and a heart and soul that the monotonous routine of pedagogueism has not at all chilled. All who come are welcome, and he receives them without apology in his home-spun coat, cowhide shoes, and weather-beaten hat, and if they will stay to dinner, the plain, every-day fare is set before them with equal cordiality.

The faces of the students are brown with toiling in the sun, but their manners frank and easy. The principle, Mr. Vehrle said, upon which they teach, is, that the peasants should learn to be highminded and refined, and yet remain simple. They are taught to follow this one good example of the Romish priesthood, to mingle freely with the people, and all that they acquire or possess of superiority to diffuse by familiar conversation and intercourse. Every young man, he said, rich or poor, *should some time labour upon the soil.*

The students take care of their rooms, and besides the work

of the field, assist in various occupations of the house; for though the school is supported by the Government, they are expected to make the expense as little as possible.

The course of instruction includes religion, German and French, geography, history, arithmetic, geometry, natural history, natural philosophy, writing, drawing, vocal music, gymnastics, architecture.

In all the normal colleges it is the same, or more extensive, and in almost every canton now there is one, and in some two, and in others three. In all Switzerland nineteen-twentieths of the children are in school, and obliged to stay there, in some till they are fourteen, and in others till they are seventeen years of age.

In every canton there is a *board of inspectors*, and minister of public instruction, and a parish board of inspectors from among the people. No young man can teach without a diploma and certificate of character from the normal college where he was educated.

But we often heard the parents complain, that the teachers were not of the high order they should be, which is one of the surest signs of progress. Where there are Catholics and Protestants, the directors are chosen in equal numbers from each; and in the normal schools no one is required to remain in the room to listen to religious instruction from those of a different denomination than his own.

In Thurgovie there are ten thousand Protestants, twenty thousand Catholics, and three Jews! They now live in the utmost harmony, worshipping in the same churches, and enjoying all privileges in common; and they agree also in allowing no Jew to live on any terms in their midst, if they can help it.

If one may credit the sermons preached in the olden time,

bad as the people are now, they are still much better than they were. In 1517, fifteen murders from drunkenness in one year are mentioned; and every species of crime is laid to their charge, by those whose duty it was to minister to them "doctrine, reproof, and correction."

We find in the chronicles of this and some other cantons the custom of allowing a murderer to do penance for his crime, and live. In 1524, it was ordained, that one who had sinned in this way should enter the church on a specified day, with eighty others, and perform penance; he should cause two masses to be said, and attend each with twelve men, paying at both twenty-five cents and a candle. He should cause a certain amount of bread to be baked for the poor, cause a light to be burnt, and prayers to be said in the church for the murdered one, a whole year; erect a stone cross, five feet high, where the relatives should direct; step aside if likely to meet any one who was a blood relation of the deceased; visit no inn, or play, or dance, where he could come in contact with them, and must pay them forty-four dollars.

There are still many of the old customs remaining, of which one of the most peculiar is the wedding, which has some of the features of those in the northern part of Germany. An orator is the bearer of invitations, who is often the village schoolmaster. He makes a formal speech before every house, which all the people run to hear. On the morning of the wedding, he accompanies the bridegroom and the groomsmen to the house of the bride, where they breakfast together; after which he makes a speech to the father and mother, recounting to them all the noble qualities of the bridegroom, and beseeching them to give their daughter willingly away, as he is sure a long life of happiness is in store for her.

A rival orator then "*takes the word*" and presents the dark side of the picture, all the difficulties of the new position, and the virtues of the bride. After this parliamentary discussion the bride departs with her betrothed for church, amidst prayers and tears and good wishes; and to keep up her spirits, musicians cheer her way with song.

After the ceremony they have a dinner, at which the bride can only eat what the groomsman places stealthily upon her plate, and must be careful that he does not in the mean time as stealthily remove her shoe, else she and her husband would be laughing-stocks. During the meal, the guests send her little presents to make sport. After it is finished, the orator makes another speech to the newly married pair, giving them advice, hoping they will receive rich gifts and be happy.

Formerly, the weddings took place on Wednesday, because the days of the week in German all end with *day* except this, which is in their language *Mittwoch*, and therefore no day at all. Now among the Catholics they are solemnized on Monday, and by the Protestants on Tuesday or Thursday.

At funerals the mourners cover themselves with long black mantles; and sometimes the schoolmaster makes a speech before the house. Black is worn a year by the relatives.

The kindling of fires on the hills at carnival was continued till the insurance companies petitioned for a law to forbid it.

The last Sunday of Lent is observed among Protestants as a *fête* day, and the first Sunday among Catholics. At the end of harvest, and when the rye is threshed, the land proprietors give a feast and rural ball, which they call the *Sichellegi* and *Pflegelhenki*—the laying down of the scythe and the suspension of the flail.

In one district is what they term a *fool's feast*. On Ash

Wednesday they repair to a castle on a neighbouring hill, and form a procession to ride through the village on horseback. They form a mock parliament, with a king at the head; and on arriving at the place of distinction, where a throng awaits them, the speaker of the day recounts the follies which have been committed in all the country round, satirizing individuals and communities. The bailiff was accustomed to send for the dinner two casks of wine, by which he escaped being numbered among the fools; and others who would procure the same favour must purchase it, sending wine or some other substantial gift.

The Christmas-tree and the Maypole are still to be seen at their respective seasons; and school children have their days of festivity.

In Thurgovie we find the spinning room as in Germany, flax being among their agricultural products : and the long webs of linen cover the grass-plots, which the women are seen sprinkling with their pretty green watering pots. Often at her marriage a maiden receives a great distaff of flax, which she is enjoined to spin off as industriously as possible. When she comes to the last layer, out fall ribbons, laces, and money, a trousseau which only her diligence can reveal.

Sometimes the dowry is an orchard of apple and pear trees, these being the wealth of Thurgovie.

Very fine laces are also woven by the Thurgovian damsels, but not in great quantities.

Of the old dress there is nothing peculiar remaining, except, with some, a sort of hat or cap made of calico, and shaped like a great plate, looking a little way off like a tray.

The houses present the same mixture of old and new as elsewhere; and in some villages they are covered with hideous paintings, the figures large as life, representing some scene in history or the Bible. But where new ones are built, they are pretty and commodious.

In no other canton is so much done for fruit, and so much pains taken in grafting. They are mostly an agricultural people, but with all the efforts of their excellent school to remove them, they still cling to the old ways from prejudice. We noticed in a journal that a course of lectures was to be given on roads, ditches, and draining ; and the number of hailstorms this season had suggested the propriety of having *hailstorm insurance companies* added to their many others.

On the borders of Zurich are many ribbon looms, and in Arbun, on the lake, they weave them of half cotton, and some that have not a particle of silk in their composition.

Only a few devote all their time to any species of manufacture, but spin and weave in the winter and rainy days, when they would do nothing else.

Their list of *savants* is very long, numbering some forty or fifty in all the different departments of science and *belles lettres*. In the days of old, many of their knights were *troubadours*. In 1192, a poem was written by *Ulric de Zazikafen*, called *Lancelot du Lac*, which is still read as one of the most remarkable in German literature. One of their *bishops* made a collection of the songs of the troubadours, and wrote many himself, but whether he tried their influence beneath the lattice of some fair damsel is not stated. He probably wrote them for others to sing.

On reading their history, it seems as if about as many authors, professors, painters, and engravers, as soldiers, have served foreign princes, and it is certainly very remarkable how many they have produced, for so small a country, and one which has the reproach of being only practical and mercenary. Few who admire the master-works in sculpture with which the gardens of Versailles and the Tuileries are filled, know how great a proportion were the work of a Swiss artist, Balthasar Keller. Will any one say, that only a land over which waves a sceptre can produce genius? In the words of another, we ask, "Has Vienna, the proud capital, absorbed in a life all material, and ministering, as it does, entirely to the senses, sent forth a tithe, a hundredth part of the great men of Zurich?" In Austria a man of genius is almost on a level with a *valet de chambre*, for there, as elsewhere, despotism only debases character and paralyzes intelligence.

CHAPTER XX.

GRAUBUNDEN.

SPLUGEN—VIA MALA—GREY LEAGUE—VALE OF DISENTIS—ITALIAN SHEP-
HERD—CASTASAGNA CHESTNUTS—ALPINE FETE—KILTGANG—ENGADINE—
DANCES.

WHEN we looked on the map to trace a route through Switzerland, and glanced upon the portion devoted to *Graubünden*, we thought, " Is it possible there can be a road, a valley, or even a footpath among those mountains, where the surface is black as if it were one vast forest ?" On looking in the guide-book we read, " No one should say he has seen Switzerland until he has crossed the Splügen."

" O'er the Simplon, o'er the Splügen
Winds a path of pleasure,"

says the poet ; and wishing to say ourselves that we have seen at least the most important parts of each canton, we look out from the back window of our room in Chur one morning, and see a coach with *Splügen* in great letters on its side, with the horses just harnessing that are to trot in that direction, and resolve to take a seat by the three respectable-looking passengers, who have already "booked themselves" in accordance with a similar decision. We send the servant to ask if there is time, and she returns to say, "In three minutes they start." But they wait three more for a passenger, and we are at the end of that time on the way. We had not then seen the Simplon or the St. Gothard, and whether it was that first impressions are the most powerful, or that the Splügen is really the most wonderful, we cannot tell, but the impression still remains, that there can be nothing more grand or sublime in nature, and nothing more marvellous in art, than is here exhibited in the course of a day's journey.

Only the *Gondo*, in the descent of the Simplon, and the *Pfaeffers*, make any rival pretensions with the *Via Mala*, but this is wilder than the former and grander than the latter, and dark and terrible beyond anything Switzerland elsewhere presents. The Rhine is rushing in invisible depths below, and the sun is shut out by the almost invisible peaks above, while we are suspended between, surrounded by the darkness of night at mid-day, winding round and round, our road disappearing the moment we have passed it, and the one before us concealed by great jutting cliffs, which we must penetrate in order to come again to the light of day. We are of opinion, indeed, that no one should say he has seen Switzerland, or a mountain gorge, till he has crossed the Splügen.

The three great roads which owe their construction to the triumphs of modern science and art, seem equally wonderful. They are built upon the same principles, and struggle with the same general difficulties, which all are equally successful in conquering. One marvels continually how the country ever became inhabited before these ways of communication were opened ; yet the Romans crossed the same mountains, and led their legions through the same valleys.

The inhabitants who peopled it are of different origin, and fled here from persecution in other lands, hiding amidst the rocks and caves from the sword of tyranny and the might of injustice.

These valleys were so secluded, that often the people of one knew nothing of those in another, perhaps for centuries, but when they were invaded, and a common danger threatened, they began to unite, and form leagues of defence against foreign foes.

Graubünden signifies *Grey League*, a name which was not adopted till the fifteenth century, and before this the country was long known as the *Ten Jurisdictions*, in consequence of another union, which had been formed; but for many centuries it was called *Rhetia*, a name supposed to be given it by the first colonists, who were *Etruscans*, and migrated hither six hundred years before the Christian era, and only a century and a half after the foundation of Rome. According to Pliny, the leader of the colony was *Rhaetus*, who thus gave the name to the whole country.

The Romans ruled it during four centuries, but they did not leave here a great work to testify to the long residence of any considerable number. No castles, aqueducts, or great highways, mark the era of their glory. But in 1786 a peasant found in digging two vases of brass, bracelets of gold and silver, *thimbles* and other utensils, and coins with the *horse of Troy* on one side, and *Venus* on the other. In 1811 were found under a rock fifty pieces of money, bearing the date of the epoch of the Carlovingian kings, and the most ancient of the hundreds of castles scattered over their heights was built in 755.

Traces of the Rhetians are to be found in all the western and northern parts of Switerland; and they formed cohorts under Roman generals, in their Egyptian conquests. The Romans were driven out by the northern barbarians, Germans, Ostrogoths, and Visigoths, till finally their country fell to Theobebert of France and his successors, who ruled it three centuries, and a bishop from among the Francs first introduced the Christian religion, and planted the cross among these wilds.

After the death of Charles the Great, German princes being rulers, the whole country was parcelled among dukes, counts, and bishops, who covered it with castles and cloisters, each assuming the right to govern those whom he found within his real or imaginary jurisdiction, till ambition and encroachments upon the domain of each other involved them in inextricable quarrels, which were ended only by the whole race being driven out, and their strongholds demolished by the people, who became equally weary of their power and their disputes.

In the fourteenth century began the alliances of different sections with other countries for protection. In the first place the bishopric of Disentis united with Canton Uri, in 1319. A few years later Disentis and two other districts formed an alliance with the three forest cantons together. Afterwards they were joined by Glarus, and two other landgravates.

In 1424 was formed the original Grey League; the name, says tradition, being given it from the grey coats or beards of the venerable delegates who formed it. They were representatives of the powerful families of the country—the lords, barons, and abbots—who swore eternal alliance for mutual protection.

Next was formed the league of the *Ten Jurisdictions*; these three being composed of districts entirely distinct from each other. But in 1471 they all united together, having seriously experienced the inconvenience which resulted from so many divisions, and needing the strength which unity and harmony would give. There was now a central lawful authority, and some form of legislation and justice. They adopted the name of *Grey League* for the whole ; and as there was never afterwards any serious division, it is retained to this day ; *Graubünden* being the German word, and the French term, *Les Grisons*, for the modern canton.

Though somewhat tedious, it is still interesting to trace the great events of history to the slight causes which gave rise to them ; and not less so, perhaps, to learn how so insignificant a thing as a name had its origin in some important historical transaction.

Besides the abbot of Disentis, two powerful lords of the country, the Counts Lax and Rhoetzuns, supported the people, finding, perhaps, that it was useless to resist them. Many others preferred to leave the country, and sold to the peasantry all right and title to their domains.

They were no longer subject to an oppressive *noblesse*, but peace and quietness were not yet. The Reformation awoke all the slumbering elements of strife and bitterness ; and bishops and ducal families who had been banished by the people now had an opportunity to be revenged ; and in no other land did the religious war rage with more violence than in this canton. The Pope and "the Great Powers" interfered in all their affairs. Their territory was disputed by Austria, France, Spain, and Italy, their fortunes rising and falling as each was conqueror or the conquered.

Yet in 1574, the day of their weakness, they had sufficient strength to enact that no prelate of either confession should henceforth meddle with their political debates.

The Thirty Years' War gave the ecclesiastics an opportunity

to attempt again to regain their power, and hundreds of innocent victims were massacred in obedience to the commands of rival authorities, and anarchy and confusion filled the land. Princes then, as now, improved every opportunity of aggrandizing themselves ; and those who were not able to defy them entirely, were tossed about between them. But Richelieu and Talleyrand did not exert their diplomacy in vain or for evil in Graubünden. Through their instrumentality a little order was brought out of this confusion ; but not till 1799, when they were united to Helvetia, had they any settled Government ; and not till 1803, when Napoleon harmonized them by his mediatorial powers, did they experience true liberty and confidence in each other. After three hundred and thirty years of unceasing warfare they were at peace, and progressed more in the " ten years of mediation," than they had in the three centuries before !

As compensation, they were obliged to furnish a certain number of soldiers to his 'armées, which then was not considered by them a great tax, had it not been for the conscription. They immediately instituted a postal bureau and communications, a savings-bank, an ecclesiastical synod for the reformed religion,— which the Austrians had entirely suppressed,—provided for schools, and formed agricultural societies.

There was a little disturbance in 1817 ; but since their constitution was elaborated in 1821, their peace has been uninterrupted, and their progress steady, though slow. In 1830, when all Europe was in commotion, not a murmur of discontent was heard in Graubünden, because they had no aristocracy to overturn, and no privileges to ask.

We often heard it remarked of this and other cantons, " They have belonged to Switzerland so many hundred years, and they are no more civilized and have no higher social life than the people in the depotisms around them. Of what use is political liberty, if it does not contribute to the advancement of those who enjoy it, if they must remain just as poor and ignorant as their neighbours in oppression ?"

We are therefore obliged to show *how* they have belonged to Switzerland, and the hindrances they have met in every attempt at progress.

The social life in Graubünden is farther advanced than in Valais. They live generally in better houses, have a better *ménage*, and fewer unseemly habits.

But each valley is distinct from the other, and separated by impenetrable and often unscaleable walls, inhabited by a clan or community as unlike those in the others as if they belonged to a different nation.

There are at least thirty of these valleys, in four of which they speak Italian, and in ten German, and in all the others Romanish (or a mixture of this with others), a language which numbers six dialects, and which no person except a philologist would ever think of learning. Though the Bible and many other books have been translated into Romanish, and there is a printing press and two newspapers in the language, it is fast disappearing, and German being universally substituted.

Of these many valleys and their inhabitants it will be impossible to say much within our space, and of many of them there would not be much to say if we would.

Graubünden is the country of contrasts in climate, soil, and people. Five-twelfths of all the glaciers in Switzerland are within her limits, there being in all six hundred and five, of which two hundred and fifty-five are in this canton. The two great rivers are the Rhine and the Inn, the latter of which receives the waters of seventy glaciers, and flows northeast to join the Danube and to swell the waters of the Black Sea.

The Rhine has two sources, the one being not far from the cradle of the Rhone, and flowing eastward, and the other far away to the south, forming in its northward course the valley of the Splügen, both uniting near Chur, or Coire, the capital of the canton.

At the western extremity of the valley of the Upper Rhine is the old *Abbey of Disentis*, the monks of which were the pioneers of Christianity, and for many centuries *princes of the empire*. Previous to the arrival of *Sigisbert*, in 1614, there was a hermitage here, but he erected it into a monastery, and by the holy fathers the people were not only taught religion, but agriculture. They extended their authority into the Urseren valley, and the first magistrate of that country was consecrated by one of their number, the abbot receiving as a sign of subjection a pair of white gloves, a token of homage which was not dispensed with till 1785.

During the early days of Swiss history they were the allies of the house of Hapsburg, and their banner occupied the van at the battle of Morgarten. But later they sided with the people, and in 1424 were among the framers of the *Grey League*, which was solemnized at Trons, beneath the spreading branches of a maple, the decayed trunk of which still stands, cloven and hollow,* but carefully preserved, and devoutly reverenced as the *Grütli* of Grison liberty. In 1778, they assembled around it to renew the oaths of four centuries before, and in 1824 celebrated with great state the four hundredth anniversary of their first league.

---

* One solitary shoot has lately put forth and bears leaves.

The abbey still exerts great influence in the affairs of the canton, though divested of its former power and magnificence. At its base clusters a little village, which is sufficiently humble to increase the imposing appearance of the monastery. The houses are of wood, two stories; small, with very small panes of glass for windows, and a stove, looking like a house by itself. Behind it is the narrow stairway that leads to the second story, where there is neither sumptuousness nor cleanliness.

The people look as if indifferent to every thought or subject that interests human beings, yet the first sound of the trumpet would see them rush bravely to battle, and the slightest infringement of their political liberties would be resisted unto death. They are their own electors, lords, and legislators; they pay no taxes,* and bow to no superiors.

In the little villages scattered here and there among the valleys, one is Protestant and another Catholic; one speaks German, another Romanish, without any one being able to say why, though we suppose it must be owing to a different origin.

Their riches are reckoned according to the number of cows they are able to winter: he who can keep two is not called a poor man, and he who can keep eight is rich. The pastures are mostly the property of the communes, and rented at so much each, the divisions comprising so large a space as will support one milk cow, or what is equivalent, either four calves or six sheep, or from eight to twelve goats. Often there is deep snow in midsummer, so that the cows must be kept under shelter many successive nights, and always after the middle of August. The barns for the hay are not built in the villages, but at the foot of the mountains, to save the trouble of transporting the hay

---

* There is no direct tax in the canton of Graubünden.

from a great distance. This is usually done on the shoulders of women, which makes them bent, and old, and haggard, when they should still be young.

The stalls for the cows are seldom warm, and straw never abundant for their beds. For each they need from ten to twelve hundredweight of hay, and allow them each day an ounce of salt. A sheep costs only a tenth or twelfth as much, and a goat still less, but they are so injurious to forests where they browse, that in many places the law forbids them to be kept at all, and in others limits the number to five or six for each family in the commune. In the summer a goat will give from two to five pounds of milk daily, but in winter very little. It is a curious sight to see them milked, which is done from between the legs behind, while they are pulling with all their strength to get away, so that often some one must stand in front and hold them by the head during the whole operation.

Among the Alpine pastures of Graubünden are several thousand Italian sheep sent for a summer residence, which pay from forty to sixty sous each a season. Their shepherds are seen lying upon sunny slopes, sleeping or sentimentalising, and when one is roused by a passing traveller, he looks up with the air of a somnambulist awakened on some perilous cliff. If he is asked for bread, he will give the best he has willingly; but this is very likely so hard that it must be long soaked in water to make it possible to break it, and he has no other drinking cup than the old hat he wears upon his head, from which he takes copious draughts himself, and not being able to make *conversazione* in his tongue, sets the wet *chapeau* upon his black locks again, and lies down in the sun. This is the climax of simplicity; we shall have nothing to relate that can excel this picture of shepherd life.

It is idylish too ; but when hunger is ravenous, and miles must be traversed before we can reach a cup of *clean* water, it is something beside !

From Chur to Chiavenna are the valleys of the *Domleschleg*, Via Mala, Schams and Rheinwald. But before we enter the Domleschleg, we pass through a valley without a name, a part of which lies west, and part north of Chur, and contains two cities and eleven villages, among which are scattered fifteen thousand people, being one-sixth of the whole population of the canton. Here are produced the best wines of eastern Switzerland, and fruits which one sees everywhere prepared and drying in the sun. In agriculture there has been very little progress. They still use the implements of the middle ages, and in this one valley, harness the cows by their heads, while in all other parts of Switzerland the yoke is placed upon the animals' necks. Now and then something is done towards irrigation ; and canals have been cut, which are rented for a few sous an hour to any one who will avail themselves of the privilege.

Haying is done first in the villages, and then upon the mountains, when all the inhabitants are seen wending their way up the acclivities with scythes and rakes, men, women, and children, leaving only a few to keep watch below. Every spire of grass is shaven from the knolls, and every herb and green thing gathered for the winter food of the cows, who after all sometimes do not have enough, and when the owners have taken all the pains in their power to preserve them, are yet compelled to see them starve, without the possibility of saving them. Many are sent to the Canton St. Gall *to board*, where they are received into comfortable stables, furnished with enough to eat, and excellent care, for fifty cents a week, which is getting boarded very cheap, we think.

Not far from Mayenfield, on a dizzy height, is the Church of St. Lucius, where they have service every year once, on Ascension day, and a rural *fête*. A little to the right is the village of Guschen, where the people have not changed in any custom for ages. But a few years since, the larger portion of them emigrated to America, and we doubt not founded one of the many Goshens for which America is famous ; and where they will certainly be clean, at least for a little time, for the "old family" dust gets shaken from almost everybody there.

Reichnau stands at the junction of the two branches of the Rhine ; and here we must relate what every traveller has related before us for half a century, that the school, which had not been long founded, was in 1793 one day visited by a lone traveller, who presented a letter to the principal, which procured him a gracious reception, and the appointment of Professor of French and Mathematics. This lone traveller was Louis Philippe, then Duke of Chartres. He remained eight months, under the name of *Chabot*, and in 1854, his Queen, Amelia, visited the castle, and wrote in the album, "*Marie Amélie, wife of Professor Chabot, the most beautiful of titles!*" Whilst here, he heard of his father's death on the scaffold, and the exile of his mother.

One would think France must be ever the true friend of Switzerland, she has been so often the home of her exiles and the asylum of her fugitives !

In the valley of the Domlesch we count twenty-two villages and twenty-one castles in the course of sixteen miles ; and here, more than in any other part of Graubünden, appears the curious alternation and intermixture of languages and religions. At Coire the language is German and the religion Protestant ; at the next village, Romanish ; at the two next, they speak German, but are Catholics; a little farther on, Romanish is the language, and the religion Catholic; then two villages where the religion of both is Catholic, but the language of one German and of the other Romanish; then several where they are Protestant and German; then several where they are Protestant and Romanish.

Our postilion speaks these two and Italian, and uses one or the other without cessation; and in the hotels we hear, in addition, French and English. For a little time we are left alone in the diligence with a young girl who speaks only Italian, and who is very much inclined to talk. Her dress is dreadfully "tattered and torn," and her countenance not less forlorn; and she seems not to have seen in her life a toilette that was better than her own, judging by the admiration she bestowed upon ours, which would have excited only the contempt of most fine ladies, being *très ordinaire*. She asks if we are *Eenglish*; and as fast as she can speak, adds one question or remark after the other: "Have got you any father—any mother—any brothers and sisters—where do you live—where are you going—what a pretty bonnet—what a fine ribbon—what do you call this (taking hold of our cloak)—and this, and this?" And then she pouted her full lips and looked down at her rags. She had on no bonnet or shawl, yet carried a well-filled purse. We asked her also where she was going, and if she had a mother. She answered as rapidly as she had asked questions, and said, "I've got a father and a mother—brothers and sisters—and a *grand*mother. I'm going home—I live in the Bernardin—I hate that postilion." And alluding to a gentleman who had stepped out to walk, she said, in her own language, "*Humpf ein Teufel*," and pouted her lips again. She was not more than sixteen, and was evidently in trouble, to which she was not very resigned.

Seeing a woman spinning on a little wheel before a door, we asked her if she could spin. " Yes, I can spin, and sew and braid straw. Yes, I can ; why not ? can you ?"

At Splügen she takes another road, but first bids us farewell very pleasantly, and says she shall not reach home till the next morning, and does not appear particularly rejoiced at reaching it at all.

She seemed to fully appreciate the scenery of the *Via Mala ;* but when we read over a bridge the inscription, which was placed there just before the great road was opened to travellers, we thought it might have been dispensed with. It says, " The road is to be opened to friends and enemies. Rhetians, be upon your guard ! Simplicity of manners and unity alone will secure your liberties, the inheritance of your fathers." They are altogether too tenacious of what they call " simplicity ;" and think it is preserving the principles of their ancestors to live in all respects as they lived at a time when there was no other way.

In the three remaining valleys of the Rhine there are only six villages, and in them all only fourteen hundred inhabitants, all of whom are descendants of regiments of Germans who were sent there in the middle ages. Those who first came would find very little to surprise them or excite their wonder if they should return.

In the documents of 1277 they are called *the free people*, and were set as the watchmen to guard the mountain passes. They have preserved their language, and changed very little in life or manners.

But we are lingering too long by the way, and must make a leap now and then, or we shall not see half the valleys.

We will take a seat under the chestnuts that form a shady grove near Castasagna. How changed the scene ! It is Sunday afternoon, and all have been to church, but now, in the cool of the day, gather together in nature's temple. Stone tables are placed around, and those who sit by them are furnished with wine, bread, cheese, and sausage ; there is also whey and goat's milk. The grottoes in the side of the hill have been converted into wine cèllars, and are well filled. There are no glasses, but large earthen *krugs*, which are passed from one to the other. The cheese is from the *Ober Engadine*, where they profess to rival the Gruyère.

There is also a *parsonage tun*, that the family of the pastor may enjoy with them the familiar hour. When the meal is finished, groups are formed for conversation ; old men to talk of the *times*, and young men and maidens to plan for the future. There is great freedom, but all is orderly though a very Babel of tongues.

They are famous in Graubünden for travelling into other lands to trade, to practise some mechanical art, or to sell knickknacks ; and when they have made what is considered a fortune in their native village, to return, and build a fine house, and enjoy the old life. So here they are, one who has frozen in Russia, another who has burnt beneath a tropical sun, some who have gathered treasures in Brazil, and another who relates his adventures in Poland. How eagerly the beardless boy listens to the marvellous tales ; and one can read on his face, " Oh, yes, as soon as I have learned the catechism I too will go out in the world." Very few are allowed to go till they have been confirmed.

There is a brown and weather-beaten man, who went away as a boy, and though he has been in many lands he looks at the pretty maiden opposite as if he were thinking, " Nowhere else have I seen any so beautiful." This perhaps is true ; for the maidens of Castasagna are of a peculiar beauty, and though they carry burdens and perform the severest labour, they remain longer youthful than in many other districts, where similar toils so early remove every trace of youth and bloom; they are graceful, and in their fanciful costume a picturesque feature of their land.

It is on the Italian borders and has an Italian clime; the lizards are sunning themselves upon the trees, and the scorpion hides his head in the wall. The luxurious fruits and flowers of the tropics add their golden hues to the scene; yet only a few steps farther, beyond the last chestnut-tree, are eternal snows, and a little farther up the valley is the village of Bondo, into which not a ray of the sun penetrates during three whole winter months.

Castasagna is the last town on the borders between Switzerland and Lombardy; and as its name indicates, it is surrounded by groves of chestnuts. It is in the valley of the Begraglia, which extends a few miles into Austria, or, as it must now be called, Sardinian or Lombardian, territory. Its population is twenty-three thousand, of which three-fifths are women, and they say, of course, many are unmarried, because the men emigrate in such numbers. Another remarkable fact concerning the same valley is, that it is the only one where the language is Italian and the religion Protestant.

The church in Castasagna is the largest in Switzerland, because it was built in 1700 to accommodate those in Lombardy who were not allowed to "worship according to the dictates of their own consciences" on their own soil. The service is very pleasantly commenced by twenty or thirty young girls forming a circle around the baptismal font, with as many young men behind them, to sing either a hymn or some rhyming verses from the

Psalms of David. When they have finished, they take their seats, and the ceremony of baptism is performed. The father comes with a relation who carries the child, attended by five godfathers, the oldest of whom holds the infant, giving the name in writing to the clergyman. The congregation sit till the prayer begins, when all rise and bow their heads. The sermon follows, by a German, who preaches in bad Italian.

In the afternoon the children are catechised by the clergyman, who stands by the font whilst they are seated in front, and answer singly and in concert, after which each one is conversed with in a familiar friendly manner. The exercise closes by singing "Psalms and spiritual songs," not artistically, as they have no teacher, but in a way to cheer the heart.

The houses are of stone, many of them white and pretty. All through the Rhine valley the patches of maize were to be seen, and the farther south we go, the more extensively it is cultivated. *Polenta* is their *daily bread,* and roasted chestnuts, which they eat with butter and salt, or with cheese, or with oil, or without anything, enter into all the compounds of their cookery. If they roast meat, the *filling* is of chestnuts, and if they fry it or boil it, chestnuts are in some way made to serve as a sauce. They know how to cook rice and macaroni, and fully appreciate the virtues of buttermilk, which stands about like water for a common drink. They also have cherry water, and wine that has experienced all the vicissitudes of a century.

Next we will visit the Münsterthal in the southeastern part on the Tyrolese border. Those who only go in thought will have no anxiety about bears and wolves, or frightful precipices, to be encountered by the way ; and those who live here know almost as little, for they are shut in from all the world by glaciers, bold cliffs, and wild forest streams. They say, in order to see their next neighbours in the Engadine, they must go eight hours up, and descend as many, which is not often done.

The name is derived from *Mestair*, a convent for women of the Benedictine order, like so many others, "founded by Charlemagne." The valley was long the bone of contention between Austria and the bishops of Coire, but since the eighteenth century the people have bought themselves free from all pretenders. Except one parish they are Protestants, and their language Romanish.

They are mostly shepherds, too, and like all shepherds, decidedly opposed to innovation. Their ambition is limited to seeing the barn full of hay, the granary full of corn, and the cattle in good condition. Their whole life is still ordered after the most patriarchal fashion, and to help one another is not less the rule than to take care of themselves. If a new barn or granary is to be built, the peasant collects his materials and all the village men come to his aid. Each one knows the use of hammer and axe, and the wood costs very little, being cut in the forests and transported on sleds. The helpers take their breakfast and supper at home, but the dinner is furnished them, and consists of bread, and milk, and cheese. Two days are usually sufficient for the principal construction, or if not, a few come the third, and are invited to stay to supper, which is luxurious for the occasion—soup, meat, rice, and chestnuts.

In the country where they grow, chestnuts are to the people what potatoes are in the more northern climes, and in the autumn, from the middle of October to the end of November, the women and children are employed in gathering them, each family storing often one hundred dollars' worth.

The fattening of snails is also another industry upon the Italian borders for those who have so many fast days and still wish abundance of nourishing food. They are placed in an enclosure upon beds of sawdust, with water not far off, and fed with leaves till their shells are thick, when they are ready for packing. From sixteen to twenty weigh a pound, and each pound is sold for two or three sous, to be retailed in Italy at one sous and a half a snail. The trade in crabs and frogs is not so profitable.

All winter the spinning rooms are in a buzz; and in the spring the scene is the same as in every Alpine land. The pastures belong to the communes, and the rents go into the common purse. In summer the women are almost the only inhabitants of the villages, and their toil within and without is very severe.

But in September, when the herds come back to the valleys, there is great rejoicing. The bailiff of the commune attends to the adjusting of the scales in the Sennhut. On the morning of the day appointed, he mounts to the pastoral counting-room, where all concerned in his operations have assembled by dawn of day; and immediately the storehouse is opened, and the contents, which have been for three months accumulating, are brought out—fat cheeses and meagre cheeses, and cheeses of all sizes and names, with great tubs and balls of butter. Forthwith commences such a weighing and reckoning, after the old style and new, as if all the world were to be portioned. When this is finished, they are heaped upon the wagons and sleds which are to transport them to the regions below. But the train is not set in motion till after dinner, which consists of bread and milk, whey and sausages.

From a flagstaff mounted upon the largest wagon floats a gay banner, not exactly like those woven in the looms of Basle and Zurich, being, not a coat, but a shawl, of "many colours," which some sugar-baker or coffee-buyer has purchased in Italy and brought home to his *frau*. There is no defect in its flutter, and it answers all the purposes for which it is designed, and is called a flag.

Every animate and inanimate thing is wreathed with evergreens and roses, and the long train moves slowly on, " with song and shout, and festive mirth." When it arrives at a designated spot, all is suddenly still—not a whisper is heard. The men bare their heads, and all fold their hands, and from every heart go up the silent thanksgivings to God, who dwelleth in the Alps, and crowns mountain and valley with his blessings. This is the custom handed down from time immemorial—this is the way their fathers did.

Before arriving at the village, two fiddlers place themselves at the head of the train, and thus with their music marshal them into town, where on the market-place they halt, and the wine cans are brought, which soon show their influence in the songs and merriment, which, however, do not last so long that the cheese and butter are not deposited in the several cellars to which they are destined, and, in accordance with the pride of Münsterthaler, before the last year's store is quite exhausted.

At funerals they have no singing, because they say, "songs are for joy." There is usually a feast in the room of the corpse, while a few remain in the meantime apart to weep and wail. The coffin is covered with wreaths, and before it is carried to the grave addresses are made, when theological students make their first attempts at exhortation. After burial there is service in church, to which the wreaths from the coffin are transported.

The *kiltgang* is called in Graubünden *hengertgehen*, and there exists a law prohibiting the custom, yet it remains. But it is no longer respectable for the visits to be made in a dark room ;

the maiden must not only have a light, but an extra candle, with the wick saturated with some ignitible substance, so that it can be easily lighted if an awkward lover snuffs out the other! The curtains must not be drawn, and the door not closed. Often, if they see a room dark where they know there is a wooer, boys enter unceremoniously, and duck him in the fountain.

Pigmies are called in some places *dialas*, in others "wild people," and "mountain-men;" and here, as elsewhere, they are believed to make cheese of chamois milk, which are cut and partly eaten, and grow again. They supply the hungry with food, and restore lost children whom they find in the woods.

But there is also a higher trust than this. An old lady lived by a wild mountain stream, and built a dam for the protection of her cottage and little vegetable patch. But the people laughed, and said, "The first rain will wash it away." The rain came, and many which men had built, and which were large and strong, disappeared in the flood, but the little structure of the widow remained, and she said, "God despises not the prayer of the poor when they call unto Him."

Union dairies are formed to make cheese of goats' milk; for in the Münsterthal they keep great herds, which are driven home every evening, and to the hills every morning. On Johannistag all the young people go with white pails to meet the goatherd as he returns to the village, and skipping from goat to goat, rob them of all the milk, which the maidens sell to buy a dress for the ball. The scolding among the *frauen* is as amusing as the singing among the maidens, when they find how they have been robbed, but there is no help.

Formerly slander was punished by clipping the tongue, and murder and adultery with death; and whoever set a house on fire, or passed counterfeit money, was burnt to ashes.

Proverbs, like "Love and beefsteak," are the same in all languages. "Slow and sure," "Lies have short legs," "Poverty is no shame," "Choose a wife and a cow from the neighbourhood," etc., are in all mouths, whether they speak English, German, or Romanish.

We must skip over the Engadine, scarcely stopping to shake hands by the way. They are a comfortable-looking people, very few of them poor, and not a beggar to be seen. They are all zealous Protestants, ten thousand in number, except two villages ; and preserve still old Bibles and Prayer-books as heirlooms, on the margins of which are recorded the martyrdoms of the period of the Reformation. They have a proverb, that next to God and the sun, the simple citizen of the Engadine is supreme. They live among the mountains, where another proverb, says, they have nine months' winter and three months' cold. Snow often falls in mid-summer, covering the valleys, without being attended by a white frost ; yet it freezes every week of the year. Seven thousand feet above the sea are pretty villages, though usually at this height are only *chalets*. The houses are better than elsewhere, because they must make them very tight and warm. The great doors are something like those in North Germany, broad enough for a carriage to enter and pass through to the stable beyond. On the side of this hall are the dwelling-rooms, often very neatly finished with a peculiar wood, having some resemblance to curly maple, being full of little knots. They saturate it with a preparation of rosin, which gives it a shining appearance, and is very agreeable to human beings and very repulsive to vermin, and therefore commendable for all purposes. The windows are very small, and set deep into the walls, which are of stone ; and often are seen pillars and pretty corridors. These are strange things among Alpine pastures; but the men of these valleys are the Swiss to be seen in all lands, engaged in every conceivable employment; but who return with their money to enrich their own valley. Many villages see in this way their property increased twenty-five or thirty thousand dollars' worth. They always reckon in Graubünden "the home and foreign resources or industry;" and at the last census ten thousand were found absent from the canton in this way, never resigning their citizenship. Their pastures are rented to Italian shepherds, and the little haying and harvesting is done by the Tyrolese.

The air is so pure that meat will keep many years; and fish and flesh are hung to dry in the sun from May till October.

The language is Romanish; but the wanderers return with all the languages of every nation under heaven.

Another Graubünden proverb is, "*One God, one coat*," and there is scarcely more in their costume—woollen coats, shirts and stockings all the year, where it is cold; and in the Italian villages, often bare feet and legs, with great straw hats, and the women in many colours, and ornaments in their braided hair.

One of the peculiar features of Graubünden is remarked in the gallows, which are seen on conspicuous heights overlooking the most beautiful landscapes, as if to make the parting as painful as possible to those who were to enjoy from them their last view of earth. They are built very strong, of stone, not poor wooden gallows by any means, to perish quickly from the earth, but as if to endure for ever. To this a good pastor of Engadine once made allusion when, according to the custom, he was called to consecrate a new one to the holy purpose for which it was built. In his prayer he said, in most emphatic terms, "*This gallows, which we erect for our children and children's children :*" but we hope without ever realizing its blessings in himself or posterity.

The valley of Davos was discovered in the thirteenth century by some hunters of the land of Vatz, who returned with a glowing description of its beauties, of the game in the forests, and fish in the seas, which induced his lordship who lived in the vale of Disentis to send people to colonize the new land, and take possession of it in his name.

Those who came are said to have been descendants of German Vallasians ; and the document which secured to them their rights is dated 1289, and calls them *free men*, who were only to pay a certain rent to him who aided them to come, in "cheese, cloth, and pigs." The lease was to be good so long as the rent was paid, and they owed no other allegiance. Not a castle ever crowned their hills ; not a lord ever set foot upon their soil.

In the other cantons we often hear Graubünden spoken of as the land where boys are kings, or where boys rule, alluding to the early period at which they are allowed to vote and hold office. Formerly it was at fourteen years of age, but now it is at sixteen, that they exercise the right of suffrage, and are held to military service ; but they cannot be elected to office till twenty.

There are no direct taxes, and no very heavy ones of any sort ; but the restrictions are very numerous to prevent the ingress of foreigners. No Jew, not born in the canton, is allowed to enter it ; and the law is not allowed to grant them the privilege. At the last census there was found to be only one residing among them.

The administration of local affairs differs in different places. In Davos the statute-books exhibit curious enactments, similar to those of the same time in northern Switzerland and Germany.

The old chronicle describes the valley as "lovely, healthy, with fish, flesh, and game, flying and swimming ;" and if there was a great hunt, every able-bodied man was obliged to go. The trophies of these excursions are still preserved in the saloon of the old *Rathhouse* in the form of long rows of skulls of wolves and bears.

If any one pulled out the beard of another, he was obliged to pay four gulden ; and in an old law-book in Austria, the penalty for the same crime was twelve gulden. This we have found in other cantons, proving that it must have been a common offence, though for what purpose it was committed one cannot imagine.

The *Kirchweih*, or *Kilbe*, was held at market-time in spring and fall, and was made known by a solemn proclamation by the *Landweibel*, saying, "My gracious lords, the mayor and council of this county of Davos command me to make known," etc. Whoever shall be guilty, during this festival, of gaming, dancing, oaths, or blasphemy, shall be fined a hundred dollars. He who cannot pay the fine will be otherwise punished.

In 1687 dancing was forbidden, as "seducing, frivolous, and injurious ;" but now they may dance in all Graubünden to their heart's content.

Whoever knew of an instance of breaking the peace, either by an offence against himself or others, was bound to inform the Government, that the offender might be punished at the next court ; but no one was obliged to inform against blood relatives or relatives at law. Also the mayor, jury, and other officers were required to make known before the high court all that they had seen or heard contrary to law, only relatives to the third degree not included. This was upon the principle that each individual, as integral part of the whole, should care for the good of the whole.

All were not only excused from informing against relatives, but were bound to stand by them "with honour, body, and goods."

Also in criminal cases no one was obliged to testify against relatives. The criminal court consisting of judge, lawyers, and other officers, was held in the open air. They were seated around a table, on which was laid a naked sword and staff of justice. The seat of the judge was a little raised, and the secretary occupied a place near him with documents.

The prisoner was conducted from the prison by the *Landweibel* and six watchmen or guard, and placed before him. When all was arranged, the mayor solemnly and earnestly addressed the court as follows, "Highly respected, noble, austere, true, honourable, prudent, wise, especially gracious, highly honoured, merciful rulers, lords and magistrates, commanded by the holy Bible and the freedom God has given our land, which is dependent on no foreign king, prince, or potentate, to secure the prisoner N. N., and appoint a day for his trial, we have set apart this day," etc. Here follow various formalities common in ordinary courts.

The judge then turns to the jury, and says, "Under these considerations I ask, if this be the time and hour, when I, as chief justice of this county, in the name of all present, shall take sword and staff in hand, and sit in judgment upon the prisoner according to imperial law and the ordinances of our free land?" * All answer, "Yes."

* Law and official terms in Switzerland are very difficult to translate, as they are different from those used by Germans, and as unintelligible to them as to those of any other nation, unless it be lawyers.

The secretary sits at the right, and on all occasions is the accuser, because he is also treasurer, and the penalties are very often fines, which are deposited with him.

Various addresses are made by the counsel for the State and for the prisoner, and judgment is found. But before it is pronounced, the judge asks if any one, man or woman, old or young, spiritual or worldly, has anything to say why favour should be shown.

If the punishment is to be death, the executioner is instructed by which form life is to be taken ; whether he shall conduct the criminal from life to death by fire, and give his ashes to water, air, or earth ; whether he shall be broken on the wheel, or whether the wheel shall pass over his neck, etc. The judge then takes the staff, and followed by the court watchmen or guard, the executioner and criminal proceed to the place appointed for the death scene.

The last sad office we need not describe ; when it is finished, he who has performed it asks the judge if he has fulfilled the duties of his office according to imperial law and just usages. He answers "Yes." The judge then asks the other officials, "If he has found judgment according to imperial law and just usages ?" "Yes." "If all concerned have acted according to the dictates of mercy and honour ?" "Yes." Then the judge says solemnly, "With God we leave his soul !" and breaks the staff. The mayor then makes a solemn address to the people assembled, exhorting the parents to bring up their children in the fear of God and in prayer and industry ; to keep them from quarrels, idleness, profanity, and all vices ; exhorts the children to obedience, and quotes many texts from the Bible, etc., and all return home.

It was contrary to common custom to break the staff after

the full execution, and entirely out of order to repeat continually, "according to imperial law," as they had never acknowledged emperor or king as lawgiver. But their statutes and formulas were probably prepared by some one who knew little of jurisprudence, and that little obtained from German codes of Charles V., which were the basis of all criminal proceedings in Germany.

CHAPTER XXI.

ARGOVIE.

ROMAN CITY—CONVENTS—QUARRELS—JEWS—DARK DAYS OF OLD—SCHOOLS —THREE CANTONAL DIVISIONS—HOMELESS PEOPLE—PEASANT DINNER FESTIVALS.

THOUGH there are traces of the Romans in every canton, in none have been found so many illustrations, not only of their power, but of their wealth, their life, and their art, as in Argovie. There was the centre of all their operations against Germany, and the *entrepôt* of their arms and commerce. This is the only place we ever heard of where an aqueduct which they built was preserved through all ages and used in modern times. It conducts the water from Mount Brunneck into the city of Vendinassa, in the same way and for the same purposes as when the famous legions had here their encampment. In the same city are the ruins of an amphitheatre, where have been found the bones of the animals who fought in the arena.

In another city is an inscription to the honour of Vespasian; and bricks have been picked up having upon them the names and numbers of different legions, coins having the effigy of Lucila, the daughter of Aurelius, mosaics and fresco paintings, marble vases, pictures and shell work, medals and monies innumerable. Near Zofingen was found a *parquet*, six hundred and twenty feet square, of beautiful mosaic, the Roman thermes, and a vase of alabaster. In many places are found the ruins of baths, castles, and camps, showing that here was almost another Rome; and the proofs are not less striking that it was plundered by Attila, and destroyed by Childebert. But why were they called barbarians? Because they pursued their enemies, and demolished their strongholds? How long since the two " most enlightened nations of Christendom " did the same ? using more deadly weapons, and followed by more inhuman consequences, and then offering *Te Deums* to the God of the Bible for their success !

The Ambrons, one of the four tribes of Helvetia, were the first known inhabitants of Argovie, and became incorporated with the hordes who came down from the north. The territory was afterwards disputed between Suabia and Burgundia ; and in the course of those disputes and conquests, the Dukes of Hapsburg, originally a noble family in Alsatia, became established in the land. The many convents which dot the hills, and were the cause of the war of the *Sonderbund* in 1847, were built by the princes of this house, and the long wars with the brave men of the forest cantons were in resistance to their unjust pretensions.

A single tower alone remains of the proud castle which was the cradle of the Imperial House of Austria. The convents, though truly Christian and benevolent institutions in their day, becoming strongholds of misrule and usurpers of unjust power, were suppressed by the Federal Government, and the property consecrated to purposes more in accordance with modern benevolence. Three for women still exist, but with many of the features of ancient nunneries modified.

The disputes between the two religions in the time of the Reformation were particularly stormy in Argovie; the French revolution kept them long in a turmoil, and not till 1852 did they succeed in forming a constitution upon a truly republican basis, when all these conflicting elements settled into harmony.

But they seem to have a peculiar predisposition to disputes. As in Schaffhausen, they improve the slightest pretence for a quarrel and especially for a lawsuit. The wit of a peasant has become proverbial, who, being asked how it had prospered with him the last year, answered, "Oh, thank God, very well; we have the means to live and a little remaining, enough to give us the amusement of a lawsuit during the winter!" This same delight in lawsuits prevails also in Tessin, while in Unterwald and Canton Vaud they will manage any way to settle a dispute rather than have the trouble of lawyers. Yet Schaffhausen and Argovie are at the extreme north, and Tessin at the extreme south of the confederacy.

Half the number of Jews in all Switzerland dwell in this canton, though she is the most illiberal in her policy towards them. No foreign Jew is allowed to enter, and the natives are confined to two or three villages, not allowed the privilege of citizenship, and subject to various restrictions which limit their means and must embitter their spirit.

The Protestants are some twenty thousand more than the Catholics; but they have learned to live in harmony, so that often the same church serves both confessions. But before this pleasant state of things was consummated, in which people agree to disagree, both parties passed through many fiery trials, and were subjected to all the troubles of those days of lawless violence.

The ministers of the reformed Church seldom displayed their

wisdom in attempting to charm their hearers, instead of endeavoring to compel them to adopt the new faith.

It is related in the chronicles of one village, that the unruly youths, not liking the restraints to which they were likely to be subjected by the pastor of the new doctrine, met stealthily in the night and tore away his grape-vines and pulled up the stakes, so that it cost ninety-three dollars and seventy-five cents to reset them. They destroyed seventy-five bundles of hemp, and stole four thalers' worth of rosemary after it had been already sold, but not removed by the purchaser; and filled the well with manure, so that the family were all made sick from drinking the water. At another time, in Passion Week, they stole the fishes from the well, carried off twenty fowls, and poisoned the watchdogs before the door.

In another place, dancing having been forbidden, before people could at all understand why or wherefore, the young men and maidens met in the forest in the night for this purpose. The good pastor severely reproved them, and was rewarded by having his orchard destroyed and his garden sown with weeds. The people restored them again, but only to see them more thoroughly despoiled, the young trees all torn up and the hedges burnt.

Two school teachers, who took the part of the pastor, were treated in a similar manner, and beaten on their way to school. One of them being a musician, found, when he attempted to blow his trumpet or similar wind instrument in church on Sunday, that it was filled with mud. Those and similar persecutions were continued, till all were obliged to leave.

These were the events of nearly two centuries ago. Now no canton exhibits the evidences of more universal cultivation than Argovie. Her school system is among the best, both for the education of children and the higher classes in the district and cantonal schools, and there are in all the large villages evening classes for those who are employed during the day.

The people are distinguished for their progress both in manufactures and agriculture. As in Zurich and St. Gall, the two go hand in hand, and those who braid straw, weave ribbons, and spin cotton, devote also a portion of their time to the soil or kindred employments. The houses of the higher and middle classes are everywhere pretty, in the midst of beautiful gardens, groves, and orchards. When we marvel at the number of fine trees in every village, by every wayside, we are told of a curious law enacted in 1806, which made it incumbent upon every man at his marriage to plant six trees, and at the birth of every son two more. Thus from twelve to fifteen thousand were planted every year.

The general features of agriculture are the same as in Zurich, and the impulse it received, and the improvements made, date to the Napoleonic period, when restrictions were removed, and tithes were abolished, which gave the profits to the labourer, and enabled him to improve his own material condition.

If there is one thing in which the Argovian takes particular pride, and in which he particularly excels, it is in the care of his cattle. They are elephants in size, and their glossy hides betoken some peculiar art on the part of their master. Not a particle of dust or straw is allowed to cling to them, and they are combed and washed as only horses are elsewhere, not with a *currycomb*, but with old cards, which, being finer and softer, are more agreeable to the animal, and improve the fineness of the hair. This receives an additional lustre by being rubbed with old flannel. They actually shine ; and the gentle creatures have an evident consciousness of their beauty, for they are careful not to soil their ashy grey and chestnut robes by lying in the mud when allowed to take a walk. Animals can acquire, if they have not by nature, a fine sensibility, and when they have once experienced the pleasant sensation of cleanliness, learn to take care of themselves.

At the farther end of every stable is a goat, who lives upon what the cows scatter about, and who is kept there also because the peasants believe if witches are disposed to exert any evil influence within their precincts, the little animal will prove a sort of *scape-goat*, and their beautiful cows pass unharmed.

Not only do they exercise this care for the person of the animal, but are at the pains of removing every feather and other unpalatable substance from their food ; and the water-troughs where they drink are kept as clean as if human beings resorted to them.

If anybody doubts the efficacy of these means, let him come and see not only how large, but how intelligent, these dumb creatures look ; how they watch every motion of those who talk to them, and listen to all they say. What an affectionate moan they will utter to welcome the milkers, who are always men, as they say, "Women tickle the cow, and never take all the milk from the udders, so that she gives less and less." It is said of them, that an Argovian will send for the doctor for his cow a great deal quicker than for his wife ! but we did not see any evidence that he was not sufficiently attentive to both.

Alas, were it not for the *eau de vie*, the distilleries everywhere in Switzerland, the people might be transformed almost instantaneously into inhabitants of an Utopia. This is their besetting sin, the one remaining curse, the blight and plague-spot of the land. They have attempted to make a law in Berne, where this evil is greatest, that the grain which is needed for bread shall not be converted into brandy. But the people consider it

15*

an invasion of rights and privileges that they should not be allowed to do what they please with their own, though it be to commit suicide and murder.

The three grand rivers, the Reuss, the Limmat, and the Aar, unite in Canton Àrgovie, and flow on together to the Rhine, which they join near Coblentz, a little town on its northernmost limits. By these four distinct divisions are made, which are indicated by the peculiar lines upon their escutcheon. The first is vertical, dividing it into two fields, the one black, denoting a fruitful land, like Argau proper. Through this crosswise a silver stream flows. The other field is blue, and three stars in its centre indicate the other three divisions. It is one of the pretiest among the cantons.

These divisions mark also a people quite distinct from one another. In the Fruckthal, where they belonged so long to Austria, not being fairly ceded to Switzerland till 1802, they have not yet become entirely Swiss in feeling. The dress of the maidens is like that in the Black Forest, while in all the rest of Argovie it is like the Bernese. In all the canton, too, they have the old German custom of watchmen, who traverse the streets every hour of the night, and cry, "Listen to my words, it is the hour. Extinguish the fires, and may God have us in his holy keeping."

There is everywhere in Switzerland a class of people whom they call *heimathlos*, or homeless people, by which they mean those who do not enjoy all, or any, of the rights of citizenship. In Argovie, not only the Jews belong to this class, but those who transact business and live in the canton without purchasing citizenship, soldiers who have formed acquaintance with Swiss in foreign service, and return with them fugitives and pilgrims. Of these last there are very many, as Argovie is the highway to

Einsiedeln, for those who come from Germany; and poor and miserable as they are, it is said they spend by the way in this canton alone upwards of five hundred thousand dollars. Many women are in their train, who come with a cradle upon their shoulders, and leave the little ones in sheds and barns, and sometimes in the open field, where they are picked up by the inhabitants and taken good care of, but still are classed all their lives among the homeless, because they were not born upon the soil. They may have a right to vote in village affairs, but not in cantonal.

Besides, there are many who are not admitted to the ordinary privileges of villagers, never having been able to pay the hundred dollars necessary to purchase citizenship, and who cannot marry till they do. They are often very poor and vicious, and it is considered a reproach upon the constitution of Argovie that she is thus illiberal to so many.

The old-fashioned houses, and those of the poor, are still very comfortless, but the modern ones are ample and commodious. Among the farmers, granary, threshing-floor, and family are under the same roof, which has the great gable end extending out many feet to act as protector to the ploughs, harrows, and other utensils which are stored underneath, and which makes the rooms very dark, but adds to their warmth in winter.

The spout of clear running water is making music in front of every door, which is a luxury not so difficult to obtain in Switzerland, as they have only to dig a few feet to find a spring, which never fails. Under the windows is usually a bench, where the neighbours meet to gossip, and a " beehive humming near."

The garden is fenced around, and the beds are in squares, measured, as we have seen them a thousand times in New England, by a man who winds a rope upon a long wooden peg, and tying the other to a similar one, places it firmly in the earth, and going to the other end makes a straight line, and then with a hoe smooths the earth against the rope, forming a pretty border. With the hoe-handle he makes a furrow for the flower seeds, which are distributed according to the taste of some fair lady who stands by to superintend. In a few weeks tulips and roses and lupins are blooming, as relief to cabbages, beets, and parsnips, and in the autumn the bright marigolds and queenly dahlias appear in a luxuriance we never saw in any land.

The beet beds are a speciality in Argovie, and are kept in producing order the whole summer. The good *frauen* have also a special way of preparing them. Besides using the tender leaves for salad, they plunge them in boiling water a few minutes, then in cold, to destroy the *herb taste* they would otherwise have, shake and wring them dry, then chopping them fine, mix them with onions, and boil them till soft.

Berries are also in the greatest abundance, fresh in their season, dried and preserved. Like the New England housewife, too, they provide for the thirst of warm days and for the sick, the delicious raspberry shrub. Meat is not an every day luxury, and their fat beeves are seldom served for their own tables. The old fashioned etiquette at a peasant dinner is also a little different from what we have seen elsewhere.

The cloth being spread, a dish of potatoes is set on, and one laid by each plate. The cook then brings a smoking pan of soup, when the family are called to dinner, and each one helps himself to a spoon from a row hanging against the wall, and standing by his chair, asks a blessing. Then seating himself, he places his elbows on the table, and guides the soup from the common dish to his mouth as skilfully as may be. After which each one peels his potato; other vegetables are brought, and pear sauce for dessert. On festival days and Sundays the *frau* brings a bit of meat, which is usually pork, and cutting it, reaches to each one a piece with her fork.

In the winter the supper is milk porridge, and in summer potatoes with salad. Now and then the children rejoice because they are to have pancakes, and on *fête* days other good things are baked at home or in the village bakery. One time, when there was a failure of crops, and bread was scarce, the Government furnished the people with rice, but they did not know how to cook it, and there was nobody to teach them, so it proved a useless benevolence.

It was owing to the efforts of a pastor of Kirchberg that fruits and berries were introduced into every garden, and among the mechanics and higher classes; the white cottages and green blinds dot the country, looking so picturesque, surrounded by orchards, or in the midst of groves, around which the little rills meander for the convenience of supplying the thirsty earth in a summer's drought, while the gardens are luxuriant with currants, strawberries, gooseberries, peaches, pears, apricots, and grapes.

Walnuts and hazel-nuts afford the children a merry pastime in the autumn in the gathering time, and all winter to crack them around the great stove in the long evenings.

In the Fruckthal there are no manufactories, and the people go over the Jura to Aarau to market. They must walk several miles, and yet seven o'clock finds them already there, with laden baskets, the productions of their orchards and their dairies, to exchange for the silk, the calico, the paper, or other fabrics for which the city is famed.

In the reign of Catholic Mary the persecuted English took refuge here, and it welcomed a colony of Huguenots, who rewarded the city for its hospitality by teaching many arts.

The cutlery is almost equal to that of Sheffield, and the founderies make bells of wondrous tone.

The people of the manufacturing towns of Switzerland are at least no more miserable than those of other places. The garrets and cellars are not crowded with a wretched class crying for food ; but those who spin and weave are, on the whole, in a little better condition than those who do not In the beautiful factory in Windegg, every room for spinning, dyeing, and bleaching, is ventilated, and contains many other pleasant arrangements that make it second to none on the Continent, not only for accomplishing all its legitimate purposes, but for securing health and happiness to those who toil within its walls.

In Wohlen are great straw-braiding establishments, which send thousands of hats to America ; and many industries of less importance are scattered throughout the canton. Argovie and Zurich are rival cantons. Being nearly of the same size, and occupying the same position with reference to longitude and latitude, standing side by side, there is no reason why they should not be equal in all things. Zurich is called the *modern Athens*, and Argovie the *culture canton*, both from the attention they pay to the advancement of education and all mental culture.

For her many societies for improvement Argovie is indebted in great measure to her historian and poet, *Henry Zschokke*, who lived in a pretty villa near Aarau, and died there in 1848, at the age of seventy-seven. He was one of the Republicans of 1830 who contributed by his writings to the great political changes throughout Switzerland, which have resulted in better Governments, and a true equality and liberty, that could be the only guarantee for order and unity.

The Argovians have produced many historians, philosophers,

and theologians. Hassler, one of their distinguished engineers, and author of eminent treatises upon astronomy and trigonometry, was in the employment of the Government of the United States from 1811 to 1843, when he died, having been for twenty years Superintendent of the Coast Survey. The beautiful paintings upon glass in some of their own cathedrals, and in other lands, were executed by native artists.

We heard an English lady ask a gentleman one day, "if Switzerland had ever produced any authors or artists of merit." He answered, "No." It seems very ridiculous to think of being obliged to prove what all people of ordinary reading and intelligence must know; but when we ventured to say, "Why, yes, very many," it was still asserted that they were all foreigners who had fled to them for refuge.

In each chapter we have alluded to a few, but to repeat their names in the little space we have to devote, is giving no true idea of their number or importance.

Music is not less cultivated in Argovie than in Zurich, and the *unions* of different societies are occasions of pleasant festivals in city and country.

Sport-loving boys light the carnival fires on the hills the same as in other cantons; and the remnants of many old customs are seen in modern dress, where the spirit of the times requires a little modifying of unseemly ways. On the first morning of May, lovers stand afar off to behold the surprise of the fair maidens, before whose windows they have erected a young fir-tree in the night, decked with ribbons and flowers, and are sure to receive an invitation to a *fête* within as a reward.

The conventionalities of the Kiltgang allow the lover to enter the chamber of his fair one, and to climb to it by the grape trellis or any other convenience from without; and if a stranger comes into their midst, and plays *kilter* with any village damsel, he is sure to be waylaid and beaten, till he is in no fit condition for many weeks to repeat his visits.

But what is called the *youth's feast* is the national *fête* of Argovie. On the evening before it is held, the children are at every door and garden fence begging flowers. The next morning they appear in wreaths and *bouquets* and dresses of white, ready for a procession, which is formed by the teachers of schools at eight o'clock, who walk with their pupils ; the parents, friends, and officials joining, as they pass, till they reach the church. The military arrange themselves in rows each side of the door, and musicians play martial music till the moment before service begins, when the organ peals forth, and the choir perform a series of solos, duets, and choruses, for which they have spent weeks in preparing. Then follows a sermon and other religious services, when two youths display their oratory in some original speeches, for which they have also been long practising ; and music again is the signal for the returning procession.

The dinners are private but festal, the church, houses, and streets being wreathed with garlands, and all labour suspended among high and low. After dinner comes the grand military review for the soldiers to exhibit their tactics, which finishes by a sham fight and siege, and of course a victory, where there is only an imaginary enemy ; when all repair to a neighbouring grove for a *picnic*, where pretty maidens are the waiters, and the tables in the gayest of all attire. Dances close the scene, in which old and young join, till it grows dark, when they disperse, the little folk having enjoyed a day never to be forgotten, and such a one as should be permitted to all children now and then; for neither in the song, or dance, or merriment, is there anything to which the most fastidious can object.

CHAPTER XXII.

TESSINO.

ITALIAN SKIES—GOVERNMENTS—CLERGY—EDUCATION—CHURCH BELLS—
PEASANT HOUSES—COSTUMES—FAIRS—MINES—AGRICULTURAL FETE DAYS
—MARRIAGES—DISTINGUISHED MEN.

WE are in Tessino, among the children of the sun, shaded by groves of chestnuts, inhaling the perfume of the citron and the orange—in the land of the olive, the fig, and the pomegranate. There is everywhere a luxuriance of foliage, and over all a mellowness of tint, and around us a softness of temperature only to be found beneath Italian skies. The language has no more the harsh gutturals of the northern tongue, but flows like some gentle rivulet over golden sands. Nature has made it a land of beauty and of glory ; what shall we find it at the hand of man !

A Swiss author, who wrote in 1797, says, " A German-Swiss pig would not enter where a Tessino family lives." This was more than half a century ago ; since then they have made many improvements. Wise and strong men have taken a seat in their councils, and vigorous measures have proved the efficiency of their government. They have had one of their own but a little while, having in 1498 voluntarily placed themselves under the protection and government of the Forest Cantons, to be ruled by bailiffs sent to them from Uri, Schwytz, and Unterwalden. Near Bellizona are the three castles which were occupied by these republican rulers, who were often as exacting and tyrannical as any delegate of Austrian despotism. As in Thurgovie, they purchased their offices at a great price, and remunerated themselves by unjust taxes and all manner of fraudulent impositions upon the peeple. This is an experience which all nations have which are governed by agents accountable to a power in a distant land, which can have no real knowledge of the wants of those over whom they rule, and never learn whether those whom they delegate, administer justice or exercise tyranny.

Before they belonged to Switzerland, they were taken possession of by cities and districts and parcelled among those who conquered them. Charlemagne passed through Locarno in 882, and gave this city as a present to his wife Engelberga. King Henry, in the eleventh century, gave Bellizona to the Bishop of Como, disposed of all the other cities in the same unceremonious manner, and afterwards kept the people in continual quarrels, as kings and bishops disputed the right to each other's possessions.

As the other cantons joined the Confederacy, they participated in the government, and each had the privilege of furnishing a bailiff for Tessino, so that it came to be ruled by deputies and bailiffs, who met every year, and formed what they called a *Syndic*, for the administration of affairs. This administration was little else than cruelty and anarchy; and towards the end of the eighteenth century we find them attempting to get rid of their foreign rulers, to form a government of their own. This was accomplished by Napoleon, by whom Tessino was invited to send a deputy to meet those from the other cantons, to decide upon the best government for the whole. The eight bailifdoms were formed into one canton ; and they immediately commenced forming a constitution, which was not finished to the satisfaction of all till 1830.

But as soon as they were delivered from a foreign yoke, under which no people ever exhibited energy and intelligence, whether it be a republican or an imperial bondage, they awakened, and proved that they are worthy of freedom in the progress they have made, though it has necessarily been slow. With the work of centuries to do in a few years, they have often excited the opposition of the people by taxes to build roads, bridges, and execute other public works, which were very expensive.

Those who have been accustomed to think of Switzerland as a confederacy for three hundred years, with the same freedom and efficiency as America possessed from the moment of her birth, will see that there is good reason, without its being a reproach, why she is far behind the republic of only half a century.

In Tessino now their greatest hindrance is the clergy, who prefer to keep the people in ignorance, and are yet too numerous and too powerful to be overcome. In 1853, the Government ventured to suppress a convent of Capuchins, who were a disgrace to their profession and a curse to the country, and, with provision for their journey, banished them from the canton. They went into the Austrian territory, and this noble, enlightened, Christian Government of the nineteenth century, visited all the Tessinians of Lombardy, in revenge, with confiscation and banishment. Six thousand people were turned out of their peaceful homes in the depth of winter, deprived of all resources ; the property which they had accumulated by industry forcibly taken possession of, and themselves driven to seek an asylum where they might. After two years' negotiations, and the paying of a stipulated salary to those infamous monks, the Lombardian territory was again opened to the citizens of Tessino.

Many people from this canton go away for a season, as in Graubünden, to exercise some trade, remaining a few months, and sometimes years, but continuing citizens of Tessino, and returning eventually to spend their days in the land of their birth.

Throngs of stone-hewers and bricklayers go to Italy in the spring, and return in the autumn, while those who sell roast chestnuts go in the fall, and return in the spring ; and also the cattle-dealers, and swarms of porters, to fill the hotels, to wait upon the English and Americans, who are seen also in throngs entering Italy in the autumn, and departing in the spring, but to spend money rather than to earn it.

They have been petitioning twenty years to have the canton formed into a distinct bishopric, but in vain. A third of it belongs to the diocese of Milan, and the remainder to that of Como, the bishop of which derives thence his principal revenues. They have also petitioned to be relieved from the observance of many festivals ; but though the people of Lombardy had their prayers granted in this respect, the favour was refused to Tessino. They have thirty more *fête* days than their neighbours, and are kept in such a round of festivities, that they are impoverished by the loss of time and waste of substance thus involved.

In 1848, when the convents of Argovie were suppressed by the Federal Government, some in Tessino were also secularised, but there are still twenty remaining, and a church for every one hundred and seventy individuals, with six hundred priests, exclusive of the monks.

It is the canton where the least is done for education; indeed, the only one where nothing is done at all. But they are now again trying to establish the system so efficiently and beneficially carried out elsewhere, with some hopes of success.

They have lately lost one of their noblest citizens, M..Franscini, who had been many years a deputy to the Federal Council, and all his life engaged in some way in promoting the good of his country. It is from his voluminous and laboriously prepared works that we glean all that is statistical concerning Switzerland. He mourned as for a lost son the degeneracy of his people. But we hope his mantle has fallen upon some one who will go forth with new strength to the great work which he began.

There are colleges in some of the monasteries; but they are mostly for the education of ecclesiastics, and the nuns in many places do something for the cultivation of young ladies; but there are scarcely five hundred youths of both sexes who are pursuing scientific and literary studies either at home or abroad.

The sound of church bells becomes almost a torture in the cities, there being in all the church towers about one thousand five hundred. Some of them ring every hour, and others at appointed times, and all every evening, till one is puzzled to know whether it is night or morning, especially as, according to the old fashion, many of the clocks still strike twenty-four times for the hours of the day instead of twice twelve, beginning the day at six in the evening, so that at seven by other people's clocks it strikes one, and at eight two, etc., by those of Tessino.

In the evening, ladies are seen promenading or riding, but all day they are invisible, unless some in long black veils are returning from mass in the early morning. Yet beauty is not all concealed beneath veils. The women who go clattering with sandals upon their feet, without stockings, and with the most *négligé* costume, are often very beautiful. They sit upon a stone or bench or under a tree all the day with their little ones in their arms, for whom they perform all motherly offices, evidently feeling that in those " holy duties " there is neither sin nor shame.

In Bellizona the houses are mostly of woods, and each family occupies one, instead of being confined to a few rooms as in great cities. The three picturesque castles which overlook the city, formerly the residences of the three bailiffs of the forest cantons, are *Castel Grand* of Uri, which is now used for an arsenal; *Castel di Mezzo* belonged to Schwytz, and *Castel di Lune*, which is in ruins, to Unterwald. The other two cities form with Bellizona an acute angled triangle, Lugano being at the point and upon the lake of the same name. Its situation is a little similar to that of Luzerno; but how differently the sloping hills are clad. Along its shores are scattered the little villages, in the midst of groves of olive, almond, and citron, which are reflected upon the crystal surface of the lake, thus presenting at the same moment a lovely landscape and a picture in *water colours* such as no pencil can trace.

The vines clothe all the southern part of the canton, sometimes being placed in regular rows in the fields, and sometimes climbing elms and mulberries, and winding their careless branches from limb to limb, while the clusters droop beneath, forming arches of gold and purple fruit. In the region of Lugano they are creeping over lattices, and sometimes formed into terraces. Opposite the city rises Mount Caprino, the base of which is full of grottoes, which they call the *Caves of Eolus*, because in summer a cold wind blows continually across. Here they have built small stone houses for their wine, where it is preserved always cool, and where they come themselves to promenade on pleasant summer evenings.

The burgher houses in the surrounding country are large, with great balconies, which they use as sitting-rooms, shaded by curtains of tobacco-leaves drying in the sun. The peasant-women are seen everywhere in bright green or yellow raw silk skirts, with many folds, and bodice of the same or different colour, laced across the bosom with cords or ribbons. The sleeves are also in two parts, tied with bows of many colours. The hair is braided, and wound into the form of a great nest, with gold or silver pins placed in a half circle around the upper part of the braid, the large heads forming thus a kind of crown. We have seen this adopted by American ladies, who call it an "Italian costume," and who might have seen it worn by an Italian princess. The men still appear in small clothes of chamois and scarlet vests; but all peculiar modes are fast giving way, even in this sunny land, to the sombre hues and plain stuffs of sober climes.

Shoes and stockings are only worn on festival days, and women may be seen bending beneath heavy burdens, wandering barefoot through the hot sand. Ornaments of gold and silver for those who can afford it, and tinsel for the poorer classes, are seen everywhere; a cross upon the breast, and a chain of garnets, alternating with buttons of gold thread, upon the neck.

The clergy preach against finery, but it is the better class that wears it; for those who do not spend their money in ways more demoralizing—in low drunkenness and revelry; while a taste for a pretty and neat attire is evidence of a little higher grade of mind and ambition.

A stone pier connects Lugano with Mendriso across the lake, which, with the bridges at the two extremities, cost one hundred and thirty thousand dollars, and was finished in 1845. It was one of the public works which the Government found it difficult to accomplish, with its new power and scanty purse; but which must in time repay them by facilitating communication with Italy for the merchandise and thousands of travellers who pass this way.

Locarno is situated on the beautiful Lago Maggiore, only a small extent of which lies within Swiss territory. This is the city from which emigrated in 1553 the persecuted Protestants, who took refuge in Zurich, and transferred their looms, and, as it would seem, all the enterprise of the town. It has never since prospered. The Pope endeavoured to increase the severity of the sentence, and commanded the Diet to confiscate their property, and oblige them to leave their children, to be educated in the Romish Church. But, as usual, the Diet refused to comply any farther than it chose with demands of pope or bishop. The Pope was enraged, and published *bans* and *bulls* against them, which they heeded in the same way. It was enough that the poor people were obliged to leave their homes, and the sacrifices were great, though they lost not all. Two centuries later, we find the descendants of these banished silk weavers extending their commerce from Germany to Lombardy, and visiting the fairs of Frankfort and Italy with the *stuffs* which should have been woven in Locarno. Another of them established a cotton factory in Piedmont in 1812, taking with him two hundred Swiss, some of them whole families. He set up his looms in an old castle, and the buzz might have aroused the old knights who once revelled there from their death slumbers, and certainly would, if awaking had been possible, at seeing such a desecration of their lordly halls. There were spinners and weavers, and dyers and bleachers, scattered among the various saloons and corridors, and though they were once nearly overturned by a landslide, attacked by soldiers, and undermined by the machinations of priests, nothing daunted them; they spun away, and when their founder died, in 1843, twelve thousand persons were employed in his *castle mills!*

Now there is a fair every fortnight in Locarno, at which appear all the costumes of the country, and all the productions of their soil. Every year in October there is also a cattle fair, the largest in Switzerland, to which are driven from all the northern cantons those they have been so carefully training, and which come in troops of hundreds and thousands, most of them over the St. Gothard, and also some ten thousand horses, to meet the purchasers from Italy.

It was instituted as early as 1513. Afterwards a rival fair was commenced at another village, that caused dissensions which lasted thirty years, but were finally settled by convention.

On all the borders of the lakes the plants which we have been accustomed to tend so carefully in greenhouses are flourishing, and in far greater luxuriance, in the open air; and the gardens of the villas are gorgeous with bloom, and made beautiful by taste and art.

But what a contrast are the houses of the poor; in many places rows of miserable huts of stone, with no mortar to cover their rudeness, no chimney, and black with soot and dust. In Germany and North Switzerland the floors are bare, but they are universally clean. Here they are carpeted with mud, which has never come in contact with water. The cattle are in separate huts, but so near that the pigs, which are red, may be often seen putting their noses in the dinner which stands cooked upon the hearth.

In the valley of Maggio and Blenio there will be rows of miserable houses for human beings, and opposite rows of very good-looking stables for the cattle.

A part of every establishment is an inclosure for drying chestnuts, where a fire must be made. There is to almost every house a patch of tobacco and of *Turkish corn*, a small species, which is sown and gathered in the course of forty days. Often over these wretched huts the acacia waves, and the fig-tree, with its luxurious foliage, tries to screen their dingy walls. To see the fruit of this tree in its green state, one could scarcely believe it could be the same as the contents of the little *drums* which we are accustomed to eat. Its shape is something like a pear, and the outer coat green, but within it is a pulp or consistency something like what children call a *mealy apple*, and of a most beautiful rose colour. But the taste is horrible. The manner of packing them for exportation would not increase the relish to those who eat them, and as we do not wish to destroy this pleasure, we leave the process to be imagined, being quite sure no imagination will exaggerate the reality.

All the implements of agriculture are after the mode which might have been in vogue before the flood,—a wooden rake instead of a harrow, and something called a plough, drawn by oxen or *perhaps by women*, with wide fringes to their skirts, long aprons, and caps like nuns.

The grain, after being cut, is not left upon the ground, but hung upon an apparatus for the purpose, that gives it the appearance of being a straw roof, with the sheaves lying one above another in layers, shedding rain readily, and exposed to the sun and wind. In fourteen days it is threshed without ever being put in barns, of which they have no need.

This picture gives the idea of poverty, but there is no reason why the people should be poor. Maize thrives better in Tessino than in Italy, yielding two or three fold more at harvest, and, where well cultivated, from eight to twelve fold. Potatoes yield eight to ten fold, and, with favourable soil and good care, from twenty to sixty fold, and this without any modern improvements of draining, irrigation, or scientific culture.

The mechanics form only an eighth or ninth part of the population, and then practise agriculture a portion of their time. Four thousand persons are absent a whole or part of the year exercising trades in other lands.

Where chestnuts grow they are often eaten twice a day, boiled or roasted, for many months. They also have *polenta* in various forms, boiled, baked, and dried, and besides, figs, peaches, pears, plums, cherries, and apricots are in the greatest abundance. Yet they grow without care, and gardens among the peasantry have no attention. They have a superstitious prejudice against flowers, but, as it would seem, none against weeds.

Every family has a red pig, and in the autumn it is slaughtered and salted for the winter, but in the summer they seldom eat meat. Sometimes a poor widow hires a few goats for their milk, and to furnish something to do for her boys. They are valued, and at the end of the time for which she has taken them, three or four years, they must be returned, or their worth in money. Fishing and hunting are everywhere free.

Besides thirty holidays more than the people of Lombardy are obliged to observe, they also have many more processions, blessings, and days when they are obliged to spend an hour or more in church, besides the daily mass, and all ordinary *fêtes*. Not to exaggerate, we may say there are five whole days and fifteen half days spent in this way by fifty thousand working people of all ages and both sexes. This makes two hundred and fifty thousand days lost to labour by the people themselves. But the working animals are also unemployed ; the hammer is still, the plane moves not, and the saw-mill is dumb. On these days they eat and drink more than on other days, and the priests confess that most of the time is spent in idleness and dissipation.

At the ceremony of baptism a great parade is made, if it be a boy, but for girls not any ! Costly gifts are made to the new mother, the bells are rung, and a procession escorts the infant to the font.

Weddings take place usually early in the morning or late in the evening, and are often solemnized between boys of seventeen and girls of fifteen. Sometimes the bridegroom, at the head of a long train of relations, knocks at the door of the bride. A person within calls out, " Who is there, and what do you wish ?" After a long parley, an old woman opens the door ; but those without are not satisfied till they enter. Being expected, the bride is arrayed for church, and with her relations joins the procession, the mother remaining at home to prepare supper. The wedding-ring is never removed from the finger.

Betrothals are public, and if the promise of marriage is not performed in consequence of fickleness on either side, a sum must be paid, which is adjudged in proportion to the wealth of the individual, and often all they have.

The *Lichtgehen* is the custom in the northern part of the canton, with the usual penalties if the lover is seen on his way, or a stranger is caught paying his addresses to one out of the village where he belongs.

When rich people are sick, prayers are said three days in church, but the poor cannot afford to pay for them. In some valleys a pound of salt is divided among all the neighbouring houses, that they may pray for the sick. At funerals there is great weeping and wailing, and many prayers for the soul of the departed. But a priest asks more for repeating the Litany aloud, less if he says it in a half tone, and a certain price if he sings it. It often requires all a poor family is worth to buy one.

There is a chapel or a cross at every corner, and daily processions to visit them and receive a blessing. If these are not attended, the peasants think "the thunder, lightning, and the rain" will destroy their crops, because the words of the prayer are, "Protect us, O Lord, from tempest," etc. If it thunders, the bells are rung for protection, or they gather under the eaves of the church, believing there no evil will come near them, and are often seen collecting as soon as it begins to be cloudy.

The carnival is held only where Bacchus can preside; and then in the usual way, as in Italy, maskers going from house to house in the evening, with lighted torches, begging, and among high and low dances and feasts. Since the facilities of communication made it possible, very many go to Milan to the theatre, instead of indulging in sports at home.

Besides these, and an indescribable number in addition, are the pilgrimages to Einsicdeln, and to the Madonna, in the Vigezzo-Thal, in Sardinia, and many a consecrated spot in their own canton.

Ghosts, witches, visions, and apparitions, are the events of every day; and if an old miser dies, they believe the earth shakes and the mountains tremble. But they say here, as in Luzerne, that spirit-rappers have not found so many supporters as in Protestant Zurich!

As we have before mentioned, they are engaged in constant litigations, though not exactly "for amusement," as they do in Aargau; and one could not expect, with their indolent habits, they would take the trouble for any reason. For this, and because of their many festivals, and also that in countries where the articles of greatest luxury are produced the people are universally the poorest, the people of Tessino are far from rich, and many of them far from comfortable. In the course of fifty years, however, they have progressed very much, and begin to feel some ambition to overtake their sister cantons in the north.

Yet their fruitful land has not been entirely barren of genius. Who has not heard of *Cetti*, who knew all the languages of Europe, besides Hebrew and Arabic? and he was born in Lugano. From the same city Napoleon invited *Soane* to be one of the thirty members of the National Institute. A Tessino surgeon was also placed by him in care of the military hospitals in Italy. Many of his profession have been distinguished in Italian cities.

Still more numerous have been her artists. *Frazzini*, who was then in Denmark, was invited by Peter the Great to make the designs for building St. Petersburg; and to *Rusca*, in the time of Catherina, both St. Petersburg and Moscow were indebted for some of the most beautiful of their structures. *Pietri* acquired great distinction in the Academy of Cadiz, and was sent to Chili to found an academy. Two beautiful edifices were designed by him in Lima. It was by the light of the genius of a Tessino artist that Moscow arose from her ashes after the great conflagration more beautiful than before. Native artists built the St. Gothard, the Bernardin, and also Mount Cenis, for the Italians; and within a few years *Fossati* has restored the mosque of St Sophia, in Constantinople.

Coldrario, who died in 1666, was director of the Academy of St. Lucas, at Rome; and *Pozzi* received the prize for painting at Parma at the age of twenty-one. The palace of Schönbrunn, near Vienna, was planned by a Tessino architect for Maria Theresa; and two others constructed the dome of Milan.

We have been accustomed to hear these works ascribed to Italian artists, because they have Italian names, and we heard an Englishman assert one day that St. Petersburg was designed by a Frenchman. We do not understand why so many who travel in Switzerland are ready to do justice to her mountains while doing so great injustice to her men.

CHAPTER XXIII.

BERNE.

INTERLAKEN—EMPRESS-MOTHER OF RUSSIA—SUNRISE FROM THE GRIMSEL —STORY OF PETER ZEIBACH—OLD CUSTOMS—BERNESE BOYS—FELLENBERG—COUNTRY LIFE.

The second time we entered Berne, it was from the south, having gone completely round the little republic, and many times across.

Interlaken is the watering-place of Switzerland. It is the concentrating and diverging point for all who ascend the mountains, cross the lakes, and thread the valleys; and for many who only wish to say they have, and to be for a little while in the midst of whirl and fashion.

We followed the example of all the world, and came to *Interlaken*, which, as the name indicates, lies *between the lakes*, and in the centre of that mountainous region known as *Berner Oberland*. From one window we look out upon a lovely valley in the midst of bloom and beauty; and from the other upon the eternal snows, which are within less than an hour's ride or walk.

It is a whirl, sure enough, a continuous throng coming and

going, with all manner of caravans and cavalcades, equipages and costumes, from those of the prince to the peasant. The Empress-Mother of Russia is this year the centre of attraction, though she herself is as insignificant a looking little "*frau*" as one often sees. We are sitting one morning on the green, with a handkerchief tied over our head, when a lady in a light blue silk tunic over a white under-dress crosses the lawn. She is followed by a troop of fair maidens, who attend her to a seat, and kiss her hand. So much for ceremony. When it is finished, they kneel at her feet, or sit on a bench ; and by-and-by comes one who has also a handkerchief tied over her head, and places herself at her side. We ask who they all are ; and first learn, that it is a train of Russian nobles, and that the house opposite is the residence of the Empress, for which she pays one hundred and fifty dollars a day.

Her daughter, the Crown-Princess of Wurtemberg, is a much grander-looking person, and affects no less state than the Queen of England or the Empress of France. When she takes a walk, a liveried servant goes before, and another behind, and her train drags nearly a yard in length on the ground, while a gaping crowd stand witness, which is evidently what she desires.

In another town we said to a Russian countess, from Moscow, something of the Empress-Mother ; and she answered : "Oh, yes, she likes to hold herself up !" and a German exclaimed, in allusion to the Crown Princess, " Every subject in Wurtemberg must live on bread and water to support this ridiculous pomp !"

But this is not our sphere ; we will change the scene.

It is the most glorious of summer mornings, and we find ourselves upon one of the distant mountain-tops ; for we rose long before the sun could find his way to such a height, in order to see him lift his head above the horizon. To what insignificance fade the crowns of princes and the pomp of courts before such a scene! What would become of all the grandeur and glory of the world if the king of light should be dethroned—if he should determine to rest for a single day, or some morning oversleep himself; or the light of his countenance be dimmed for a moment whilst we are watching his awaking? We have never before been so impressed with his majesty and that of all the starry hosts.

But again we must bring ourselves back to earth and ordinary mortals; and, alas! in the fulfilment of our mission, expose the chambers of a human mind and heart from which the light of the Sun of Righteousness has been shut out, and the darkness become like that which would fill the world if the Author of light should veil his face.

Three centuries ago, a hut was built upon the Grimsel to accommodate those who wished to pass from Canton Uri to Valais, and a man called then, as now, a *spitler*, was placed there to attend to weary travellers. Those who could afford it paid for the attention they received; and those who could not, were not less hospitably cared for. Contributions in all Switzerland, which were collected in winter, supported the humble establishment, which was very little enlarged or improved during a hundred years. Often in the spring it was found covered with snow and mud, and had to be dug out and made habitable, as then no one thought of remaining all the winter, the travellers being few or none who passed that way after the snows covered the hills.

When travelling became the fashion, and the glaciers greater objects of attraction than galleries of art, the Grimsel presented almost every day a scene like an assembly, so great was the throng upon its heights, nearly seven thousand feet above the sea. Thence paths led in many directions to the glaciers and valleys of the four cantons.

In the early part of this century the house was fitted up by the inhabitants of Hasli Valley, and rented to a man who took all the risk and trouble, and paid a stipulated sum to the owners. In 1836, being obliged to give it up, it was rented to his son-in-law, Peter Zeibach, who had shown himself a worthy, energetic man during all his life, and whose wife and daughters were well fitted for the responsible household duties of such an establishment.

It was soon proved that the choice was not ill made. Peter enlarged and improved the premises, till the "*Hospiz*" was one of the best in Switzerland ; and by his attentions and just dealings he made himself renowned in many lands. The travellers'-book was filled with his praises in every language. A German artist had covered it with designs ; a professor had written whole stanzas in Greek ; students had scribbled much good and bad wit ; and English, American, and French verses showed the appreciation the authors had of good fare, if they could not sing like Homer and Byron.

It was to study the neighbouring glaciers that Agassiz and his companions built their tents upon the ice, where their ruins still stand, and they numbered Peter as not among the least of the natural curiosities with which they became acquainted, and the name of the philosopher and host were linked in many a complimentary verse.

The peasant never put off his costume or assumed the pretensions of a gentleman. Unless sought for counsel or to interpret, or settle disputes with guides, he was seldom seen, the higher official duties being left to his son, and the daughters in the pretty Bernese costume superintended the household. They spoke German, French, and English, were always in the dining-room to be sure that every want was attended to, settled the bills, attended to the sick, and made each one feel that he was in a pleasant family instead of a mercenary inn.

There were in summer fifty servants; dining, reading, and sitting-rooms; and good lodgings for more than a hundred people. Thirty or forty cows supplied milk, butter, and cheese of the best quality, many horses were kept for guides, pigs for fresh meat, and more than a hundred goats.

Justice and integrity were the special characteristics of Peter. In all troubles which arose he was arbiter, and no one found fault with his decisions; he prospered as the wicked rather than the righteous are usually seen to do, and became rich, though he entertained gratis at least six thousand poor who every year came to his door. No one who ever heard it will forget his "God protect thee!" which was so seriously and heartily uttered to all who left him to tempt the dangers of the snowy depths below. Would that he had always uttered it as earnestly for himself; then surely God would not have forsaken him in the hour of temptation and darkness.

It was on a cold November night that the flames were seen enveloping the snowy peaks of the Grimsel, and the next day the Government and Council of Ober-Hasli were informed of the calamity by Peter, who said that a stranger had lodged there that night, and probably through his carelessness the fire had originated. The house was insured in Berne for five thousand dollars, and the furniture for four thousand. It was the duty therefore of the Government to inquire into all the particulars of the catastrophe, and they immediately sent a committee to examine the premises and ascertain the extent of the loss.

No evidences that any one had perished in the flames appeared, and various things led to suspicion that accident had not been the cause of the fire. Further examination revealed that many things had been hidden in the hay and buried in the ground; wine, beer, vegetables, and cheese were found where only care could have placed them.

As soon as suspicion was awakened, the servant who had been left there for the winter had fled; and when a second deputation went to search the ruins, they met Peter and his son just returning from Canton Valais with wood to rebuild the house. When asked about the articles which were buried, he said it was his custom, in order to keep them from freezing; but he had forgotten to mention them in making his statement. But in a day or two were found many more; doors and windows concealed behind rocks, boxes of glass, furniture, kitchen utensils and stores. The judge, pointing to them, said in a friendly tone, "Peter Ziebach, you are an unfortunate man."

He saw that he was ruined, and stood for a moment sunk in deep thought; then rushed wildly down the steep, and plunged into the sea. They dragged him from the water and restored him to life; alas, for what? That he might spend twenty years in a solitary cell!

He was placed on a horse, and by a strong guard brought to Meyringen. How often our thoughts turned as we traced the same wild solitary way to the grey-haired man of sixty-two, who had lived a long life of honour and probity, and now in age had covered himself with infamy, and plunged his innocent wife and children into irretrievable misfortune. Strange mystery is the human heart.

No suspicion rested upon his family, and he had in no way involved them by communicating to them any of his plans.

We will go back and trace the power of temptation in an honest mind. Peter had five brothers and sisters, and lived in a secluded valley of Ober-Hazli, where his father had a patch of land which he had helped to cultivate in summer, and in winter learned the beautiful art peculiar to this valley, of carving articles in wood, which he and his brothers sold in the hotels of Interlaken, the Rhigi, and Lucerne to visitors, and returned with the money to their parents.

Reading and writing were the extent of his education, and in 1826 he married the daughter of Leuthold, who spent his summers upon the Grimsel, and in the winter manufactured perfumes and carved wood. Peter was received as a son, and made partner in each department of business, all of which prospered till the family were no longer poor, but among the affluent of the land.

In 1821, there were only ten beds in the Hospiz, and at the time it was burnt, in 1852, there were a hundred; three communes had been added to the property, and the interest had increased threefold. Peter often took three thousand dollars in a season, and spared not his own means, and shrank from no care or labour that could add to the pleasure and comfort of his guests.

But in 1853, his lease would end. In October he had tried to renew it for twenty years upon conditions more favourable to himself, but had not succeeded. He had reigned as king on the mountain for sixteen years, and acquired a reputation which placed him among the first and most honourable of Swiss innkeepers. In the hotels of every canton his name was heard, and in his native valley he was considered a benefactor, and looked up to with respect. He could not endure the thought of resigning it. The mountain air was his element, and the bustle and business of the hotel his life.

Then came speculations concerning means of retaining it, or becoming the owner. The house belonged to the company, but if it were destroyed, with a little aid he could rebuild it, and it would be his for ever. The train of thought can be easily imagined now that we know the end. Two months before the fire he came to the bed of his wife in great agony, crying for help, but soon became quiet, and could not explain what was the trouble. It was the struggle between the good and the evil principle within him, and the evil at length prevailed. He flattered himself with the thought that the wrong would not be so very great where no lives would be endangered, and resolved also to do great good if he should be owner of real estate, a man of property and influence. The new house should correspond with the times, and the Grimsel should fill the land with renown.

The two servants were induced to accede to his plans by the promise of three hundred dollars. Six pounds of sulphur and five bottles of gas were purchased and placed in different parts of the building, besides wood covered with fat. Peter attended to the packing himself, and when all was ready on the 5th of November, went home. The men drank, to give them courage, and one took a light and kindled each place through a hole which had been made for the purpose. In three hours the house was burnt to the ground.

On the 13th of May, 1853, the old man, now bent and sorrow-stricken, stood with his accomplices before the Assizes of Berner Oberland, in Thun. The accusation was read, and he was then entreated to give a detail of the events. This he refused to do ; but said, as far as he was concerned, it was just, only harshly expressed, and in some things exaggerated.

Pausing with a deep shudder he said,— " I know I have brought upon myself and family the deepest misfortune. There is for me no justification. I have sinned, and pray all men to see in me henceforth a warning. After having devoted my life to industry and economy, and striven to promote the honour of my children and the good of my country, through one sin I have brought disgrace and misery to them, and must myself sit down for ever in darkness and the shadow of death. There are many here who have known and respected me, and the judge will commit and punish me against his will and love for me; but I deserve the full punishment of the law—dungeon and death. For myself I could not ask the sentence mitigated, but for the sake of my family I pray it may be lightened; and to my companions I ask you to be merciful."

By the law he was adjudged to death; but the Federal Council commuted the sentence to twenty years' imprisonment and chains. The two principal accomplices were sentenced to twelve, and the other to eleven years in solitary confinement. Only seven of these years are passed, and still thirteen remain.

Whoever studies the records a hundred years hence will no doubt think this a severe punishment under the circumstances, as we do many that were inflicted a hundred years ago. It was a crime, but it was the only one of a life, and was deeply repented. The judgment of God will be more merciful.

Berne has been always a ruling power, disposed to conquest and to tyranny, until the last revision of her constitution and the formation of the present Federal Government. The oligarchists are for the present in the minority, but the gall and wormwood are in their hearts, and having lost their power, they make it up in exclusiveness, in boasting of superiority which is no longer otherwise visible. One hears continually of the "seven patrician families" who have kept themselves entirely pure from all plebeian connections and relationships; and it is true they have isolated themselves so entirely from the world for fear of contamination that they have adopted about as little of the world's progress as the inhabitants of Spitzbergen. The patricians of Philadelphia would be amused to find a *field bedstead*, with all appurtenances thereunto, the principal furniture of a saloon among those who would not admit into their presence a person who could not count ten generations.

When the great Haller wished to publish his history in the city, and walked among them prince of poets, orators, philosophers, magistrates, and physicians, they could not tolerate his having been *humble born*, and could not allow that Berne should stand upon his title-page. This was in the eighteenth century, and if they had the power they would use it in the same ridiculous manner now. They do not allow any marriages to take place out of this charmed circle, and have thus intensified stupidity to the very last degree. The ridiculous pretension of the little German courts is not quite so ridiculous as that of these Swiss patricians, which are not confined to Berne alone, as we have elsewhere said.

We find very early among the statutes of Berne attempts to restrain the guilds, with the avowal that it is for the purpose of preventing their ever acquiring the influence they did in Zurich. In 1363, they were forbidden to assemble without four members of the Government present; and any who should form a guild without permission should pay four hundred dollars, and be banished for ever from the city.

Before this many of the nobility had become impoverished and resorted to handicrafts, and when they came by their trades to be members of guilds, they wished also to retain their position and influence, but they had soiled their hands with labour, and could no more sit down with princes.

But their efforts did not entirely succeed. A century later great troubles arose with the butchers, who rebelled against the restrictions, and the bakers did not like that the Government should fix the price of bread. But instead of heeding their petitions, they were restrained within narrower limits, and all old laws concerning apprentices and master workmen were renewed. No apprentice was allowed to have more than seven dollars and a half in his pocket at a time.

In 1467, a clothmaker was obtained by the Government, and supplied with house, dyeing materials, kettles, shears, etc., and all foreign clothes forbidden to be sold. All that were made were examined weekly, to be sure no fraud had been practised, and carried to the city sale-house. The richest people dressed in grey homespun till the sixteenth century.

A French tailor was banished so late as 1798; and not till 1798 did they get rid of all privileges and restrictions in trade and mechanics.

1366.—It was ordained that all grain must be brought to the market in Berne. This was a Government monopoly; but when there was a scarcity, and the corn-house was empty, the Government felt obliged to fill it; and in time of famine, in 1477, they sent to Strasburg and procured nine hundred thousand pounds, the transportation of which cost them six thousand Rhenish gulden (two thousand seven hundred and fifty dollars).

In 1487, an apothecary was appointed, with a salary of ten dollars a year and eight wagon-loads of wood.

In 1394, twenty-one *brunnen* were finished, it being a very dry summer. Since then many others have been added. The designs of the statues and masonry are curious specimens of the olden time. One is an ogre eating a child, half of which hangs out of his mouth, and several are peeping their heads out of his pockets and hanging to his girdle, waiting the dictates of his appetite. Another is the figure of a bear standing on his hind legs, dressed in a coat-of-mail, and wearing a helmet, in one hand a banner and in the other a sword.

The streets were paved in 1399, and *fines* were mostly appropriated to improving and adorning the city. If a wall was to be built, or tower, or public-house, all the citizens helped, and it was soon finished.

Duels were, in the thirteenth and fourteenth centuries, authorized by Government; a place appointed for the combat, and judges to attend to the ceremony. They fought within a ring, and he who first ran out was considered vanquished. Women who were slandered had also the privilege of proving their innocence by single combat, though the arrangements were a little different. The man was obliged to stand in a ditch to his waist, and defend himself with a club, while the woman pelted him with stones. A woman thus vindicated her honour in 1288, and came off victorious.

At all entertainments the men and women were obliged to sit as far apart as possible; and in 1602, great consternation was produced at a wedding by young ladies entering the room with gentlemen, and sitting promiscuously at table. The Government immediately set itself to correct such a scandal, and ordained that in future there should be no sitting by each other among gentlemen and ladies, and that two officers should be present on all occasions to see that this order was obeyed, and cause a fine of fifty dollars for each offence. Exactly how far apart they were obliged to remain is not stated, nor whether they were within speaking distance.

A wedding is mentioned of a rich heiress, at which a great supper was given, and the bride and bridegroom had a roast peacock. Henry von Luttermann performed the office of *femme de chambre* for the bride, and her morning gift was a gold chain.

No citizen of Berne could marry a woman from another state unless she had a dowry of fifteen hundred dollars.

A shoemaker was fined fifteen dollars for making shoes a finger's length longer than the foot. Ladies were forbidden to have *tails* to their dresses, or to wear caps more than two-thirds of a yard high, with fringe hanging to the bottom of the dress behind. The nobility bordered their dresses with ermine, "but could not be consoled for the loss of their *beloved tails*."

In 1577, it is recorded that a noble lady of Berne bore her husband the twenty-sixth child. In 1542, an innkeeper was forbidden to ask more than four sous for a good meal of fish and meat. At a wedding only one kind of roast and salad was to be set before the guests, and only six could be invited. Women and girls could have a simple soup, but boys nothing. Those who wished to entertain men could set before them one dish of meat and a pint of wine ; and the hostess must be careful to have it ready by ten o'clock in winter, and at eleven in summer, so that they could get through at four and go home.

We find the Government issuing mandates concerning caps and trains till the end of the eighteenth century. Many efforts were made to create a national dress. Young men who went abroad and returned in the costume of another country, must lay it aside within six weeks, and dress according to law. Clergymen must wear their cloaks to conceal their gaiters, other gentlemen to cover their hips, and women to hide their ankles ; and servants must not wear velvet, or silk, or hats, or shoes with heels.

Coffee-houses were introduced about the year 1700, by a Frenchman, but forbidden by the Government. Twenty-five years later an attempt was made to form a society where tea and coffee should be the beverage, and playing cards and conversation the amusement, but the Government forbade it. At the same time this same Government allowed the formation of a society called the *Golden Lause*, to which belonged more than fifty members of the *Great and Little Council*, which required of the members to get drunk every day of the week ! Those who mourn the degeneracy of the present times, and especially of democratic rulers, can pause and consider.

In 1737, it is mentioned that a new and peculiar feature had appeared in Bernese society, not at all productive of virtue or good manners.* Young girls from eight to ten years of age formed themselves into a society or "Sunday Union;" and without any supervision from older persons, spent the evening in "wild sports and junketing;" and when they arrived at the age of sixteen or seventeen, young gallants were added to their members, who were as destitute of good manners as themselves. Officers from the garrison entertained them with stories of their amours and revels, which were not of a nature to refine their manners or purify their minds, and furnished them with books of doubtful character, all of which had the most deleterious influence on the whole family life and general society, which remains to this day.

The author does not say how long these had existed ; whether they originated in Berne, or were adopted from some other country, or were introduced, as were many of their customs, by some of the swarms of foreigners who were always fleeing to them for refuge. But he proceeds to lament the consequences of these *coteries*, which separated the members of families, alien-

---

* History of Berne, by Von Zilller.

ated affections that should be cemented, and exposed the young to evil influences which parents and guardians had not the power to counteract because they were ignorant of them ; and created a stiffness in manners and society which prevents cordiality, and is inimical to good feeling.*

In the beginning, two hundred and forty-three families formed the oligarchy, and the "Great and little Council" could be formed from those only. They assumed all lucrative offices, and arrogated to themselves all privileges. The "*Burgher*" and "*Bauer*" were alike contemptible. It was this aristocracy and arrogance which led to the "war of the peasants" in 1513. They were conquered, but not extinguished, and one after another, in each canton where oligarchism prevailed, there was a succession of revolutions,—in Lucerne in 1570, in Basle in 1591. In 1652, Berne changed the value of her currency, so that he who had ten dollars yesterday, had only one to-day. A similar ordinance appeared in Lucerne, and was the signal for universal rebellion. "Of what use was it," said the peasants, "to abolish the old slavery and impose a new one? Those oppressions are insupportable. Where is the beloved justice of the ancient Confederacy? Berne indeed makes very good laws, but they are never executed."

For the tumults, wars, and massacres which followed, we have not room. They continued till the nineteenth century in some form, and ended only with the abolition of caste and privilege. Vaud and Argovie struggled till they became free ; and Berne was obliged to yield all her conquered territory, except Bienne, and part of the ancient bishopric of Basle.

In 1830 the aristocratic government was overturned for the

* We have described them more particularly in Canton Geneva.

last time, and the constitution based upon the utmost freedom. The "two hundred and forty-three families" have dwindled to a very few; but their hatred, revenge, and bitterness, are intensified in proportion; and the manner in which they foster their pride, and affect to despise "new people," is infinitely amusing. The next generation will perhaps get a little Christianized and modernized; for, in spite of all the bars and bolts of conventionalism, new ideas do now and then creep in. The schools will soon send forth one generation which must have learned a little of the true Christian and liberal spirit, if they are taught the history of their country as written by their best authors, and imbibe the spirit of patriotism and enthusiam as sung by their poets.

We have never anywhere seen so many fine-looking, manly, and well-behaved boys as in Berne. The first day we returned to the city, we visited the play-ground, from which we could always overlook the exercises of the gymnasium, where were held also school exhibitions. We should like to know the future of some fine little fellows, who show us their prizes and certificates with eyes that sparkle like fire, and a manifestation of pride and emulation that proves their appreciation of an honourable name. We made many friends among the little folks, and found it dreary enough in our walks when it became too cold for them to run, and jump, and scream on the lawn. But we remained long enough to see them slide down hill; and if American boys would know how this feat is performed in Switzerland, we can tell them—exactly as it is in America! The sleds are of all fashions and sizes, and they begin at the top, and wheel around a long, winding way, sometimes losing their balance, and tumbling heels over head, as we have seen them on a thousand hills at home. Sometimes there are girls also, whom the boys politely draw up the steep places, and guide the sled carefully again on its way down. We are only sorry they cannot remain always frank, true, open-hearted Swiss boys, instead of being trained to the falsehood, narrow-mindedness, and bigotry, which their conventionalisms require.

But we did not remain always in Berne capital. It was the first canton where we saw the peasantry in their villages and homes; and in no other do they seem to be so rich and prosperous; or rather, in no other do we see those who seem so rich and prosperous. The distinctions are greater between the rich and poor.

After their heroes, the name and life with which we were best acquainted in Switzerland before we came, was that of Fellenberg. When we came to Berne, our first inquiries were for his institution, and some one answered, "Oh, it is in ruins. Since he died it has not been kept in operation." But this did not deter us from wishing to see where he laboured.

The work he accomplished is known to all the world. His school was patronised by every nation in Europe; and with him originated the noble ideas concerning agriculture as a science and means of elevation for the masses, which are now those of all men. He purchased two thousand acres of land a few miles from Berne, known as Hofwyl, and devoted it to experiments which should prove the theories he advanced. He established a manufactory of instruments adapted to the different fields they were to till, and showed how a knowledge of the chemical nature of soils, of the physiology of plants, of natural history, and kindred subjects, enabled the farmer to overcome obstacles, and reap a thousandfold for his labour. But he did not instruct by precept alone. He toiled with the peasant in a peasant's frock, and often accompanied visitors around the establishment, who did not suspect him of being the great man himself. His pleasant voice and cheerful smile were everywhere, as must always be the case, with those who would make any impression upon the people they would elevate.

He established also a school for orphans and the poor, where the teachers acted upon the same principle. They not only taught books and read homilies, but laughed, and played, and worked with the children.

We visited the grave of the noble man, and thought "how strange and how sad that there should have been none on whom his mantle could fall when he ascended to heaven." The ruins do not testify to the impracticability of his system, but those who inherited the property had no taste or talent, and especially no heart for such a work. The schools are still in successful operation, but the farms are no longer an agricultural school ; though the Federal Government has lately purchased a portion of the land to found a college and carry out the principles which there originated.

In Thurgovie, at Kreuzlingen, at Hauterive in Friburg, and at Glarus, are institutions which are the offspring of Hofwyl; and agricultural societies were formed throughout Europe which are also the fruits of his labours. What a waste it would have been, indeed, of such a mind and soul to spend them in the idle and ridiculous ceremonies of European diplomacy !

The peasantry in the villages around Hofwyl are also proofs of the refining influence of a cultivated Christian man in their midst. The country is beautiful as fairyland. The fields with their rich harvests stretch away in broad prairies, dotted here and there with a smiling village, an ample farmhouse, or a humble cot, with orchards and gardens that speak of profusion, and the perfection of rural happiness. We entered a village store, a village schoolhouse, and the village church.

The preacher was an old man, and like the Lutherans in Germany, he wore a gown and little black velvet cap. The church, like most of the Protestant churches in Switzerland, was plain to severity. The services began at eight o'clock, in order to finish while it was cool, and before we should get sleepy; they were nearly the same as in America, except the baptism of four little babies, with their godfathers and godmothers dressed in black satin, with the white chemisette and silver chains which characterise the Bernese costume, and the little ones rolled up like mummies in white, handed on cushions. There was evidently quite an attempt at display on the part of the mammas, and they were not so entirely absorbed with the solemnity of the rite that they could not glance around to see if they were sufficiently admired.

The schoolhouse was a two-story, square building, painted white, as we have since seen so many. Their school system is not old enough to admit of decayed buildings; but it is now old enough to be well established and good. A century ago a teacher in the city received four dollars a year! Now there are schools in every commune, four high schools in the city, and one or two in every prefecture of the canton.

In the Emmenthal, in the northeastern part, the villages are large and handsome, and those who are still called peasants are bankers and merchants, and extensive landowners. We do not know what position or dignity one must acquire in order to relinquish the title of peasant. We asked a young lady, who considered herself a patrician, if she knew any of the people in these fine houses, and she said, "Oh, no, we have nothing to do with peasants."

We should have stopped at Brienz on our way from the Grimsel to Interlaken to describe the beautiful carvings in wood which are now so celebrated. An old man first cut little articles for his amusement, without any idea of selling them, and had no idea of design. Others soon imitated him, and made little things for ornament. Now it is a great industry, which supplies all the world, and the artists must have the genius of the sculptor. In a year, they delivered at a single market between thirty and thirty-five thousand dollars' worth. The articles are everything that can be imagined for use or ornament, in carved work, and mosaics of different coloured woods. Tables are bordered with the national colours and costumes of the twenty-two cantons. We asked how much such a one would cost. The man answered without hesitation, "We will deliver it in New York for twenty dollars." We had that moment arrived, and had not mentioned New York or America. So skilful they become in detecting the representatives of every nation.

We were rowed over the lake by some pretty maidens, and saluted at the foot of the foaming Giesbach by a troop with cheerful song. Thirty years ago, a traveller mentions the same salutation, and we learn that a family on the opposite shore have been trained from generation to generation for this purpose. Before the steamer arrives, one collects the centimes, which reward them for their pains. Whilst this is being done, two travellers are chanting their prayers so loud that it causes a little disturbance. They evidently consider themselves bound to recite so many every morning, and not having risen early enough to accomplish this task in private, they seize these few moments of waiting, and thus inform a large company of their devotion, as we do not understand what other purpose is answered by reading the Prayer-book aloud in public, instead of softly ; and think, also, that what had been put off till the eleventh hour might have been deferred a little longer, or that the lips might have breathed a few words which would have been as acceptable to Him " Who knoweth the heart from the beginning, who heareth in secret, and rewardeth openly."

We cross the Lake of Thun, where we are again encircled by a snowy wreath, and though only an hour's ride from Brienz, presenting a combination of mountain, glacier, and gorge, as different as if they were in two hemispheres ; but from no point is the great chain of Alps so imposing, so grand, so beautiful, as from Berne. We return to them as to familiar friends, and say a long and last farewell, with a pang scarcely less poignant than that which the snapping of some human tie will cause. We recall a thousand scenes with pleasure—the lovely gardens on Zurich's banks, the villas reflected in Leman's blue waters, the rude features of Lucerne, the panorama from the Rhigi, like a living picture, which needs no art to keep it for ever present to our vision. We still tremble as we think of the *Via Mala*, and the proud pinnacles of the *Gallenstock;* but Berne, had she only a mirror to reflect her beauties, would combine them all in one; so gracious and enchanting are her sunny summer landscapes smiling at the feet of those eternal snows.

CHAPTER XXIV.

CONCLUSION.

ATTACHMENT OF THE PEOPLE TO THEIR GOVERNMENT—FEDERAL ASSEMBLY—COUNCIL OF STATE—FEDERAL COUNCIL—TRIBUNAL—CONSTITUTION—OFFICIALS—POSTAGE—NATIONALITY.

WE have traced the history of Switzerland from the beginning even to the end. We have seen the little band of brave mountaineers, a little handful, expand into a great and prosperous nation ; and the union which was at first that of only three men, and then of three states, became a confederacy of twenty-two sovereign cantons. The homes they swore to defend were, at first, only a few rude huts of the wilderness, and their country bounded by the visible horizon. He who would know into what this wilderness has blossomed, and these homes expanded and beautified, must ascend the Rhigi, and looked abroad upon a picture more lovely than anything pencil has painted, or dream of poet conceived. He who thinks Switzerland is less dear to her people as it is than as it was, can have very little idea of the tenacity with which they cling to a birthright which not all the gold of princely coffers could buy when it seemed scarcely more than a mess of pottage, and which they would not now barter as long as there was left a living soul to shed the last drop of blood in her defence.*

We have sufficiently shown that the incessant revolutions and convulsions to which Switzerland was for centuries subject, were in no measure owing to the liberty she enjoyed ; but, on the contrary, to some defect in the *Charter of Freedom*, which kept them in constant clamour for *more*. They could not be content whilst fettered by a single bond. There was in their union some strong cementing principle, else it could not for ages have resisted the assaults from without and the oppressions from within which caused the fabric so often to totter, and by which it was so often shattered, but never destroyed.

For a long time the cantons presented scarcely more than a series of broken links, without the genuine family tie, the true spirit of brotherhood, which could make them one, not only in name but in reality. The federal league was indissoluble, but it was weak. It did not secure to them nationality, neither the character abroad nor the strength at home which alone could enable them to take their place among the nations. This was their condition till 1802,† when Napoleon interfered, and per-

---

* Our sheets go to press during the discussions concerning the annexation of Savoy and the neutral provinces on the Lake of Geneva. Some journals think it is very amusing and ridiculous that Switzerland should think of asserting and defending her rights, with her limited territory and limited means, but we do not understand why, when she has never yet failed to do so, never when lacking union and strength. We have had many a long conversation with the most mercenary and time-serving of her people, and verily believe there is not one who would not sacrifice the last centime for her glory, and whichever of the "great powers" begins a contest with her will find it interminable, for though many times conquered, they never have been, and never will be, subdued.

† The following table contains a list of the cantons, with the number of square miles in each, the population, and the date when each canton joined the Confederacy. It will be noticed that the first league was composed of three cantons in 1308, and that the Confederacy was not united or powerful until 1803, under the mediation of Napoleon, and was not joined by all the cantons until 1815. The country was finally organized under

formed for them the master-work of his life, grand because it was also good, the most glorious because it was the best. In France he insisted upon maintaining the unitary system, because he believed no other adapted to his people ; but in Switzerland he respected the federal principle, and made it the basis of the *Act of Mediation,* which took place February 19th, 1803. The

a constitution binding upon the whole republic, in 1848. The struggle for independence, freedom, and union has lasted through a period of five hundred and forty-five years :

Cantons.	Square Miles.	Population.	Date.
Aargau, or Argovie...............	511	190,000	1803
Appenzell.......................	149	54,000	1513
Basle...........................	192	66,000	1491
Berne...........................	2,576	440,000	1352
Friburg.........................	564	95,000	1481
St. Gall.........................	744	172,000	1799
Geneva..........................	92	65,000	1815
Glarus	276	32,000	1352
Graubünden, or Grisons...........	2,961	92,000	1798
Luzerne.........................	595	128,000	1332
Neuchatel.......................	297	66,000	1815
Schaffhausen....................	117	35,000	1501
Schwytz.........................	340	48,000	1308
Soleure.........................	255	65,000	1481
Tessino...	1,044	114,000	1803
Thurgan, or Thurgovie............	266	92,000	1803
Unterwalden.....................	266	25,000	1308
Uri..............................	426	14,500	1308
Valais	1,667	80,000	1475
Vaud............................	1,186	203,000	1798
Zug..............................	8	16,500	1352
Zurich...........................	683	280,000	1351
Total...............	15,315	2,400,000	

The comparative size of Switzerland may be better known by reflecting that the area of the State of New York is three times greater—the former having 15,315 square miles, and the latter 45,658. Switzerland is not quite equal in surface to that part of New York lying west of the Hudson River and north of the Mohawk, including Oneida and Oswego counties, the difference being only about one hundred and ninety square miles. But while this part of New York supports only about 600,000 people, Switzerland supports four times as many. Switzerland is also more mountainous, and more northerly, lying between 45 deg. 60 min. and 47 deg. 49 min. north latitude, while all this part of New York lies between 43 and 45 deg. Hundreds of square miles of Switzerland are covered with perpetual snow and ice, while northern New York is every year relieved of its winter burden. If northern New York were crossed by good highways and railroads, it might become the Switzerland of America.

ten years which followed were the most prosperous Switzerland had ever enjoyed. They then first learned to govern themselves. Tithes, restrictions, and prohibitions were abolished, and industry, commerce, and agriculture awoke from their long slumber, to open a horn of plenty, and pour broadcast its treasures. For the benefits which he conferred, the great conqueror required much treasure and much blood, yet they pardoned this and the ruthless devastation of his armies, in consideration of the good he did. Everywhere the "period of mediation" is spoken of as the golden era of their modern existence. When Napoleon fell, and the "great powers" again became arbiters, they destroyed the beautiful structure merely because it was the work of Napoleon. Again the common good was sacrificed to cantonal and individual interest; again they were tossed by convulsions and torn by dissensions. For fifteen years jealousies and rivalries between the different states put an end to progress, and threatened the existence of the confederation. But now they learned thoroughly the evils of dissension, and the year 1830 saw the formation of the new constitution* for the good of the whole, and the revision of nearly every cantonal constitution better to promote their individual interests.

They are now united in the *Swiss Confederacy*, and we must consider a little more minutely the different parts of the edifice which has proved so far to be exactly adapted to the wants of the republic, and promises for the future a glorious prosperity, which may well make the despots around them tremble, for it will demonstrate incontestably that freedom is the only state in which a people can become truly great or remain truly satisfied.

The Federal Assembly is composed of two houses, "*The*

---

* This was drawn up chiefly by M. Rossi, the distinguished jurisconsult of Geneva.

CONCLUSION.

National Council," and the " *Council of State.*" The former is composed of deputies chosen from among the people, one to every twenty thousand inhabitants. For there every man who has reached the age of twenty years is entitled to vote, provided he is not incapacitated by crime or otherwise from exercising the rights of citizenship in his own canton.

The *Council of State* is composed of forty-four deputies, two being elected from each canton, without reference to the number of inhabitants. The consent of both houses is necessary in order that any measure become a law, and the members vote without instructions.

The *Directorial Authority* and *Superior Executive* is vested in a *Federal Council,* composed of *seven members,* each from a different canton, and retaining his office for three years. A president *pro tem.* is chosen from these seven counsellors, who enjoys a salary of about two thousand two hundred and fifty dollars,* and each of the other six members receiving during his term of office something under two thousand dollars per annum. Their duties are to watch over the good of the nation collectively, with reference to its external and internal affairs ; and when the assembly is not in session they can raise troops, if necessary, but with the reserve of convoking immediately the councils, if the number of troops raised exceeds two thousand, or if they remain in service more than two weeks. They render an account of their proceedings at each meeting of the assembly.

There is also a *Federal Tribunal* for the administration of federal justice, and a court for the trial of penal offences.

The two chambers in session elect the Federal Council, the

* Half as much as a county official in Bavaria.

commander-in-chief of the federal army,* and the major-general. They contract foreign alliances, declare war, and conclude treaties of peace and commerce, take measures for external safety, the maintenance of independence and neutrality, and guarantee their territory and constitutions to the cantons.

There are one hundred and fourteen articles in the federal constitution ; but we have sufficiently illustrated their provision and spirit in the course of the work to make repetition unnecessary. Each canton retains its own legislation, its civil and penal justice, its system of taxation, and public instruction, decides its relation between Church and State, and the disposition of its military.

The system of rotation in office is the same in Switzerland as in America. There is not one office which is for life, if the people choose to change it. The judges are not only elective, but also very far from being chosen among the law-learned. They say the fitness of judge and jury depend on qualities of the heart rather than the mind ; and though monarchists, judging from theory, without any real knowledge of the facts, contend that it is impossible the duties of any office can be well performed without experience and knowledge, it does not appear that all public duties are not as well executed in Switzerland as in any neighbouring land. No man thinks of an office of any kind as a means of livelihood. It is merely an honour which he enjoys for a little time, and he then quietly lays down his staff to take up his trade again. When parties change, the principal incumbents are removed, as in America, which is in some respects an evil, but no greater, one would think, than a system which compels a whole phalanx of officials to swear truth and

* At present General Dufour, who served under Napoleon, and is considered one of the ablest officers in Europe.

fealty to whomsoever may be in power, whatever their name or principles. Those who had taken the oath of fidelity to king and emperor in Russia and Austria, hesitated not to take the same to Napoleon when the fortunes of war gave him the right to rule over them. In France we see a similar body promising to be true to the king in 1790, and a few years later crying, "Down with the king, and long live the republic." On their offices depended their daily bread; and when Napoleon seized the sceptre, they were as ready to crown the emperor as to dethrone a king, and when his fortunes waned, to support the restoration.* Those who received a staff from Charles X. or Louis Philippe were just as ready in 1847 to wield it for the republic, and now are not the less loyal to the Third Napoleon. They are only true to him who will secure to them the means of life, by whatever name he may be called. They do not profess to have either principles or opinions. They are merely part of a vast machinery, turned by something more fickle than the wind, and ruled by something stronger than iron. This is an evil which those of a republic have not to fear. If they suffer from the instability of their official corps, they have not to dread the more fearful stability of a large and well-organized class of men embodying a power secured only to that of the army, ready at any time to perjure themselves and sell their country to any usurper who will promise them in return the pittance which is to keep them from penury and starvation. Any one who has experienced their immobility and indifference to everything except government interest, might be ready to pray for almost any revolution that should give them a little more sympathy with humanity.

* " The king is dead, long live the king," is the expression the moment one is dead and another is proclaimed.

The military system * was illustrated in the history of Neuchâtel, and the school system of each canton in connexion with the development of its resources.

The prosperity of the little republic in commerce, manufactures, and agriculture, is known to all the world ; and a very common subject of reproach is their mercenary spirit, their materialism, and the absence of all that is poetic and artistic. One author, who likes them on the whole, says, "There is a little too much of the money-making spirit of North America." Exactly what this means we have never been able to learn, as we have never yet found people of any nation to differ very much in this respect. The difference consists in the means to which they apply themselves to arrive at the same end, and the capacity they bring to the accomplishment of it. The same freedom in every country of Europe that exists in America, England, and Switzerland, would awake to the same life the stolid, stupefied, slumbering populace. But there would then be lacking the resources of America, which open a path to every human effort and conception, and to which, quite as much as to her people, the great wealth and prosperity are owing. These might be multiplied even in Europe by removing the trammels and opening the ways now made inaccessible to trade and commerce by tariffs, taxes, and prohibitions. Nothing annoys an American so much in the Old World, as the *littleness* in all business transactions, from the manufacturer to the *concierge*. They know nothing about doing things on a grand scale. Everything is bought and sold by the ounce, and this is according to a settled system of things, for the

* The whole expense of the military is at most $555,000
The amount of salaries paid to officials 555,000
The united revenues of the Federal Government and Cantons . . . 845,000
The whole expense of the Government, including military, manufacture of powder, coinage, debts, etc. $3,539,850

purpose of supporting several grades of intermediate personages, who have no other means of livelihood than a species of menialism, such as these very people would consider it the lowest degradation to practise in America. It would take no more time for them to learn the science of honourable commerce and industry than the petty details of fraud and exaction, and it would add infinitely to their nobility of character ; and if they spent a hundredth part of the *calculation* in making dollars that they do in saving kreutzers, centimes, and sous, their souls would expand accordingly. We have never found them otherwise disposed towards British or American gold than to get as much of it as possible, and however lavishly expended, it is by no means despised.

This pettishness and dishonesty are no more characteristic of the Swiss than any other Europeans. We are of course speaking of the lower classes. They have more energy, are more original, and more inventive, because there are more incitements, and a better reward for their labour. The great corps of officials and soldiers who are supported in other countries in idleness, are here engaged in remunerative employments. Their government is not expensive, they are not restrained by prohibitions, there is no direct taxation, and no tariff * that is felt as the least weight upon the people. In commerce they are next to England, though they have not a mile of sea-coast ; and, as we have elsewhere said, there is no other country where agriculture yields so great profits, though the land is divided into almost infinitesimal parcels.

If there are persons still who would depreciate the Swiss in respect to intelligence and sentiment as compared with those

---

* The highest duty for luxuries is about three dollars per quintal.

around them, the statistics concerning newspapers, letters, and telegraphs may influence their opinions, if these may be taken as any criterion by which to judge. Those are likely to create the greatest facilities for promoting the culture of the mind and heart who most highly appreciate it.

The Federal Government did not assume the direction and expense of the post-office department till 1850 ; and during the five years which succeeded this change, the number of letters and packages increased more than a million, and the number of newspapers and travellers more than doubled. One sou is the lowest, and three sous the highest, postage for a letter from one point to another within the limits of Switzerland, and packages are in proportion. We give the number of letters transported in five different countries during the year 1856.

Great Britain	. 778	millions—to each person		17·25
France . .	. 252	"	"	7
Prussia . .	. 110½	"	"	6·42
Austria . .	. 54	"	"	1·77
Switzerland	. 23¾	"	"	9.88

It will be seen that Switzerland is next to England in the number of letters passing through her post offices in proportion to her people.*

Newspapers are not subject to a stamp, and the postage is

---

* A single telegraphic despatch to any part of Switzerland is twenty sous, and Prussia, with eight times as many inhabitants, sends not so many messages by several thousand. We append the number of stations in different countries of nearly the same size :

Belgium 42	Netherlands 23	Saxony 25
Sardinia 59	Wurtemberg 22	Switzerland 107
Bavaria 29		

lower than in either of the countries mentioned, amounting in a year—

In Switzerland for a daily sheet weighing an ounce and a half	2 75
" Germany for the same amount and distance	7 75
" France	14 60
England, including stamps	32 86

It is the principle of the government to secure the welfare of the whole, rather than luxuries for a few. There are at present no palaces and no castles except those of Nature's adorning, but the establishments for the poor and sick are truly princely ; and no object of benevolence fails for want of interest or support. The Swiss are accused of being cold and heartless —and we have seen those who deserved the accusation richly— but that the simple, unsophisticated people are less warm, cordial, and generous than those around them, we did not find. They do not talk sentiment so fluently as some, but sentiment is very far from being heart ; and we have seen it proved abundantly, that an appreciation and cultivation of the fine arts is no proof of mind or elevation of character. Yet that there are no immense galleries, not so much of the artistic in architecture, is no evidence, in Switzerland or America, that art is not appreciated. The Swiss demolished the castles, not because they were beautiful, but because they were to them associated with tyranny, barbarity, and everything base and contemptible in humanity. This is the motive which has destroyed them in every country. Those who built them and inhabited them were the veriest boors that ever crossed a threshold. Art could not be to those who knew them, and cannot be to any one who has studied the history of nations, the representative of the highest civilization ; but without any appreciation of it there must certainly be lacking one of its most important elements. The proportion of artists which Switzerland has produced is certainly very great ; and the greatest number of the dreamy wanderers among the ruins and galleries of the Old World are English and Americans. When they are so far civilized in Europe as to dispense with standing armies and standing officials—without which at present no throne could be sustained a day—they will see their material interests advance in geometrical ratio ; but, as a consequence, art need not fall backward, nor the people understand or admire it less.*

Those who infer from the noisy and disputatious elections in Switzerland that they are a turbulent, law-defying, and discontented people, depart as widely from the truth. They are very tenacious of the privilege of "speaking their minds," and of exercising the "right of suffrage ;" but, like Americans, when they have done this, if defeated, they submit and wait till the next opportunity for victory. With their government and institutions they are perfectly content.

It is said there are many traitors in their midst, who would much prefer to become the subjects of France, or some other princedom, to remaining the simple citizens of a republic ; who would not hesitate to deliver their land to pillage, and see their brethren torn by wolves, in order to be rewarded with the gilded trappings of a court, and an empty title that would designate them as the parasites of a throne ; and there are a few of

---

* The army of France costs exactly the same as the whole American Government; while the sum expended for education is the same as that appropriated for the one city of New York—six millions of francs.*

In the State of Ohio the tax for education is twelve per cent., and this does not include the fund from the sale of lands devoted to this object, while in England the tax for educational purposes is only two per cent.

* Report of the Minister of Public Instruction.

this class we know, but a few so worthless that they do not deserve to be numbered with the Swiss people, who are one and all the loyal subjects of the Confederacy, and would at any moment sacrifice for it their "lives, their fortunes, and their sacred honour."

It is said also that kings and emperors have not yet given up the strife—have not ceased to intrigue, especially at Geneva and Neuchâtel, with the hope of gaining, either by gold or diplomacy, these coveted provinces; and that if not successful, ere another year a French army will stand on their borders to demand what they will then not have the power to refuse. For ourselves, we do not believe Napoleon III., ambitious and wily as he may be, is capable of such baseness; but if he is, we can only say let him try; he will have a fruitful soil the next year, watered with the blood of thousands.

APPENDIX.

I.

It is to be regretted that there is no comprehensive and popular history of Switzerland in the English language, and until within a year there existed none in any language. English readers are familiar with a few important events, which the guide-books have transcribed from German authors, though we have seldom found them correct in facts or dates, and much less in opinions. For the material of the following summary we are indebted to the folio volumes entitled "La Suisse Historique," and "La Suisse Pittoresque," published lately in Geneva; the chapters concerning the different cantons being furnished by various learned men and popular authors from each. We have also consulted the twenty volumes of Chronicles in German, entitled "Gemälde der Schweiz," recording the minutest particulars of history, chronology, and statistical information concerning every canton. The attention just now attracted towards Switzerland has led us to believe that the connecting links we here furnish will be traced with interest by all who wish thoroughly to understand her position and resources.

The people of Switzerland, considered in any light, cannot be understood without a knowledge of their history. What they are we cannot at all appreciate without knowing what they were. And if any author, centuries since, had given us in detail the life of the "shepherds on the hills," we might transcribe it almost literally; for those who watch the herds and tend the flocks have not changed, and hundreds of years hence will probably see them nearly the same. Unless by some strange convulsion these mountains should be levelled into plains, or man should no more require flesh and milk for food, the Alps must ever present the same scenes; for no other inhabitants can people their solitudes, and in no other way can they be made to contribute to the support of human life.

Two thousand years before Christ, some parts of the country were inhabited, but anything definite concerning the people cannot be known until the Romans became their masters. They were accustomed to denominate all who dwelt to the north beyond their own limits, *Hyperboreans*, and the mysterious regions which the Alps hid from their view and protected from their aggressions they believe to be the workshop of *Cyclops*, where blazed continually his mighty forge.

There are many evidences that their religion was that of the Druids.* They worshipped a God whom they called "*All Fater*," Father of All, and whom they believed to be omnipotent and omnipresent. They worshipped also the sun, and moon, and stars as his agents. They believed he lived in the forests, and would be angry if they were destroyed. But to kill the ferocious animals who peopled them was a proof of heroism which was pleasing in his sight. Among the Alps animals were regarded with a kind of homage, but not as gods. Fire, air, and water were also invoked as mediators, which was the case among all simple people. Where the mind is uncultivated, and the power of the spirit not in the ascendency, something tangible and which their eyes can behold is needed, which leads them to the *Great Invisible!*

Some of their relics, and many of their customs, indicate a Scandinavian origin, and there are also traces of the Persians and the people of the East. In the time of Julius Cæsar they were no more in number than the present population of one of their cities. Yet in their earliest history are discovered the elements of a confederacy; and some have ascribed to each canton a tribe, or clan, and over each a chief, who ruled by military force. They may have originated in many countries; those who settled in the North perhaps in Germany; in the south-east are many traces of the Etruscans, and in the south-west, of the Celts and Greeks. Old chronicles say, Francus descended from Priam, son of Troy, and the Helvetians from Hell, son of Gomer, grandson of Japhet: or Franc may be from a Greek word meaning sincere, and the Helvetians, sons of Hell, from their ferocity.

They were found divided into classes; nobles, including those who belonged to the religious or military order, and plebeians, who had been slaves but were now either entirely free, or having been made so, experienced still some restraints.

---

* Not the least curious of these testimonies to the existence of this curious order of priesthood are what are termed the *Druid's foot*, a symbol in the form of two equilateral triangles linked together thus △, and which are to be seen on some of the old houses in cities still, bearing the name of the Druid's foot, though those who placed it there probably did not know what it meant, and those who now walk out and in beneath it know still less. Like the Penates of Rome, it is preserved as a link with the days of old, and reverenced for some virtue their forefathers supposed it possessed.

It was a century before the Christian era that the Romans sent to explore Helvetia, and on the shores of Lake Constance was fought the first battle, when *Diviko* was the Helvetian hero. To trace the progress and consequences of Roman conquest is not necessary; they were the same everywhere. But in the words of one of their own historians, "though often conquered, they were never subject, for a civilization perfected under a yoke and in chains has no sure foundation."

Traces of the religion, laws, manners, and customs of the Romans are abundant. Both Basle and Geneva were Roman colonies, and the names of the family of Cæsar will be seen on milestones from Valais to Vevay, Villeneuve, and Zug.

Towards the end of the second century the Germans drove the Romans from the northern part of Helvetia and established themselves as permanent possessors. Their religion taught the sacrifice of human victims, and the first Christian missionaries found the hands of the people of Zurich imbrued in human blood. So late as 640 were still found traces of these heathen altars, and the fires are still kindled on their mountains, which form one of the links in the chain to prove the faith of their fathers.

The inhabitants of the south-eastern part were more peaceful in their nature, and became, in a measure, incorporated with their conquerors, consenting to live under the same laws and to speak the same language. So early as the second century there were flourishing Christian communities on the banks of Lake Leman, and, long before this, they believe their soil to have been hallowed by the footsteps of Paul, who stopped in Geneva on his way to France, where he built a church; and Peter to have preached the Gospel in Valais. Their disciples were scattered everywhere, and in some cantons earned the glory and the crown of martyrdom.

But the Christian religion was an essential auxiliary to the policy of France, and it was after her conquests and during her reign that Christianity was propagated throughout Helvetia. Burgundian, German, Gothic, and Lombard became subject to France, and later, when Charlemagne was their king, here was the centre of his vast empire and the radiating point of his influence. Switzerland abounds still more than Germany in traditions, legends, and authentic histories concerning him. He was obliged to cross their mountains on his way to Italy, and brave Swiss are said to have formed his advance guard in his transalpine conquests, and for their courage and fidelity to have received the famous trumpets which have played so conspicuous a part in their own historical battles, called the bull of Uri, the cow of Unterwald, and the horn of Lucerne. Their popular songs are full of recitals which refer to his exploits, and though many be only legendary, it is matter of history that he built churches, established monasteries, and patronized science. He modified the feudal system, which had been introduced by the German invaders,* and with him ended the reign of unbridled barbarism. His missionaries taught at St. Gall, Zurich, and in Valais.

* Feudalism existed in Switzerland in all its phases as it did in Germany, but it would be unnecessary to enlarge upon it here.

It was under the Carlovingian princes that the first settlements among the high Alpine forests were made. Those who would fell the trees and cultivate the land were promised special privileges. They were to be owners in their own right of the soil they cleared, and to choose their judges from among themselves. The people of the plain and low countries, subject to lords who reaped the fruit of their labours, were thus induced to incur the perils of the wilderness, and were also out of the way of the hordes of barbarians who were continually infesting the land. They at first followed the courses of the large rivers, and then of those which led them into the lateral valleys, ascending the mountains by degrees, gradually increasing in numbers, till they were a strong power by themselves, ready to defy those who pursued them. In these solitudes, and by this mountain air, was matured that spirit of liberty which all the despots of Europe have not been able to crush. Though they fell by thousands and tens of thousands in their battles, they rose again from their ashes, with increased strength and a more terrible might, not only to resist but to endure.

Uri, Schwytz, and Unterwald, were long known as the Forest Cantons, thus indicating the nature of the country and the position of the people who inhabited it. So early as 857, we read that " the herdsmen of Uri met those of Glarus in the high pastures of Unerhoden."

But it was under the Dukes of Zaringen, a powerful race of Burgundian nobles, that flourishing cities were founded, and prosperous villages began to dot the till then desolate plains of Helvetia. Being defeated in their wars with the German emperor, in the twelfth century, and humbled by the Bishop of Geneva, they turned their attention to Switzerland, and attempted to gain power and influence by promoting the interests of the people. They built cities, which were speedily filled with an enterprising population, whose trade and commerce were great sources of revenue. The *burghers* were ever oppressed, and therefore ever at war with the feudal lords, and this new prosperity became new source of dissension. But the people of the surrounding country united with the citizens, and they were soon able to brave the power of their haughty masters. The *commune*, or village, was the commencement of the modern canton. Helvetia had been divided into *gaus*, or districts, by the Romans, and which they called *pagi*, and Western Helvetia parcelled by the Burgundian kings; but this was only for the purpose of levying taxes and supporting armies. No privileges were enjoyed except by the conquerors; the people being mere slaves to obey their mandates. But now, while Frederic Barbarossa was employed in crusades and quarrels with the popes, the principle of *communal liberty* which was taking root in the soil he scarcely thought worth his attention, and these germs served as the *beginning of the constitutional freedom and legislative codes of modern society.* Here were the seeds of the tree which now casts its protecting shadows over the land. But the lords and bishops did not long slumber over this new state of things. They saw the danger which threatened their supremacy, and during the temporary absence of Berthold V. assembled their forces to conquer and take possession of his kingdom.

But he returned in season to defeat their plans ; and having now become so powerful by the multiplication, not of armies, but of peaceful subjects, he was considered worthy of the imperial crown, which was offered him by the Guelphs. This he refused, and after long struggles with the prince of Savoy and the death of his two sons, he returned to his castle in Friburg, in Brisgau, where he died, February 14th, 1218, the last of the Zäringen dukes, and with whom terminated their reign in Switzerland. It was now again united to the German empire. But the immediate government was entrusted to counts and landgrafs, who by inheritance and conquest soon became rich and powerful enough to vie with the emperor whose vassals they were.

The most illustrious of these families, whose history is most intimately connected with that of Switzerland, were those of the counts of Alsace and Argovie, usually at that time denominated *Hapsburg*, from a castle they possessed near Aarau, in the canton of Aargau, and who owned vast estates in Helvetia. Rudolph II., fifth heir of his line, inherited in 1240 all these lands and titles, with an ambition still more grasping and insatiable, and which was at length rewarded by the imperial crown, after years of long and bloody wars with the equally aspiring house of Savoy. Having at first neither time not power to subdue them, he made continual concessions to the people of the Forest Cantons, who were ever complaining of encroachments upon their rights. Whilst he lived there was no serious revolt, but immediately upon his death, and the accession of his son, they began to talk of unions and associations for mutual protection. The first proposition was made by Zurich, and seconded by the Forest Cantons. Their first written treaty of alliance is a memorable document, which was not discovered till the end of the last century, when a Latin copy was found among the archives of *Schwytz*, and a German copy in *Stanz*, Canton Unterwald, both bearing the date August 12, 1291. We give it entire :—

"In the name of the Lord. Amen.

"This is to protect our honour and to watch over the public good, to consolidate peace and tranquillity. Be it then known to each and all, that the people of the valley of *Uri*, the general assembly of *Schwytz*, and the mountaineers of the lower valleys, considering the crisis of the present time, have promised in good faith, in order to be better able to defend their persons and goods, to afford reciprocal aid with money and arms, within and without the valleys, against those who shall do violence to one or all, or any wrong whatever to their persons or goods. We renew by the present act our ancient form of confederation, in such a manner, however, that each of us who has a lord shall be bound to render him obedience, and to serve him conformably to his condition and duty.

"We have resolved unanimously not to receive or to admit into our valleys any judge who has bought his office with money, or who does not dwell among us, and is not our countryman. If there should arise any dissension among the confederates, the most prudent among them shall interfere to reconcile the parties, and if in any case one shall reject the decision, the others shall oblige it to submit. These ordinances are to establish our good, and contribute to our prosperity. In testimony whereof this present act has received the seal of the three communities and valleys aforesaid."

By this is proved that they had no idea of anything but continuing subjects of the empire, and their league was merely to protect themselves against the tyranny and usurpations of inferior agents, who resided in their midst, and could not endure to see them enjoying rights and privileges which everywhere else were considered the peculiar prerogatives of what they termed "rank and birth." The emperor himself often disapproved of the acts of the bailiffs, but so far away could not control them.

These transactions took place towards the close of the last crusade, which had fanned the spirit of liberty in every part of Europe.

On the death of Rudolph of Hapsburg, the imperial crown was again disputed between his son Albert and the house of Nassau, and in this contest Switzerland was divided, Berne and Zurich preferring the latter, and the other principal cities choosing to remain subject to Austria. But in the developments of the projects of the family of Hapsburg they soon learned that they had no permanent good to expect from their rule. Albert, having several sons, wished to provide them all with a domain suitable to their rank, and formed the plan of subduing Helvetia entirely to his will, to be dismembered and parcelled as he pleased. He also wished to control the Alpine passes, in order to open a free way for his army into Italy. He at first attempted to treat with them, but unfortunately his emissaries were coarse and vulgar, insulting the people whom they came to conciliate, and hastening the strife they were sent to appease.

It is here that the story of Tell and Gessler appears, which has been published in every spelling-book and primer since spelling-books and primers were known.. The beautiful drama of Schiller has made all their contemporaries and the events of the time familiar in every language, and the stage has given them a reality that makes them seem not things of the past but of the present—a part of our own experience. There have been those who denied the truth of the story of Tell and the apple—denied the existence of Tell at all; and one author wrote a treatise to prove that the whole was merely a legend, and very similar to one prevalent in Denmark. The Government ordered all the copies to be collected and burned. In every cottage the picture of the "three men of Grütli" hangs upon the wall. Like the Declaration of Independence, with its thirty-one signers, in America, it is a household god. It is the first story the mother teaches to her lisping child, and the watchword with which every son is inspired to bend the bow and point the arrow. It it in every school-book, the title-page of every almanac, and decorates the council chamber, the rich man's parlour, and the village inn. We often tried the effect of doubting it, and were always amused with the indignation with which such an idea was received. "Do you really suppose there were any such persons, and that these things actually happened?" "To be sure we do; we know it very well. It is in our history. Why, indeed, it is all true; we know exactly where they all lived." We soon learned that if we wished for any favour in their eyes, we must not even for our amusement express any doubts about one of those heroic deeds of which they are still so proud; and not having really any doubt about them ourselves, we did not care to incur their ill-will for nothing. It would have been about the same if any one had said to us, " Washington was a tyrant, or anything less than the greatest and best of men." Whoever should say it in earnest might never again hope to be the friend of an American. And we really think any person who should, on Swiss soil, deny any portion of their honour to the men of *Grütli* would be banished without mercy.

Gessler was one of the bailiffs sent by Albert of Hapsburg either to pacify or subdue the people, and said "he would soon make them so tame and soft that he could wind them round his little finger." His castle was in *Küssnacht*, on the north side of the *Waldstätter See*. As he was one day returning from Uri, he passed through Steinen, and saw the house of *Werner Stauffacher*, who was one of the chief men of Canton Schwytz, and one whom Gessler knew to be a friend of freedom. Hating him, and wishing to show his power, he said, "The house was too fine for a peasant; he could not allow that the people have houses like the lords of the land." Stauffacher, knowing that it was meant for a threat, was dispirited, and on returning home his wife noticed the change in his usually pleasant countenance. She asked of him the reason, and heard the insult which he had received—he had been called a clown; and this was not enough, he must live like the brutes in his stalls. She was still more indignant, and exclaimed, "Why do men bear these things? How long shall pride laugh and humility weep? Of what use that houses are inhabited by men? Shall we mothers raise sons for beggars, and daughters to be slaves to strangers?" Her husband did not answer, but went out silently, and crossed the lake from Brunnen, to his friend, *Walter Fürst*, who lived at *Attinghausen*.

Henry an der Walden lived in the valley of Melchthal in Canton Unterwald, and owned also large fields, which he cultivated. The Bailiff of Landenberg, upon some slight pretence, accused him of disrespect, and confiscated his property. One day, while ploughing his field, his oxen were seized and led away, at which he was so exasperated that he entered the castle, struck the servant of the bailiff in his face and fled. A messenger came to seek him, and his father said he was not at home, and he knew not where he was. He also had taken refuge in Uri with Walter Fürst. In revenge, they bound the aged Melchthal and dug out his eyes.

One of the lieutenants of this same bailiff of Landenburg was one day passing the house of a peasant near Engelberg, who had a beautiful wife. For a pretence, he ordered her to prepare him a bath, which she dared not refuse, and whilst doing so he insulted her. She fled to her husband, Conrad, who, enraged, entered the house, and struck the wretch with his hatchet. He too was obliged to flee, and sought refuge in Uri: and the house of Fürst was the general rendezvous of those who experienced similar indignities. These became so frequent, that endurance was no longer possible to their chafed spirits, and they began to talk seriously of revolt.

The three principal men, Walter Fürst, Werner Stauffacher, and Arnold an der Walden, held secret and serious council, and in order to be secure from intrusion and the spies of their enemies, chose a spot which then was far from any human habitation, and distant from any path man would be likely to tread.

The lake of the Forest Cantons, or in the language of the country, the *Vierwaldstaetter-See*, stretches during its greatest length exactly east and west; but at Brunnen, suddenly turning a bold promontory, it forms a right angle, which gives to the remaining portion the direction of north and south. This southern arm is sometimes called the *Bay of Fluelen*, from the port at its extremity, where it receives the Reuss, which, having come down from the St. Gothard, flows through the lake and on to where it joins the Rhine. About a mile below the promontory, at the foot of a rocky ledge, is a little spot conspicuous from the bright green of its verdure. This is Grütli, or Rütli, the secret place, where the three met whom history calls " honest conspirators," to talk of what could be done to free the land from their oppressors. Each agreed to enlist ten from his own canton, and thus form a little band to be ready in any case of emergency, or at the appointed time to attack the castles, and banish the whole train of foreign bailiffs from among them.

The castle of Ratzberg was the first among the doomed ones to fall. A young damsel who was servant to its lord had a lover among the conspirators, and it was agreed that she should admit him by a ladder at night to her room; and through his aid several of his companions ascended in the same manner. On the next morning, January 1st, 1308, the devout proprietors being at church, unaware whom they had left to "keep the castle," it was taken possession of, and after delivering the goods and chattels to the proper owners, destroyed by fire.

It was the custom to make the Lord of Landenberg presents on New Year's morning of goats and kids, poultry, grain, and whatever they had, the produce of their labour. The peasants resolved to observe the custom with a more generous offering than usual; and so a large party came with their gifts, that when the doors were opened they entered without resistance. There is something a little revolting in such treachery, which can only be excused by considering the worse than treachery they had experienced.

The oath to which they were all bound, was " To remain true to each other till death; not to act separately; to protect their ancient rights and freedom; and also not to harm the people, cattle, or goods of the Count of Hapsburg; to banish the bailiff and dependents; to shed no drop of useless blood;. but the freedom and rights they had received from their fathers to transmit undiminished to their children.

Thus remarks a Scottish author: "These poor mountaineers in the fourteenth century furnish perhaps the only example of insurgents, who, at the moment of revolt, bound themselves as sacredly to be just and merciful to their oppressors as to be faithful to each other, and we may add, who carried out their intentions."

In the pictures of the " *Three men of Grütli*," they are represented as clasping the left hands and holding the right aloft with the thumb and two fore-fingers raised, the others shut into the palm. Their dress is the skins of animals fashioned differently, according to the idea of the artist.

Tell had married the daughter of Walter Fürst, and thus being the son-in-law of the chief conspirator was of course admitted to their councils. His name is said to signify rash, or to talk without reason, which corresponds to the English signification, a similarity whch is very striking between many of the Swiss and English words. In the history of *Tell*, his character seems to have acquired for him the name, or else the name was given him in conformance to very early exhibitions of an impulsive nature, or it may have been by accident, as often happens, though no great occasion reveals it to the world. But whether he was rightly named or not, his rashness came very near marring their well-planned scheme. He lived in Burglen, in Canton Uri, not far from Attinghausen, and became one of the thirty who were to surprise the castles.

The tyrant Gessler had observed, or his fears led him to think he had, certain signs of discontent among the people, which prompted him to put their loyalty to the proof. It being market-day in Altdorf, which is between Attinghausen and Burglen, and was probably the centre then of the scattered population, he caused a pole to be erected, upon which his cap was hung, and all who passed by were commanded to pay it homage. An unusual number were gathered together, and Tell at length observed a commotion in the crowd, which attracted him to the spot where the pole stood. Pretending not to see it, he marched proudly by, making no signs of doffing his cap as the others had all done. This being remarked, he was seized and ordered to bow to the signal, or the dungeon would be his punishment. This he refused, and the tyrant drew near, evidently not displeased with an act of disobedience which would give him occasion to exercise his power, and fill the people with terror. Suddenly the thought struck him that Tell was a famous archer, and a fiendish smile crossed his coarse visage as he said: "You are renowned in the land; you shall buy your freedom with your skill. They say at a distance of a hundred paces your arrow never fails. The distance being measured, you shall cleave an apple from the head of your son." On hearing this, the whole multitude uttered an involuntary cry of indignation at the heartless cruelty of the tyrant; and the bold forester who had never known fear, and for himself would never have prayed for mercy, threw himself upon his knees and begged with tears that he might not be made the murderer of his child. But he stood before one who had never known mercy, and though aged men offered their lives to save their friend from so revolting a deed, it was only the more triumphantly commanded;—the greater the suffering he could inflict, the more he exulted. All remonstrances being in vain, the arrows were selected, the paces counted, and the little boy placed at the end of the line beneath a linden-tree, to which he refused to be bound, saying, "He would not move or wink, and had no fear, for he knew he should receive no harm from his father's hand." Still the father hesitated, made weak by his love and horror of the crime he feared to commit. Three times he bent the bow and let it fall unstrung. The stillness of death reigned in the circle of strong men, while hearts that never beat before with terror, throbbed convulsively. Mothers wept and clasped their children in speechless agony. Every eye was strained to painful intensity. Every spirit breathed a prayer to heaven. At length a wild shout proclaimed that it was finished. The arrow winged its way unerringly, and the father raised his eyes to heaven and cried : " O God, I thank thee !" The next moment the boy was pressed to his bosom. As he knelt, a second arrow fell from its hiding-place in the folds of his vest of chamois, and Gessler coming near demanded to what purpose it had been destined. Fearing a repetition of the terrible command, the tongue of the brave archer faltered. " Nay, tell me the truth, why have you concealed this arrow ?" Now standing erect, and with a glance which made the tyrant cower, he said, " To pierce thy heart, monster, had I killed my child."

He had promised life if the shot did not fail, and this promise he did no*, dare to break ; but he said, " I know your rebellious spirit, and will bind it in chains which no man can loosen. You shall live, but in a dungeon so deep that neither sun, nor moon, nor stars, can penetrate its darkness." Amidst the muffled execrations of the populace, he was seized and bound, no one offering again remonstrance or interference, and taken to the little skiff which lay moored in the Haven of Fluelen. The day of retribution was near; they had not long to smother their wrath.

But scarcely had they embarked, when a wild storm arose. The sea was lashed into fury, and the boatsmen plied their oars in vain. " We are lost !" they exclaimed. The darkness of night spread over the scene, and the flashing lightning and echoing thunder seemed to the simple people the voice of God denouncing judgment against him who was, in the eyes of One who searcheth the heart, a murderer. They asked that Tell might be set free, for he was as skilful in guiding the helm as in bending the bow, and his arm might yet save them from a watery grave. Their prayers were at first in vain ; but the storm becoming more fearful, and death, the grim messenger before whom the guilty, however mighty, must tremble, seeming evident, the cords were commanded to be cut. The strong, brave man was free. He took the oars, and strange it seemed to the old mariners, who had resigned them in despair, as they beheld the boat obey him like a thing of life. It darted like the arrow he had so successfully winged, but not to its destined port. Unheeded, he neared the shore, to where an opening in the cliffs made it probable to him to secure a foothold on the rocks, and by a sudden spring, he leaped and stood defiant before them on land, while the boat was tossed back upon the waters. Only an instant he remained fixed upon the spot, and bounded into the forest. The little bark danced at will upon the waves till the storm abated, when they guided it into port at Brunnen, and took their way over the mountains to Kussnacht.

But an unquenchable thirst for revenge was kindled in the heart of the injured father. With the stealth of the Indian he tracked his foe, who had scarcely arrived at his castle when the unerring arrow transfixed his heart.

This has been called a stain on the Swiss revolution, as it was an unnecessary deed, and committed more to avenge a private wrong than to achieve freedom for the people. Yet no one believes an instant that an indignity, which was merely personal, could have received this punishment. The whole land was groaning under a sense of insulted and outraged honour, and

APPENDIX. 413

this last act had shown them that they had nothing to hope from obedience and the most abject submission. The only reproval Tell received from his compatriots was, that they feared he had frustrated their plans. And whatever the cool judgment may say, the heart involuntary approves. No tyrant has been more thoroughly execrated, and no hero more applauded.

II.

When the emperor heard of the banishment of his agents, and the destruction of their castles, he prepared immediately to punish the insurgents, and marched towards Switzerland with a powerful army. But scarcely on its borders, he was defeated by a traitor in his own ranks.

His nephew, instigated by private wrongs, with the aid of two or three accomplices allured him across the river, which would separate him from his camp and place him beyond the reach of aid, and there struck the deadly blow which branded him through all time as the midnight assassin. Almost beneath the walls of his own castle the proud emperor was left to die alone. But a peasant girl passing by, soothed his last moments, and carried the intelligence, without knowing his rank, to the castle.

The murderer escaped, but a thousand innocent persons became the victims of the haughty queen's revenge, which she afterwards repented, and spent fifty years in a convent, endowed by their confiscated estates, in prayers and fastings to atone for her crimes.

Several of the immediate successors of Albert continued to the Forest Canton their privileges, preferring to retain them as friends rather than convert them into foes. But at length the family of Hapsburg determined to renew their pretensions, and the next two centuries present us only a continued series of battles and skirmishes between the princes of this house and the Swiss mountaineers.

Western Switzerland was not involved in this struggle, their position and interests uniting them with France, Burgundy, and Savoy. From the time of the oath in Grütli, and the revolution of the Forest Cantons, Switzerland is divided, till the Reformation gives them again a common cause.

At Morgarten, in the Canton Zug, 6th December, 1315, was fought the first battle that acquired for the Swiss a name which attracted the attention of Europe to their affairs. Here they showed that they were not mere wild rebels of the mountains, but brave in war as wise in council, and no contemptible opponents for the disciplined corps of princes. A few days after this victory they renewed the solemn oath of *Grütli*, meeting at Brunnen, for this purpose, and assuming the appellation of *Eidgenossen*—confederates— *leagued by the same oath.*

They had eight years before expelled the Austrian bailiffs, but without resistance. Now they had baptized their cause with blood. Thirteen hundred shepherds, who had never seen a battle, gained a victory over twenty thousand armed men, commanded by king and nobles. Their renown filled the land, and the three little cantons became the centre around which rallied in a few years the remaining states of the Confederacy. Lucerne joined them in 1332, Zurich in 1351, Glarus and Zug in 1352, and Berne in 1353.

Henceforth they are the eight cantons, and instead of Helvetians we find them adopting the name and escutcheon of the little canton whose heroes had so distinguished themselves in the battles and councils of the republic; whether by definite agreement or common consent is not known, though it seems a pity that the Federal arms should not have been characteristic and significant.

The Swiss Confederation, as we have seen, did not begin, as in Germany, by the union cities. The first efforts for freedom were by shepherds and agriculturists. The cities which had received charters and privileges, remained long indifferent to the brave Forest Cantons, and not till they were joined by Lucerne, thought of granting them either aid or encouragement.

As commerce and industry increased, the *bourgeois* gained influence, and an aristocracy of wealth took the place of the old one of birth and blood. These, as in ancient Rome, formed the *patriciat*, and by degrees through associations, acquired an influence in public affairs. Thus we see a constant antagonism between the *noblesse* and the *communes* in all the Zaringen cities, among which Berne was always conspicuous. It is curious to observe the wrestlings and never wearying struggles of the people against their oppressors, the princes of Hapsburg, who had the nobility always on their side; yet during all these two centuries the people were, with scarcely an exception in small or in large expeditions, victorious. On one occasion, a Bernese noble made the impious exclamation, "that God must have turned *burgher*."

The battle of Lauffen, in 1337, which the people of Berne fought against the *noblesse* of Western Switzerland, increased their self-reliance, and gave them a consequence which admitted them to the Confederacy. But Lucerne had been long a member before her sons were called to martyrdom, and the name of *Sempach* enrolled beside that of *Morgarten*. Seventy-one years after Leopold of Austria led his army into Helvetia, his son experienced a defeat as inglorious, in the same unworthy cause. Here the King, six hundred nobles, and two thousand soldiers fell before an army which at the beginning was not fourteen hundred strong. Every battle is commemorated by a chapel with rude paintings upon its walls. On those of Sempach appears conspicuous *Arnold of Winkelried*, from Unterwald, who seeing they were in danger of being overcome, and wishing to inspire them with fresh courage, exclaimed, " Protect my wife and children ; I go to open a path to freedom," and rushing forward gathered in his arms as many lances as he could grasp, and plunged them in his bosom. As they bore him from the field, they asked him if he had no message to his friends. "None," was his remarkable answer, "but say to the people, never allow a bailiff to remain in office more than one year." This was in 1386, about five hundred years ago, and a striking testimony to the corrupting influence of power, and the necessity for a free people who would retain their liberty, to change often their rulers!

One after the other every canton becomes the theatre of battle, and sees some little spot bathed in the blood of her martyrs. But, alas, when we have recorded one more, the pure spirit which pervaded their councils and inspired their courage is dimmed. Success and power have not been without their influence on them. The rigid respect for the rights of others, which has hitherto characterized their victories, is mingled with a love of conquest and a wish to exhibit their bravery, whether it be in a good or an evil cause.

The battle of *Naefles*, in Glarus, 1389, is the last of those conducted purely on defensive principles, in which their glory was without a shadow. With this terminated their fear of Austria; their liberties were consolidated, and the *noblesse* began to respect and court the alliance of the *bourgeois*.

Yet in other parts of Switzerland were enacted nearly the same scenes, as they threw off the yoke of the nobles and emancipated themselves from feudal despotism.

So early as 1378 the Suabian cities had formed a league with Constance, the city of the lake, and the bourgeois of St. Gall had been permitted to unite with them. Appenzell prayed for the privilege of placing herself under the same protection, and was denied, because they feared their strength would not be equal to the opposition they should experience. She then appealed to the confederate cantons, and on deliberating upon it in their assemblies, only three were in favour of receiving her. But Schwytz would not consent to refuse to others what they had so gladly accepted for themselves; and offered to form with her a partial league, giving her all the aid in their power. Thus strengthened, they broke out into open revolt, resisting the nobles and destroying the castles on their own territory, and marching their armies across the Rhine, till even Austria trembled at their approach. In one campaign they devastated twelve cities and sixty-four castles, freeing themselves entirely from a foreign yoke. The indignities which they experienced were the same in character as those inflicted upon the people of every country subjected to feudal authority. Their bailiffs were the same coarse, vulgar boors, as we have seen in the Forest Cantons.

Upon one of the mountains of Schwandi, a castle was tenanted by an agent appointed by the abbey of St. Gall. He liked to sit in his tower and look down upon the lovely valley, and watch the people at their toil, the subjects over whom he possessed absolute power. But a little boy, who passed every day on his way to the Alps, attracted his special attention. His father lived in the Rachentobel, and was a miller and baker, with a large family to support. The little boy brought milk and whey from the pastures. One day as he passed, the nobleman called to him, and said, "What is your father, and what does your mother?" "My father bakes unpaid bread, and my mother mends old clothes." "Why do they do this?" "Because you take all the money!" On hearing this the bailiff threatened to set his dog on him.

The little boy ran home and related his adventure, and the father told him next time he went to the mountain to put a cat in his pail. No sooner did the nobleman see him coming on the following day than he called out, "Now, you jackanapes, can you tell whether a magpie has more black feathers or white?" "More black." "Why?" "Because the devil has more to do with tyrants than with angels." Immediately the dog was set loose, but the same instant out jumped the cat, and, as was very natural, the fight was between the animals, whilst the boy ran laughing home. The nobleman had him brought back by force, and thrust his spear into his side, telling him to be careful in future of his tongue. The miller related the event to his neighbours, and they gathered together from all the hills and attacked the castle. Its possessor, having no power to resist, fled to a neighbouring mountain; and when he looked back, saw his proud fortress in flames. The men of Schwandi have been ever peculiarly honoured; for though this was the beginning, they did not stop till every stronghold of these hated tyrants had met a similar fate.

In the Grisons, now denominated Graubünden, the work was more fearful still, because the feudal lords were almost as the trees of the forest for multitude. The ruins of more than one hundred and sixty castles may still be counted upon their mountains; and not till a century after the men of *Grütli* had become free from all feudal tyranny did the people of the Grisons begin their struggles. They, too, were at first exasperated by the same insults. A beautiful peasant girl in the valley of the Engadine attracted the admiration of the Lord of *Gardoval*. He had watched her as she went on some household commission from her village of *Comogask*, and went forth to meet her. She promised to return to him if he allowed her to go home first and apprise her father, who would be anxious at her absence. Thinking it safer to trust her, he extracted a formal oath, and she hastened home. The father said, "You have promised, and must keep your word; but I will go with you." He communicated his purpose to a few trusty friends, and the daughter arrayed herself in bridal attire to meet her lover. When they were near the appointed rendezvous the father concealed himself in a thicket, and the fair maiden went on, and was greeted with a joy the greater because of the partial distrust in spite of her promise. But in another instant the father had plunged a dagger in his heart, and at a given signal his companions appeared and destroyed the castle.

John Chalder has been called the *Grison Tell*, and the bailiff to whom he owed allegiance another *Gessler*. He saw one day the horses of his master turned to feed in his corn, and killed them on the spot, for which he suffered a long and gloomy imprisonment. The dungeons of those days are described elsewhere. One almost wonders how the people could be betrayed into any crime that should doom them to live within their dark and narrow walls. One day after Chalder was released he saw the bailiff passing his house whilst they were at dinner; and wishing to atone for his former rashness, he invited him politely to partake of their meal. Upon which this polished nobleman "spit in the soup," thinking the dungeon had tamed its victim to unresisting meekness. Quick as thought, the peasant grasped him by the throat, and plunged his head into the steaming dish, saying, "Now eat the soup you have seasoned." The universal war which followed left few lords or castles in their midst.

At every step is some memorial of these struggles, some monument of these victories, some festival to keep the deeds of their fathers in remembrance. They are related still around the fireside, and become familiar to every child before he leaves the parental roof, though they may not know that they are recorded in a single book.

But they had been so long in the field, that war had become a passion; and when no longer obliged to defend their legitimate soil, they became the aggressors. The castles of Hapsburg and their broad domains in Aargau and Thurgovie they determined to add to their possession, and coveted also the inheritance of other princes lying on their borders. They were not less successful in conquering than in defending, and soon became enriched by large additions to their territory. But they did not give to the conquered people the rights which their fathers had bought "with so much treasure and so much blood." They were treated as subjects, and not allowed to choose their own bailiffs; the privilege which they had considered so precious, and for which they had sacrificed so much.

In these conflicts they became embroiled with each other, and rival princes enlisted Swiss against Swiss. The Reformation commenced, and popes, and cardinals, and clergy added their quarrels to those of kings, nobles, and soldiers. It was during the session of the great council at Basle, that occurred the most famous of all their battles. They were at war with Germany, and France was the ally of the Emperor. The Dauphin, afterwards Louis XI., came with an army of thirty thousand men to aid the Emperor, and with the hope of throwing consternation into the council, in revenge for their having deposed Pope Eugene. The Swiss in their haste could assemble only fourteen hundred men. They met just outside the walls, and the battle lasted ten hours. The French remained masters, because the Swiss resigned it with their death, only ten being left to tell the story. It was considered disgraceful that they did not die, and they were not permitted to return into the cantons. This was the battle of St. Jacob, 1447, and they call it the Thermopylæ of their history.

It was their bravery on this occasion which led Louis to say, it was better to have such a people for friends than enemies, and to propose, instead of protracting the war, that they should become his allies. This was the date and origin of that long period of "foreign service" which has been so reprehended, so misrepresented by their enemies, so regretted by themselves, and only this year come to an end. Whilst we write, it is announced that the regiments which are in Naples, and which have been long the only ones remaining in the pay of a foreign prince, are returning home; and the Government has passed a law, that whoever again enlists as a soldier under any but his own country's flag, loses his citizenship, and is henceforth an outlaw. They have long endeavoured to bring about this result, but like many another evil, it was easy to plant it, but very difficult to root it out. In the day of its beginning, war was the one glorious occupation for men of all ranks, and labour a degradation. Those who could not engage in agriculture had no other resource, and they saw that, by becoming the ally of France, they should secure protection against their increasing foes, and avert evil from their country. It was not the custom then to look forward to results, and there was yet for centuries no united, harmoniously-acting Government to control the people. What was attempted by one canton was resisted by another, and the emisaries of every despot in Europe were constantly intriguing in their councils.

Later, when there, was a little respite from war, young men enlisted for a series of from four to five or six years, as a means of gaining a little money to render their homes more comfortable. Being allowed to visit their friends every year, a communication was kept up, and the love of their country kept bright. Austria, at one time, paid the Canton Graubünden one thousand dollars a year to preserve peace with the Tyrol. Francis I. paid during his reign more than three millions of dollars to Switzerland for soldiers. Louis XIII. paid them a million and a half of dollars, and from 1474 to 1774 they received fifteen hundred millions from France. In the course of this period eight hundred thousand men fought in the battles of French kings, and six hundred thousand were slain. One of the ministers of Louis XIV., who disapproved of employing the Swiss, said to him, "Sire, with the thalers which have been paid to the Swiss, a high-road might be paved from Paris to Basle." Marshal Stuppa, from Graubünden, being present, replied, "Yes, and if the blood which has been shed for France by Swiss were poured into a channel, we might sail in ships from Paris to Basle."

"Point d'argent, point de Suisse" (No money, no Swiss), has been repeated for centuries to their reproach. We saw in one of their journals this summer an explanation to their honour, and one which seems quite as probable. When the Duke of Sforza said to the captain of a Swiss regiment, after a victory, "Help yourselves like knights, for I have no money;" the answer was, "This we cannot do; where there is no money there can be no Swiss," meaning that they could not serve without honourable reward, as plunder was not to their taste and not their custom—a scruple which it is well known few knights of the same period were wont to entertain.

Under the several governments which they have served, the Swiss attained to the highest military honours. They have furnished marshals and generals to Austria, France, and Holland, to Spain, Portugal, and Italy; and on account of the fidelity which never swerved when they had sworn allegiance, they were ever entrusted with the most important and honourable posts. Who has not shed a tear over the fate of the noble phalanx which Napoleon kept as his choicest reserve at the battle of Waterloo, and who has not regretted that when he ordered them up as a forlorn hope he did not place himself at their head! He would have died gloriously, had he fallen where they fell!

Still we must record it against them, that when America, struggling for liberty, appealed to them for aid, they refused; and though we find in their chronicle a reason which they deemed sufficient, to us it seems but a vain excuse. It would have made a bright page in their history had they stood side by side with the heroes of Bunker's Hill, Monmouth, and Saratoga.

By allying themselves with France they incurred the enmity of the Burgundian princes; and Charles the Bold, to avenge this alliance, invaded their country, and gave them an opportunity again to display their valour on Swiss soil. In those wars their military renown reached the highest point, and then ended the heroic period of their history.

The battles of *Grandson* and *Morat* have no rivals in any country, among any people; but one of their own historians says, " This glory was dearly bought, for venality and corruption among their chiefs and counsellors were its attendants. The people had fought, but the rulers had profited." The Swiss had a beautiful custom of kneeling in silent prayer on the battlefield. And it was in this position that they were surprised on the plain of Grandson, it being taken for one of submission; but it enabled them to use their lances to greater effect among the cavalry of their enemies, and evidently gained them the victory. At Morat, a town not far from Berne, a linden-tree was their council-house, which is still standing, and now with its spreading branches might shelter an army instead of its chiefs.

Byron and Cooper have made these spots familiar to all English readers, and the costly hangings of the Burgundian camp, and the gold and diamonds of their princes, are still present among other curious relics of the sacristy of the cathedral of Berne. They are among the most beautiful specimens of the costume and manufactures of those days. Money and jewels were poured into the hands of the Swiss soldiers, for the duke fled almost alone over the mountains, leaving his wealth to the victors.

It was after these battles that the *diplomats* of every country came with their gold and their flatteries to secure the little republic as their ally. There were not wanting good men and true, who had protested against selling themselves in any way to become the servants of princes; but bad men had gained the ascendency, and held the reins of government.

Nicholas von Flue is the name of one of those patriots who appeared a burning and shining light in the midst of the corruption of those evil times, and standing up boldly and earnestly to speak in their councils, prevailed against the machinations which had nearly dissolved the Confederacy.

December 22d, 1481, a new treaty was formed at *Stanz*, in *Unterwald*, for the purpose of better regulating their internal affairs, that civil dissensions might not make them a reproach and by-word among the nations; and the same day Friburg and Soleure were admitted to their union, but not to the full privileges of their government.

Still each canton had the power to call a diet, which made them of almost ridiculous frequency and insignificant importance. One attracts our particular attention. It took place in 1492, in Berne. The year that Columbus with his little fleet was groping his way over the yet trackless ocean, to find that great unknown world, here was assembled a federal council; but before these turbulent political elements had fairly settled into harmony, America had become a nation, with her *diplomats* in every court of Europe, her vessels on every sea, and her flag fluttering on every breeze.

This diet was to deliberate upon the Austrian and French alliance; and we find a little spark of that fearless spirit, which had never been quite extinguished, in the answer of the then Secretary of State, when the Bishop of Mayence exclaimed, " Give your support to Austria, or by this pen I hold you will be made to do it." The reply was, "Others have attempted to force us with halberds, which proved as powerless as your goosequill." The Emperor Maximilian I. attempted to win them by flattery, and when this did not succeed, to conquer them again by force, attacking them simultaneously on all the frontiers of the north and east. But being everywhere repulsed, and finally beaten at Dornach, they retired forever with their unjust pretensions.

Three more cantons were now admitted to the Confederacy, Basle, Schaffhausen, and Appenzell, making the whole number thirteen; though the eight original cantons still preserved to themselves some exclusive rights.

With this period begins the Reformation, the events of which are too familiar to need more than an allusion. Zwinglius and Calvin, Œcolampadius and Forel, where the great Swiss reformers; and the strife of parties was in this not less bitter, and the religious wars not less devastating, than those of conquest and ambition.

In the works of their authors, we find curious remarks concerning the different characters of the good men who were conspicuous in these struggles.

Zwinglius, they say, was a man of the world, and had learned what human passions were by mingling with men in all the relations of life. When curate at Glarus, he went with his parishioners to Italy, and stood by their side in two successful battles. Though not less good and noble himself, he was not so censorious and exacting as some of his compeers.

Luther had lived all his life the tenant of a cell, and knew nothing of the world; his judgment was formed from the abstract idea of things, a metaphysical conclusion without comparison. When Zwinglius attempted to arouse the pride and love of country of the people by patriotic appeals, Luther condemned him, saying the preaching of the Word was sufficient; a sermon was better than the sword; and whilst he was drinking his beer with his companions, he felt that the truth he had set forth was at work in the hearts of the people.

Calvin said Luther had been spoiled by flattery, and the people thought he (Calvin) was too speculative, and not sufficiently republican. The doctrine of election *was not a democratic doctrine, and they could not listen to it!*

Here Western Switzerland appears again in the drama, and the wars between Catholic and Protestant deluge the land with blood. It was in one of those that Zwinglius fell, having accompanied the Zurich regiments as their chaplain. His body was burnt with barbarous inhumanity by the fanatic soldiers. Yet these very fanatics were the sons of the noble men of the Forest Cantons, and for a whole century we see those who should have been brethren, thus opposed in deadly strife, each fighting for what he believed to be his country and his God. Alas, what crimes to be committed in the name of the Prince of Peace!

But when these struggles were ended, there followed a long peace in the cantons, the longest they had ever known; and now we see them continually ruffled by little feuds concerning rights and privileges. The Forest Cantons were always jealous of the cities, and feared the consolidation of power.

Zurich, seeing a tendency in the Government to concentrate and form an aristocracy of birth, assembled her citizens to the number of six hundred, and demanded her rights at the point of the bayonet. They were granted without hesitation before the sword was unsheathed.

In Basle it was an aristocracy of wealth which threatened ; in Berne, Soleure, Friburg, and Lucerne, the ascendency of caste and party. Thus, for another half century, we find Switzerland without any of the characteristics of a nation ;—the nobles tyrannizing over the citizens, and the cities tyrannizing over the peasants.

But a brighter day is dawning, and in the midst of all this evil there is much good. Industry flourishes in the country, and in the cities art and learning have awoke from their slumbers. The press is free, and opinion untrammelled.

The next period is one of philosophy and thought. We see stormy debates in their councils ; but there is a grandeur in their motives. If the aristocratic majority prevails, the influence of the stormy minority is always good. In the convulsions of their government we behold the travail of thought and the springs of action. There were then, as now, *old fogies*, who mourned the " good old times," and opposed all innovation ; but the liberal and the progressive obliged them to yield.

The democratic tendencies of the writings of Rousseau and Voltaire aroused the elements of another party strife, and the aid of Louis XV. was invoked by the aristocrats to crush the fruitful germ of democracy ere it had taken root. He sent an army to surround Geneva. In a council, one of his generals said to a deputy from Zurich, " Do you know that I am the representative of the king, my master ?" " And do you know," replied the fearless Zurich deputy, " that *we* are the representatives of our *equals* ?"

In Neuchâtel they had a dispute with Frederick of Prussia about imposts ; in Lucerne a quarrel about succession ; and, in 1770, still another revolution in Geneva about naturalization ; but all were the throes of Liberty in the various stages of her development.

Order had in some measure settled herself in the land, and plenty began to crown the labours of the husbandman and artisan, when the French revolution swept like a whirlwind over Europe. Switzerland prayed to remain neutral, but kings and emperors had not forgotten the bravery of her sons ; and the peasantry, in the midst of their rural toils, remembered at the first sound of the tambour that they were warriors. Again their soil was drenched with human blood, their government shattered, and their free institutions overthrown. These little republics, which seemed scarcely able to support themselves, were taxed and despoiled to the amount of more than twelve millions of dollars in money alone.

But Napoleon had the discernment to see that they could never be retained as a province of France, and offered a partial restoration of the old order of things. He sent for deputies to meet at Paris from all the cantons, and listening respectfully to their opinions, and as respectfully expressing his own, they formed a new government, which secured them ten years of peace, and is known as the *period of mediation*. Six new cantons were added, making now nineteen, and all on an equality, which they had never granted to each other. The administration of internal affairs was left to themselves, and their president of their own choosing. In return they were to furnish Napoleon twelve thousand men. His overthrow placed them again at the mercy of the allies. But their experience had not been without its use. They had learned that "union is strength." We see them in future more willing to sacrifice personal and cantonal interest to the good of the whole.

Geneva, Neuchâtel, and Valais, who had long been allies, were incorporated into the Confederation, making the number twenty-two; and the old treaty of alliance, offensive and defensive, was renewed with many improvements. Each canton was sovereign in its own affairs, and *subjects* existed no more on Swiss territory.

The general government was called a *Diet*, and consisted of deputies from each canton. Still there existed privileges which kept a portion of the people restless, and in two or three cantons caused a division. In Basle the country separated from the city; the great ground of complaint being the inequality of representation in the general assembly. The Canton Appenzell was already Outer and Inner Rhoden; the one being Catholic and the other Protestant. Discontents in many others led to the subject of a revision of all their constitutions.

During all the years from 1815 to 1848, we see them in constant ferment, which had in more than one canton broken out into civil war, and as yet the federal authority was not sufficiently strong to quell these petty disturbances.

In 1847, took place the famous war of the *Sonderbund*, in consequence of the suppression of many convents, and the banishment of the Jesuits. The influence of the priesthood in the little cantons where the Catholics were a majority was a continual hindrance to progress in what concerned the general good. The equal distribution of rights and privileges affected their position and revenues, and they opposed with all their strength the supremacy of federal power.

The year 1848 saw the final triumph of general over individual interests. A grand Diet assembled at Berne, all the cantons being fully represented. The degree of federal authority was still the bone of contention. What should be the title of the President, the extent of his power, whether there should be one chamber or two, and the principle of representation, kept them in stormy discussion many weeks. At length, one hundred and one cannon booming from the neighbouring heights announced the completion of their work. The large majority of fifteen cantons had united for the adoption of the federal constitution, and chosen Berne to be the seat of the Federal Government. For the detail of their enactments we have no space, but to all who doubt the power of a people to govern themselves, we commend their constitution; and those who think it possible to grant too much freedom to a people, may compare the statistics of law and order in any part of Switzerland with those of the countries which surround them.

The great marvel is, how through all these convulsions they have preserved their existence; and though we hear it often prophesied, by those in whom the thought is a wish rather than a conviction, that they will not remain long independent, we believe there are not a hundred men in Switzerland who would not stake life and fortune in defence of their country, and their country's freedom.

APR 15 1861.

www.ingramcontent.com/pod-product-compliance
Lightning Source LLC
Chambersburg PA
CBHW030549300426
44111CB00009B/911